SOCIAL RIGHTS AND THE CONSTITUTIONAL MOMENT

Chile's constitutional moment began as a popular demand in late 2019. This collection seizes the opportunity of this unique moment to unpack the context, difficulties, opportunities and merits to enhance the status of environmental and social rights (health, housing, education and social security) in a country's constitution.

Learning from Chilean and international experiences from the Global South and North, and drawing on the analysis of both academics and practitioners, the book provides rigorous answers to the fundamental questions raised by the construction of a new constitutional bill of rights that embraces climate and social justice. With an international and comparative perspective, chapters look at issues such as political economy, the judicial enforceability of social rights, implications of the privatisation of public services, and the importance of active participation of most vulnerable groups in a constitutional drafting process.

Ahead of the referendum on a new constitution for Chile in the second half of 2022, this collection is timely and relevant and will have direct impact on how best to legislate effectively for social rights in Chile and beyond.

Volume 28: Human Rights Law in Perspective

Human Rights Law in Perspective

General Editor: Colin Harvey
Professor of Human Rights Law
School of Law
Queen's University Belfast

The language of human rights figures prominently in legal and political debates at the national, regional and international levels. In the UK the Human Rights Act 1998 has generated considerable interest in the law of human rights. It will continue to provoke much debate in the legal community and the search for original insights and new materials will intensify.

The aim of this series is to provide a forum for scholarly reflection on all aspects of the law of human rights. The series will encourage work which engages with the theoretical, comparative and international dimensions of human rights law. The primary aim is to publish over time books which offer an insight into human rights law in its contextual setting. The objective is to promote an understanding of the nature and impact of human rights law. The series is inclusive, in the sense that all perspectives in legal scholarship are welcome. It will incorporate the work of new and established scholars.

Human Rights Law in Perspective is not confined to consideration of the UK. It will strive to reflect comparative, regional and international perspectives. Work which focuses on human rights law in other states will therefore be included in this series. The intention is to offer an inclusive intellectual home for significant scholarly contributions to human rights law.

Recent titles in this series

Investment and Human Rights in Armed Conflict: Charting an Elusive Intersection
Daria Davitti

Specifying and Securing a Social Minimum in the Battle Against Poverty
Toomas Kotkas, Ingrid Leijten and Frans Pennings

Protecting Human Rights and Building Peace in Post-Violence Societies
Nasia Hadjigeorgiou

Collective Trauma and the Armenian Genocide: Armenian, Turkish, and Azerbaijani Relations since 1839
Pamela Steiner

The Times and Temporalities of International Human Rights Law
Edited by Kathryn McNeilly and Ben Warwick

Social Rights and the Constitutional Moment: Learning from Chile and International Experiences
Edited by Koldo Casla, Magdalena Sepúlveda, Vicente Silva, and Valentina Contreras

For the complete list of titles in this series, see 'Human Rights Law in Perspective' link at www.bloomsbury.com/uk/series/human-rights-law-in-perspective/

Social Rights and the Constitutional Moment

Learning from Chile and International Experiences

Edited by
Koldo Casla
Magdalena Sepúlveda
Vicente Silva
and
Valentina Contreras

•HART•
OXFORD • LONDON • NEW YORK • NEW DELHI • SYDNEY

HART PUBLISHING

Bloomsbury Publishing Plc

Kemp House, Chawley Park, Cumnor Hill, Oxford, OX2 9PH, UK

1385 Broadway, New York, NY 10018, USA

29 Earlsfort Terrace, Dublin 2, Ireland

HART PUBLISHING, the Hart/Stag logo, BLOOMSBURY and the Diana logo are trademarks of Bloomsbury Publishing Plc

First published in Great Britain 2022

A catalogue record for this book is available from the British Library.

A catalogue record for this book is available from the Library of Congress.

ISBN: HB: 978-1-50995-189-5
ePDF: 978-1-50995-191-8
ePub: 978-1-50995-190-1

Typeset by Compuscript Ltd, Shannon

Contents

List of Contributors

Alexandra Barrantes is a Senior Social Policy Specialist and Head of Social Policy Unit at Development Pathways with more than 20 years' experience in social protection, poverty reduction, inequality, and economic and social rights. Before joining Pathways, Alexandra was a UNICEF social protection consultant in Latin America and led the Organisation of American States' (OAS) Equity and Social Protection Unit. She has formed part of several international technical working groups on poverty, social protection and Sustainable Development Goals with the World Bank, the International Labour Organization, UNRISD and others.

Juan Pablo Bohoslavsky was the United Nations Independent Expert on Debt and Human Rights between 2014 and 2020. He worked at UNCTAD and as a consultant for ECLAC, OHCHR and the Argentine State. Bohoslavsky holds a PhD in Law from Universidad de Salamanca. He was Hauser Fellow at the New York University Law School. He has written extensively on finance and human rights, and he co-edited *Pinochet's Economic Accomplices: An Unequal Country by Force* (Lexington, 2020).

Koldo Casla is a Lecturer in Law and the Director of the Human Rights Centre Clinic of the University of Essex. Before joining Essex, he was Research Associate at the Institute of Health & Society of Newcastle University, where he co-drafted the first Bill on Economic, Social and Cultural Rights in the UK (2017–19), Policy Director of the UK social rights NGO Just Fair (2016–19), and research consultant for Amnesty International, authoring four reports on the rights to health, education and housing in Spain (2013–19). Casla holds a PhD in European and International Studies from King's College London.

Valentina Contreras Orrego holds a Law Degree from the University of Chile, and an MSc in Human Rights from the London School of Economics and Political Science (LSE), and is the representative in Chile of the Global Initiative for Economic, Social and Cultural Rights (GI-ESCR).

Verónica Delgado Schneider holds a Law Degree from the University of Concepción, and a PhD in Law from the Università Tor Vergata Roma, Italy. She is Associate Professor in the Department of Economic Law at the Faculty of Legal and Social Sciences of the University of Concepción, where she teaches Environmental Law, Urban Law and Environmental Water Law. She is the author of several publications on environmental and water law. In 2019, she was part of the Water Roundtable, the Oceans Roundtable and the Ecosystems and Biodiversity Roundtable of the Chilean Ministry of Science, Technology, Knowledge and Innovation, in the context of the UN Climate Change Conference COP25.

Delphine Dorsi is the Director of the Right to Education Initiative (RTE). She is a lawyer specialised in human rights and has been working for more than ten years in the field of the right to education. She holds a research Master's in Human Rights from the University of Strasbourg.

Karinna Fernández holds a Law degree from Valparaíso University, a Master's in International Public Law from the University of Chile, and an LLM in International Human Rights at the University of Essex. She has served as an advisor on international criminal cooperation and extradition for Chile's Public Prosecutor's Office and as a consultant with the Inter-American Commission on Human Rights. Currently, she is a legal advisor of Londres 38 in Chile and Forest Peoples Programme in the UK.

Alfonso Henríquez R. holds a PhD in Law and a Master's in Moral Philosophy. He is a Lawyer and teaches at the Department of History and Philosophy of Law of the University of Concepción. He is also a visiting professor of the Programme in Law, Environment and Climate Change of the University of Concepción. He has taught various postgraduate courses on judicial enforcement and protection standards on economic, social and cultural rights, policy and regulatory framework for educational leadership in Chile, and political philosophy.

Dominique Hervé Espejo holds a Law Degree from University of Chile, a LLM from University College London (UCL), and a PhD in Law from the Universidad Católica de Valparaíso (Chile). She is Associate Professor in the Department of Public Law at the Faculty of Law of the University Diego Portales in Santiago, where she teaches Environmental Law. She is the author of several publications on environmental law and climate change.

Jody Heymann, MD, PhD, is founding director of the WORLD Policy Analysis Center at the University of California Los Angeles, and Distinguished Professor at the UCLA Fielding School of Public Health, Luskin School of Public Affairs, and Geffen School of Medicine. She has worked with a wide range of intergovernmental organisations, including the WHO, ILO, WEF, UNICEF and UNESCO. Heymann has authored more than 430 publications, including 18 books. Selected titles include *Advancing Equality: How Constitutional Rights can Make a Difference Worldwide* (University of California Press, 2020), *Disability and Equity at Work* (Oxford University Press, 2013), and *Making Equal Rights Real* (Cambridge University Press, 2012).

Sandra Liebenberg, BA LLB (UCT), LLM *cum laude* (Essex), LLD (Witwatersrand), is HF Oppenheimer Chair in Human Rights Law and Distinguished Professor in the Faculty of Law, University of Stellenbosch.

She also serves as Extraordinary Professor at the Centre for Human Rights, University of the Free State, South Africa. She previously served as Chair of the Technical Committee advising the South African Constitutional Assembly on the drafting of the Bill of Rights in the 1996 Constitution of South Africa. Liebenberg is a former member and Vice-Chair of the UN Committee on Economic, Social and Cultural Rights.

Eduardo Marchant holds a Master's in Law from the Universidad Austral de Chile. He is currently a Law PhD student at the same university. His research interests are related to the rights of persons with disabilities, in particular to reasonable accommodation, political rights and the participation of people with disabilities in the Chilean constitution-making process.

Pablo Marshall is Assistant Professor of Law and Vice Dean of the Law School at the Universidad Austral de Chile. He holds a PhD in Law from the University of Glasgow. He edited the volume *Citizenship and Disadvantaged Groups in Chile* (Lexington, 2018), and he has edited and authored five other books on constitutional law in Spanish.

Gonzalo Moreno is a Senior Research Analyst at the WORLD Policy Analysis Center, where he is one of the leads of its Constitutions database. He has more than 10 years of experience supporting the creation, analysis, and dissemination of quantitative databases on laws and policies that matter to persons with disabilities, including constitutional protections, workplace legislation against harassment and discrimination, and equality in education. He has previously written or presented on the evolution of non-discrimination in constitutions, on gender-based discrimination at work, and on paid leave policies. Moreno is the co-editor with Stein and Heymann of *Disability and Equity at Work* (Oxford University Press, 2013).

Francisca Moya is a Lawyer and Graduate in Legal and Social Sciences from the University of Chile (2012) and holds an LLM in Public Law from London School of Economics and Political Science (2018). Currently, she is PhD candidate in Law at the University of Glasgow. Before her postgraduate studies, Moya served as a law clerk at the Constitutional Court of Chile and as a legal advisor to the General Secretariat of the Presidency of Chile.

Vivian Newman Pont is Executive Director of the Center for Law, Justice, and Society Dejusticia. She has a postgraduate degree (DSU) in Administrative Law from the University of Paris II Panthéon-Assas in France, a Master's degree (DEA) in Domestic Public Law from the University of Paris II Panthéon-Assas and a Master's degree in International Aid for Development from the University of Barcelona in Spain. She graduated with a JD from the Universidad Javeriana in Colombia. Newman Pont coordinated the Public Law Department at the Universidad Javeriana and taught Administrative Law at the same university.

Viviana Ponce de León is Assistant Professor of Law at the Universidad Austral de Chile and researcher of the Núcleo Interdisciplinario sobre Desigualdad y Derechos Humanos. She holds a PhD in Law from the Pontificia Universidad Católica de Valparaíso.

Amy Raub, MS, is Principal Research Analyst at WORLD and responsible for the translation of WORLD's comparative policy research into findings for policymakers, citizens, civil society, and researchers. Raub has been deeply involved with the development of WORLD's databases on constitutional rights, laws, and policies since 2008, and is a co-author of *Advancing Equality: How Constitutional Rights can Make a Difference Worldwide* (University of California Press, 2020).

Julieta Rossi is the Director of the Human Rights Master's Program at the National University of Lanús and Associate Professor and researcher at the Justice and Human Rights Institute at the same university. She is also Professor at the School of Law and the Human Rights Master's Program at the University of Buenos Aires and at the Human Rights and Democratization Master's Program at the National University of General San Martín. She is a legal advisor at the Federal Prosecutor's Office in Argentina. Rossi was the Director of the International Network for Economic, Social and Cultural Rights (ESCR-Net) and a member of the Board of Directors and director of the programme on Economic, Social and Cultural Rights at the Center for Social and Legal Studies (CELS).

Constanza Salgado Muñoz is a Graduate in Legal and Social Sciences from the University of Chile (2009), holds an LLM in Regulatory and Tax Law from the Universidad Católica de Chile of Chile (2014) and PhD in Law from the University of Edinburgh (2020). She has authored and edited a number of books on water, property, fundamental rights and constitutional law.

Magdalena Sepúlveda, PhD, is the Executive Director of the Global Initiative for Economic, Social and Cultural Rights. She is also a member of the Independent Commission for the Reform of International Corporate Taxation (ICRICT) and of the High Level Panel on International Financial Accountability, Transparency and Integrity for Achieving the 2030 Agenda. From 2008 to 2014, she was the United Nations Special Rapporteur on Extreme Poverty and Human Rights.

Vicente Silva Didier is a lawyer, currently working as the Latin America representative of the Global Initiative for Economic, Social and Cultural Rights (GI-ESCR). He holds an LLM in International Human Rights Law from the University of Essex.

Sebastian Smart is Regional Director for the Chilean National Human Rights Institution and Lecturer at Universidad Austral de Chile. He holds a PhD in Latin American Studies and Human Rights from University College London and a MA in the same university. He holds a Law Degree from Universidad Católica de Chile, and has published several articles on human rights. He co-edited *Pinochet's Economic Accomplices: An Unequal Country by Force* (Lexington, 2020).

Aleta Sprague, JD, is Senior Legal Analyst at WORLD and an attorney whose career has focused on advancing public policies and laws that address inequality. She has co-authored a range of publications examining how laws and policies shape racial, gender, and socio-economic disparities, including most recently *Advancing Equality: How Constitutional Rights can Make a Difference Worldwide Worldwide* (University of California Press, 2020).

Michael Ashley Stein is the co-founder and Executive Director of the Harvard Law School Project on Disability, and a Visiting Professor at Harvard Law School since 2005. Stein participated in the drafting of the UN Convention on the Rights of Persons with Disabilities, and has collaborated with civil society groups and international organisations. He has over 200 publications and nine edited volumes, and has been supported by fellowships and awards from the American Council of Learned Societies, the National Endowment for the Humanities, and the National Institute on Disability Rehabilitation and Research.

Pam Stek, PhD, is a Writer and Editor at WORLD. She is a historian with a background on how public policy shapes equity and equality.

Verónica Valenzuela holds an LLM in International Human Rights Law, University of Essex, and a Bachelor's degree in Judicial and Social Sciences from Universidad de Talca, Chile. Her LLM dissertation focussed on the justiciability of social rights within Chile's constitution-making process. She has worked on human rights for different Chilean human rights institutions, including the National Institute for Human Rights, the Human Rights Program at Under-Secretary of the Interior, and Under-Secretary for Human Rights. Since 2014, she has been involved in litigation, particularly in the investigation and criminal prosecution of the gravest crimes committed during the Chilean dictatorship.

Alejandra Zúñiga-Fajuri, PhD, is a Professor at Valparaíso University in Chile and a researcher at CIFDE-UV. She has developed projects in political philosophy, distributive justice and bioethics. She has published three books and numerous articles in *The Lancet*, *Child & Adolescent Health*, *Bulletin of the World Health Organization* and the *International Journal of Health Services*, among others.

List of Cases

LIST OF STATUTES AND CONVENTIONS

1

Introduction: Social Rights and the Constitutional Moment

KOLDO CASLA, MAGDALENA SEPÚLVEDA, VICENTE SILVA AND VALENTINA CONTRERAS

I. CHILE'S CONSTITUTIONAL MOMENT

IN THE 1990S, Bruce Ackerman defined 'constitutional moments' as historic milestones of intense deliberation and change in a country's politics, change that reflects in the country's constitutional settlement.[1]

Since October 2019, Chile has been going through its own constitutional moment, a moment that began with popular resistance against rising public transport fees in the capital, Santiago. The uprising went on for weeks, and was initially answered by force. A research team from the UN High Commissioner for Human Rights spent three weeks in the country in November that year, and they detailed extensive allegations and examples of torture and ill-treatment by police against people held in detention, as well as cases of arbitrary detention; official figures in late 2019 reported more than 28,000 people detained within weeks and no fewer than 26 deaths in the context of the protests.[2]

The turbulent unrest was only appeased with an agreement between the government, the majority of political parties and civil society groups to channel social demands through a participatory process of constitutional reform. The issues brought to the fore by the mobilisation of late 2019 included the increasing cost of living, low wages and pensions, lack of quality education, and a poor public health system;[3] in other words, social rights.

A plebiscite was held in October 2020, in which 78 per cent of citizens confirmed their support for the launch of the process to reform the constitution, and 79 per cent favoured the creation of an ad hoc constitutional convention to

[1] B Ackerman, *We The People: Transformations* (Cambridge, Mass, Harvard University Press, 1998) 93–94.

[2] UN Office of the High Commissioner for Human Rights, *Report of the Mission to Chile: 30 October–22 November 2019*.

[3] Centro de Estudios Políticos, *Estudio Nacional de Opinión Pública No 84* (December 2019).

that end. The 155 members of the constitutional convention, 17 seats on which were reserved for indigenous people, were elected in May 2021. Chile's became the first constituent assembly with guaranteed parity between men and women.[4] The convention's proceedings began in July 2021, and it is expected that an entirely new constitution will be put to the people in a referendum in late 2022.

Despite being amended several times, to this day Chile's democracy continues to be built on a constitution written under Pinochet. The regime adopted the 1980 Constitution as an attempt to provide a veneer of legitimacy to the dictatorship. The 1980 Constitution contains a number of problematic procedural requirements, such as preventive constitutionality control by the constitutional court, or super majority requirements in both chambers, particularly insurmountable with the anti-proportional electoral system in place until 2018. So-called 'authoritarian enclaves' made it difficult – if not impossible – for progressive governments to bring about law and policy changes, let alone constitutional amendments.[5] For example, between 1990 and 2005, despite electoral defeats, the right-wing opposition enjoyed a majority in the senate thanks to a sizeable group of non-elected senators.[6]

The 1980 Constitution is also the embodiment of the neoliberal model: it prioritises private property and a market-driven economy, but it does not guarantee education, healthcare and social security for those in need. Chile signed and ratified a number of international treaties that proclaim economic, social and cultural rights, but by and large these rights have not been incorporated into domestic law. The 1980 Constitution, in Articles 19 and 20, recognises only the freedom to choose between different providers, for example, in relation to health and social security, but it does not ensure a minimum content for these rights; the right to education and the right to a healthy environment are not justiciable, and the right to adequate housing is nowhere to be found. That is why, in 2016, the UN Special Rapporteur on Extreme Poverty and Human Rights concluded that 'the formulations used (in the 1980 Constitution) do not generally conform to international standards and are not firmly anchored in the language of rights and obligations. The methods of implementation envisaged are relatively open-ended and non-empowering and do not explicitly include judicial action' in relation to social rights.[7] Alongside the United States, whose constitution is completely silent about them, Chile is the country in the Americas that has so far most resisted the constitutionalisation of social rights.[8]

[4] V Undurraga, 'Engendering a Constitutional Moment: The Quest for Parity in the Chilean Constitutional Convention' (2020) 18 *International Journal of Constitutional Law* 466.

[5] MA Garretón, 'Chile 1997–1998: The Revenge of Incomplete Democratization' (1999) 75 *International Affairs* 259.

[6] J Couso, 'The Possibilities and Limits of a Constitution-Making Transnational Legal Order: The Case of Chile' in G Shaffer et al (eds), *Constitution-Making and Transnational Legal Order* (Cambridge, Cambridge University Press, 2019) 275.

[7] UN Special Rapporteur on Extreme Poverty and Human Rights, *Report on his mission to Chile*, UN doc A/HRC/32/31/Add (2016), para 25.

[8] R Gargarella, *Latin American Constitutionalism, 1810–2020: The Engine Room of the Constitution* (Oxford, Oxford University Press, 2013) 145.

Under the 1980 Constitution, social rights are not a matter of public service; they are instead tradeable goods available only to those who can afford them. And affordability is very unevenly distributed as a result of high levels of inequality. As reported by the UN Economic Commission for Latin America and the Caribbean, 'wealth in Chile is highly concentrated. While the poorest 50 per cent of households owned just 2.1 per cent of the country's net wealth in 2017, the richest 10 per cent held two thirds (66.5 per cent) and the richest 1 per cent accounted for 26.5 per cent'.[9] The gap between the average income of the richest 10 per cent and the poorest 10 per cent of the population is 20 to 1, one of the highest rates in the OECD.[10] Chile has the second highest Gini coefficient of income inequality in the OECD,[11] and the second lowest rate of public spending in relation to the GDP.[12]

Chile's constitutional moment unfolded in these socio-economic conditions. The constitutional moment was institutionalised through the mentioned constitutional convention in a process agreed upon by the government, opposition parties and civil society. For Verdugo and Prieto, one of the unique features of the Chilean constitution-making process is that it is 'both a bottom-up process pushed by groups favoring a constitutional replacement and an elite-driven bargain that includes rules designed in a top-down way by political parties, which tried to channel the social demands via representative institutions'.[13] Following the mandate of the plebiscite, the constitutional convention was set up ad hoc, called to coexist with parliament (national congress), which continued with its own business while the convention focused on the drafting of the future constitution. Chile may be an example of what Arato called the 'post-sovereign paradigm of constitution-making', where 'none of the actors, institutions, or organs involved in the several stages could claim to fully embody popular sovereignty'.[14]

Negretto identifies four factors that explain constitutional replacements in democratic regimes,[15] and Chile displays all four of them: (1) the need to implement significant changes in the basic structures of the state to further democratization, and – in Chile's case – to revise and remove the remaining authoritarian enclaves mentioned earlier; (2) a context of political crisis, in Chile's case the social unrest in late 2019; (3) a shift in electoral allegiances

[9] ECLAC, *Social Panorama of Latin America 2018* (2019) 58.

[10] OECD, *Society at a Glance 2019: OECD Social Indicators* (OECD Publishing, 2019) 98.

[11] 'Income inequality' OECD Data: https://data.oecd.org/inequality/income-inequality.htm.

[12] 'Government spending' OECD Data: https://data.oecd.org/gga/general-government-spending.htm.

[13] S Verdugo and M Prieto, 'The Dual Aversion of Chile's Constitution-Making Process' (2021) 19 *International Journal of Constitutional Law* 149, 150–51.

[14] A Arato, 'Beyond the Alternative Reform or Revolution: Postsovereign Constitution-Marking and Latin America' (2015) 50 *Wake Forest Law Review* 891, 893.

[15] GL Negretto, 'New Constitutions in Democratic Regimes' in GL Negretto (ed), *Redrafting Constitutions in Democratic Regimes: Theoretical and Comparative Perspectives* (Cambridge, Cambridge University Press, 2020) 4–7.

and/or balance of power, as a result of which existing institutions no longer serve the interests of those with the power to change them; and (4) the need to modernise and potentially harmonise existing constitutional rules, which in the case of Chile were adopted for and by a regime that was very different from today's democracy.

When it comes to constitution-making, active participation can be as significant as the future content of the constitution; citizen engagement in constitutional processes can have a strong positive effect on deepening society's democratic credentials.[16] The democratic legitimacy of a constitution depends on the extent to which the opinions of those most affected by it are taken into account. In a democracy, only when participation is open, transparent, and meaningful, do citizens have reasons to see a constitutional settlement as their own, to take ownership even when they may not necessarily agree with everything the constitution says.[17] Beyond the symbolic or normative argument for direct citizen participation, the way the established political class, in government and in opposition, respond to the challenge matters enormously as well. Negretto's comparative analysis of constitutional reforms in democratic contexts shows that the combination of popular and elite-driven approaches can determine the success and sustainability of the democratic settlement after the adoption of a new constitution:

> Inclusive constitutional agreements at the level of representative elites not only establish legal limits on state action but may also provide opposition parties and citizens alike with the means to make institutional constraints on executive power and civil liberties effective.[18]

Chile's constitutional moment is a time of potential transformation for the country. In the 1970s, Chile became the first theatre of operations of neoliberalism.[19] In 2021, however, a majority of the elected members of the constitutional convention pledged to advocate for structural changes in the economic and political system and to support social rights, while right-wing parties obtained less than a third of the seats, diminishing the chances of a blocking minority.[20] Gender equality, better recognition of indigenous people, social rights, the protection

[16] TA Eisenstadt et al, *Constituents before Assembly: Participation, Deliberation, and Representation in the Crafting of New Constitutions* (Cambridge, Cambridge University Press, 2017).

[17] K Casla, 'The Democratic Case for Social Rights in Chile's Constitutional Moment' Petrie-Flom Center Harvard Law School (August 2020), https://blog.petrieflom.law.harvard.edu/2020/08/24/chile-constitution-social-rights-health/.

[18] GL Negretto, 'Constitution-Making and Liberal Democracy: The Role of Citizens and Representative Elites' (2020) 18 *International Journal of Constitutional Law* 206, 207.

[19] N Klein, *The Shock Doctrine: The Rise of Disaster Capitalism* (London, Penguin, 2007) ch 2.

[20] N Massai and B Miranda, 'La mitad de la convención: 77 constituyentes electos provienen de listas que impulsan cambios radicales al sistema' *Ciper* (May 2021), https://www.ciperchile.cl/2021/05/17/la-mitad-de-la-convencion-77-constituyentes-electos-provienen-de-listas-que-impulsan-cambios-radicales-al-sistema/.

of the environment and the deepening of democracy were particularly prominent among the 32,000 measures proposed by the 1,400 candidates standing for election to the convention.[21] As observed by Verdugo and Prieto, the 'aversion towards the economic model of the Pinochet Constitution also overlaps with the transformative undercurrent of the Chilean constitutional movement and its emphasis on social, economic, and cultural rights'.[22] Such democratic impetus shows that the defence of human rights in general, and social rights in particular, need not be solely the business of lawyers, academics, NGOs and international human rights bodies. In other words, Chile's constitutional moment is also the moment of the democratic case for social rights, where the constitutionalisation of social rights may represent the will of the people, in stark contrast with the 1980 Constitution, where neither social rights nor the will of the people mattered for the regime.

II. THE CONSTITUTIONALISATION OF SOCIAL RIGHTS

Social rights are proclaimed in a number of international human rights treaties, the most significant one being the 1966 International Covenant on Economic, Social and Cultural Rights, signed and ratified by Chile and more than 170 countries around the world. As a matter of international law, states have a responsibility to show how they give effect to these rights in their domestic legal order, including the provision of legal and judicial remedies.[23] Also, as a matter of international law, states may not invoke their internal law as a justification or an excuse for their failure to abide by their international human rights obligations (Article 27 of the Vienna Convention on the Law of Treaties).

Social rights can be made directly enforceable, just like any other human right, either via constitutional procedures or in ordinary courts. In addition to judicial enforceability, there are at least three other types of social rights provisions in comparative constitutional law. First, social rights can be constitutionalised as guiding principles of public policy, or non-enforceable policy commitments for public welfare. Second, constitutions may recognise social rights in such way that, although not explicitly made non-justiciable, judges nonetheless interpret them as not intended to create individual entitlements to judicial remedy. And third, social rights can embed the very formulation of the type of state, such as a 'social republic' (France) or a 'democratic and social state' (Germany

[21] Observatorio Nueva Constitución, 'Análisis de las propuestas constitucionales de los (as) candidatos (as) a convencionales ¿Cuáles son los principales temas del debate constitucional?' (May 2021) https://www.observatorionuevaconstitucion.cl/2021/05/13/observacion-n3/.

[22] S Verdugo and M Prieto, 'The Dual Aversion of Chile's Constitution-Making Process' (n 13) 156.

[23] UN CESCR, *General Comment No 9: The Domestic Application of the Covenant*, UN doc E/C.12/1998/24 (1998).

and Spain).[24] These types of provisions are not mutually exclusive. International and comparative practice shows that, even when social rights are not constitutionalised as directly enforceable rights in court, social rights can symbolically represent the rejection of a neoliberal agenda, and can provide an interpretive guidance for the application of private law (for example, in the case of the social function of private property when regulating the private rental sector).[25]

In 2013, at least 160 constitutions contained at least two economic and social rights, 26 of them as aspirational rights, 75 as justiciable rights, and 59 with a mixture of both. In 2016, environmental rights were present in 68 per cent of constitutions and were justiciable in 42 per cent, up from 53 per cent and 29 per cent respectively in 2000. In 2016, the right to health was judicially enforceable in 74 countries, 20 more than in 2000. The right to housing is present in 42 per cent of constitutions. Child protection, education, health and social security appear in more than two thirds of the world's constitutions, and are justiciable in at least 40 per cent of them. The right to education is present in 81 per cent of constitutions and is justiciable in 59 per cent. This is why Rosevear, Hirschl and Jung conclude that economic and social rights 'are not only more present in constitutions but they are also more likely to be justiciable than ever before'.[26]

One of the criticisms of the justiciability of social rights, particularly in the Latin American context, has been that giving judges power to adjudicate social rights has little transformative power, and may even be counterproductive. The critique argues that justiciability tends to favour those who are relatively affluent and have access to court, and does nothing or very little to address structural inequalities. The critique deserves to be taken seriously, and requires the appreciation of nuance, as each country is likely to present a very different reality in this regard. After all, as observed by Landau, 'we may continue to gain a more fruitful understanding of judicial politics by viewing judiciaries as integral parts of their own political regimes'.[27] At the same time, the literature on the welfare state has shown that the support of the middle-classes is essential to the sustainability of public services; similarly, broadening the base of support for universal social rights may require striving towards the combination of both less and more transformative outcomes from the justiciability of social rights.[28]

Liberal egalitarianism and autonomy-based arguments have been used to justify the need for social rights in the terrain of political theory. The proposition

[24] J King, 'Social Rights in Comparative Constitutional Theory' in G Jacobsohn and M Schor (eds), *Comparative Constitutional Theory* (Cheltenham, Edward Elgar, 2018) 159.

[25] Ibid, 166.

[26] E Rosevear et al, 'Justiciable and Aspirational Economic and Social Rights in National Constitutions' in KG Young, *The Future of Economic and Social Rights* (Cambridge, Cambridge University Press, 2019) 40.

[27] D Landau, 'Socioeconomic Rights and Majoritarian Courts in Latin America' in C Crawford and D Bonilla Maldonado (eds), *Constitutionalism in the Americas* (Cheltenham, Edward Elgar, 2018) 214.

[28] D Landau and R Dixon, 'Constitutional Non-Transformation?' in KG Young, *The Future of Economic and Social Rights* (Cambridge, Cambridge University Press, 2019) 125.

is that everyone needs access to certain material essentials that can enable him or her to become a free and autonomous individual, autonomy understood as the ability to make reasonable and rational decisions based on certain conceptions of standards of adequate behaviour.[29] King, for example, argues that the agency threshold:

> requires a bundle of resources and opportunities that gives persons a 'real possibility' to engage in basic life planning, including the capacity to frame and achieve long-term goals. The most abstract statement of the social minimum is that it must provide a material foundation of self-respect by making its attainment a real possibility.[30]

On the other hand, champions of the so-called democratic critique contend that constitutionalising social rights – giving judges too much power to adjudicate on social rights – presents a fundamental conflict with the separation of powers in a democratic society. In their opinion, judicial review of social rights is 'democratically illegitimate', as the substance of rights should be determined by democratically elected and accountable bodies; the legislature – and potentially the executive – would be best placed to resolve substantive disputes and conflicts of interest in society.[31]

The democratic critique of human rights is powerful, and it should be taken seriously by advocates, academics and policy actors involved in constitution-making. Two immediate responses are pertinent. First, besides ensuring the material conditions of freedom, the universal satisfaction of social rights can ensure that individuals can become citizens and make meaningful contributions to the community of which they are part. In this sense, in the 1940s, TH Marshall introduced the notion of 'social citizenship', presenting social rights as essential ingredients of citizenship and advocating for an egalitarian form of welfare based on reciprocal responsibilities between members of society.[32] More recently, Benhabib argued that a society that takes human rights seriously requires both a liberal defence of rights – understood as limits to state power – and a civic-republican vision of rights – as accountable power representing the will of the collective; 'Without the basic rights of the person, republican sovereignty would be blind; and without the exercise of collective autonomy, rights of the person would be empty'.[33]

Second, constitutionalising social rights does not take the authority away from democratically elected bodies. On the contrary, the fulfilment of social rights requires the involvement of all powers of the state, not only the judiciary.

[29] K Möller, 'Two Conceptions of Positive Liberty: Towards and Autonomy-based Theory of Constitutional Rights' (2009) 29 *Oxford Journal of Legal Studies* 757.

[30] King, 'Social Rights in Comparative Constitutional Theory' (n 24) 150.

[31] J Waldron, 'The Core of the Case against Judicial Review' (2006) 115 *Yale Law Journal* 1346.

[32] TH Marshall, *Citizenship and Social Class and Other Essays* (Cambridge, Cambridge University Press, 1950).

[33] S Benhabib, 'Reason-Giving and Rights-Bearing: Constructing the Subject of Rights' (2013) 20(1) *Constellations* 38, 46.

Countries exploring new forms of legal or constitutional enhancement of social rights should be encouraged to apply an incrementalist approach to judicial adjudication, so that all powers have the chance to enter into a form of dialogue over the merits and limits of judicial review of social rights. Such incrementalist approach requires caution and restraint from legal operators, particularly at the beginning, and sincere collaboration between judiciary, executive and legislature.[34] King's metaphor of social rights as capstone is a helpful one:

> I would argue that the idea of social rights as human or constitutional rights must be the crowning piece, the finishing touch (structural, not ornamental) on a broader institutional structure and system of supporting values that will make the real enjoyment of social rights a reality. The scholarly study of constitutional social rights in my view needs to be joined up to the fields of social policy, to political economy, to related fields of law such as labour, private and tax law and to a political philosophy that is a bit more elaborate about the questions and institutions for distributive justice than is even contemporary liberalism.[35]

That is the very spirit of collaboration, interdisciplinarity and epistemic humility that inspired this book.

III. THIS BOOK'S CONTRIBUTION

This book seizes Chile's constitutional moment as an opportunity to reflect about the contexts, merits and difficulties of enhancing the status of social rights in a country's basic text. This edited volume arose from collaboration between the Global Initiative for Economic, Social and Cultural Rights, the Human Rights Centre of the University of Essex in the UK, and the University of Concepción of Chile. In 2020 and 2021, this partnership brought together practitioners and academics from Chile and other countries (Argentina, Brazil, Canada, Colombia, Ireland, Mexico, South Africa, Spain, the United Kingdom and the United States) to share and learn from international and comparative practice with the goal of informing the ongoing process of constitutional reform in Chile. More than 30 contributions were compiled and submitted to members of the constitutional convention and other public authorities in Chile in September 2021.[36] The following chapters present an extended version of a selection of those essays.

Even today, the majority of comparative constitutional studies in the English language tend to focus on the United States and Europe, and the analysis of

[34] J King, 'The Future of Social Rights' in KG Young, *The Future of Economic and Social Rights* (Cambridge, Cambridge University Press, 2019) 317.

[35] Ibid, 315.

[36] Global Initiative for Economic, Social and Cultural Rights, Human Rights Centre of the University of Essex and University of Concepción (ed), *Derechos sociales y el momento constituyente de Chile: Perspectivas globales y locales para el debate constitucional* (GI-ESCR, 2021).

peripheral legal systems, when it exists, can be found only on the sidelines as a more or less blatant afterthought.[37] Unlike common practice in comparative constitutional law,[38] this book is anchored in Latin America, in Chile. The specific legal and political opportunity created in this country since 2019 is the very reason for the existence of this edited volume.

The first two chapters are devoted to the political economy of human rights. Bohoslavsky, Fernández and Smart trace the links between Pinochet's regime and the beneficiaries of today's structural inequalities in Chile. The authors show that the benefits of the Chilean economy were unevenly distributed and concentrated within a small and privileged minority. The dictatorship imposed and reproduced radical inequalities that were not challenged on democracy's return. In fact, income, wealth and power inequalities took root solidly during the transition and they are still standing: the economic accomplices of the regime benefited from past and present inequalities. Such a socio-economic outlook explains, in the authors' opinion, why the 1980 Constitution is one of the weakest in the region in terms of the recognition and protection of social rights. Bohoslavsky, Fernández and Smart argue that the current process of constitutional reform requires a profound reconsideration of the distribution of resources as a matter of accountability of the economic accomplices of Pinochet's dictatorship.

Moya and Salgado also look at the relationship between economic policy, the constitution and human rights. The authors focus primarily on the role that the 1980 Constitution – and its interpretation by legal operators – played in the development of neoliberal economic policies in the last four decades. Moya and Salgado end their chapter with a proposal for a new and open constitution for Chile.

Alongside the lessons to be learned from Chile's rich constitutional history, trends in constitutional drafting globally can offer valuable insights for the country's process of constitutional reform. Sprague, Stek, Raub and Heymann present conclusions from a large cross-national comparative analysis of different approaches to the constitutionalisation of the right to equality around the world. Their chapter provides a global overview of the different strategies pursued in 193 countries to recognise equality and non-discrimination in relation to sex/gender, race/ethnicity, language, religion, socio-economic status,

[37] Very good exceptions must be noted: R Gargarella et al (eds), *Courts and Social Transformation in New Democracies: An Institutional Voice for the Poor?* (Farnham, Ashgate, 2006); V Gauri and DM Brinks (eds), *Courting Social Justice: Judicial Enforcement of Social and Economic Rights in the Developing World* (Cambridge University Press, 2008); D Bonilla Maldonado (ed), *Constitutionalism of the Global South: The Activist Tribunals of India, South Africa, and Colombia* (Cambridge, Cambridge University Press, 2013); C Rodríguez-Garavito and D Rodríguez-Franco, *Radical Deprivation on Trial: The Impact of Judicial Activism on Socioeconomic Rights in the Global South* (Cambridge, Cambridge University Press, 2015); D Landau and H Lerner (eds), *Comparative Constitution Making* (Cheltenham, Edward Elgar, 2019); P Dann et al (eds), *The Global South and Comparative Constitutional Law* (Oxford, Oxford University Press, 2020).

[38] M Tushnet, 'Comparative Constitutional Law' in M Reimann and R Zimmermann (eds), *The Oxford Handbook of Comparative Law*, 2nd edn (Oxford, Oxford University Press, 2019).

disability, migration, sexual orientation and gender identity. The chapter uses cases from around the world to highlight how constitutions have been used to advance equality for people at the margins, identifying where countries are making progress towards achieving equal rights and where progress is stalling or critical gaps remain that undermine equal opportunities.

The next three chapters draw lessons for the judicial enforceability of social rights in South Africa, Colombia and the Inter-American human rights system, respectively. First, Liebenberg reflects on the aspirations, achievements, disappointments and lessons from the constitutionalisation of social rights in South Africa. The country's 1996 constitution was enacted with the aim of laying the foundations for the construction of a post-apartheid society based on social justice, improving the quality of life of all citizens, and unlocking the potential of each person. Central to this aspiration was the inclusion of a set of judicially enforceable socio-economic rights in the constitutional bill of rights. Liebenberg's chapter tracks the debates and struggles surrounding the inclusion of socio-economic rights in the South African constitution, the achievements, as well as the limitations of their constitutional entrenchment. The author draws a set of conclusions regarding what constitutional projects such as Chile's, which for some shares a similar transformative aspiration, can learn from South Africa's unfinished experiment with justiciable socio-economic rights.

Newman focuses on one of the youngest rights in comparative constitutional law: the right to access information. Colombia's 1991 constitution recognised this right for the first time not only as a fundamental right in itself, but also as an instrument to participate, seek accountability and guarantee other human rights, including social rights. Relying on both Colombian and Inter-American case law, Newman presents the transit of access to information from an ordinary right in administrative law to a fundamental human right. The author shows the significance of access to information for social rights in a case study by concentrating on the value of transparency in the criteria of beneficiaries of a social assistance programme in the midst of the Covid-19 pandemic. This example evinces, the author contends, that by making information available to the public, citizens are empowered to question schemes called to protect and fulfil social rights, holding public authorities to account over the implementation of such schemes.

Rossi looks at the evolving case law in the Inter-American human rights system in relation to the justiciability of economic, social and cultural rights, and its impact on domestic legal systems in the Americas. The author identifies different phases in the Inter-American jurisprudence with a particular focus on *Lagos del Campo v Peru* (2017) and *Comunidades Indígenas de la Asociación Lhaka Honhat (Nuestra Tierra) v Argentina* (2020). In these cases, the Inter-American Court of Human Rights changed direction from its previous approach, and declared the violation of Article 26 of the American Convention on Human Rights, on economic, social and cultural rights, which traditionally had not been considered directly justiciable. Rossi's chapter presents some of the ups and downs in the evolution of the Inter-American approach to the justiciability of socio-economic rights, including the opportunities and challenges to translate this evolving jurisprudence onto the domestic legal contexts in Latin America.

The following two chapters pay attention to persons with disabilities, one of the latest social groups to be recognised by international law as particularly vulnerable to human rights abuses. Moreno, Stein and Heymann provide a global overview of the different strategies that national constitutions in 193 countries take to guaranteeing equality and non-discrimination, social rights and other human rights for persons with disabilities. Using the UN Convention on the Rights for Persons with Disabilities as the normative framework, the chapter evaluates the current state of constitutional protection for persons with disabilities worldwide, describing how these protections have changed over time, and emphasising both success stories and remaining gaps. To make it most relevant for Chile's ongoing process, the chapter focuses especially on changes in countries that have enacted new constitutions after ratifying or acceding to the UN Convention, adopted in 2006 and in force since 2008. The chapter also includes a selection of cases from courts around the world to illustrate how constitutional provisions have been used to advance equality, highlighting the importance that constitutional guarantees, or their absence, have for the implementation of rights and freedoms for persons with disabilities.

For their part, Marshall, Ponce de León and Marchant address the conditions for effective political participation of persons with disabilities in Chile's constitution-making process, as well as the potential of such process to achieve a more inclusive constitution for persons with disabilities. On the basis of the UN Convention on the Rights of Persons with Disabilities, the chapter introduces the conceptual framework that identifies the opportunities and difficulties that such participation entails. The authors reflect about the possible outcome of a constitution-making process that includes norms advancing the cause of inclusion, respect, support and accessibility for persons with disability.

The book concludes with a selection of chapters that delve into what the constitutionalisation of social rights may mean in relation to laws and policies on education, housing, health, social security and the environment.

Henríquez offers an overview of the main transformations in Chile's educational laws over recent decades to contextualise the constitutional debate and the origins of the education system in place. The author focuses on three milestones: first, the changes introduced during the dictatorship in the 1970s and 1980s; second, the approach to education of the first democratic governments in the early 1990s, characterised, according to Henríquez, by a continuity policy; and third, the modifications introduced under President Bachelet (2006–10 and 2014–18). The author finally presents a series of proposals that could strengthen the role of the state as a guarantor of the right to education.

The national focus is complemented by the international analysis presented by Contreras, Silva and Dorsi. Their chapter explores the potential impact of implementing in Chile the 2019 Abidjan Principles on the human rights obligations of states to provide public education and to regulate private involvement in education. The authors' review of international human rights standards and comparative constitutional practice examines the possibilities of enshrining the right to a free and public education of excellent quality in the next constitution.

Casla and Valenzuela concentrate on the right to adequate housing as part of the right to an adequate standard of living. The first section presents the content and significance of this right in light of international and comparative law, with examples from Mexico, Spain, Germany, the Netherlands and the UK. In the second half, the chapter explores some of the legal and policy implications of enhancing the status of the right to adequate housing in Chile's new constitution, specifically in relation to the responsibilities of housing developers, the legal recognition of the social function of housing and homeownership, and the need to protect tenants with strong habitability standards and security of tenure in the private rental sector.

Zúñiga-Fajuri makes the case for the constitutionalisation of the right to healthcare as a social right. The author argues that health efficiency principles cannot be used in all decisions concerning the allocation of health-related resources, as such an approach leads to greater health inequalities. Based on an analysis of the evolving approaches to health theory and practice in the country, Zúñiga-Fajuri defends a liberal egalitarian model for the distribution and application of health resources, which in the author's view, will make it possible to introduce the required changes to achieve the objectives of equity and efficiency.

In her chapter, Barrantes explores the potential opportunities of incorporating social security as a right into the new Chilean constitution. Relying on international human rights principles, Barrantes examines the role social security can play through its redistributive capacity, contributing towards wellbeing, poverty reduction, increased cohesiveness and social inclusion. Together with a comparative look at constitutions in other Latin American countries, the analysis draws a series of recommendations within the particular context of Chile.

Although institutional progress has been made in recent years, Delgado and Hervé argue in the last chapter that policy efforts have fallen short in the protection of the environment. The difficulties and challenges Chile is facing are not mere issues of good governance. The authors contend that the issues will not go away with ad hoc legislation on water resources, glaciers, biodiversity, land management, forestry or fisheries. The current constitutional framework and interpretations have undermined the necessary reforms. To bring about a truly transformative shift in society, Delgado and Hervé write, Chile requires a fairer, greener constitution.

2

Yesterday's Accomplices, Beneficiaries of Today: The Knots of Inequality Tied by the Dictatorship

JUAN PABLO BOHOSLAVSKY, KARINNA FERNÁNDEZ AND SEBASTIÁN SMART*

I. INTRODUCTION

THE 1973 MILITARY coup, the consolidation of the dictatorship government and the atrocities that it committed had the purpose of creating the necessary conditions for the implementation of economic policies that would benefit a minority in the country and abroad, and consequently, would be rejected by a large part of the population.[1] The rationale of the dictatorship was primarily economic, with a view to the reconfiguration of social and labour relations. The strong redistributive bid that started all over the world in the seventies, exacerbated by the implications of the Cold War for the region, became a reality in Chile.

In this chapter, we will explore the role that both national and foreign key economic actors played during General Augusto Pinochet's dictatorship; how and why the economic policies implemented during the dictatorship reconfigured the country's economic framework, facilitating and deepening the levels of inequality still present in Chile; and why and how the new constitution should untie this knot in order to guarantee accountability, reduce the levels of inequality and ensure the fulfilment of economic and social rights of the whole of Chile's population.

The importance of discussing economic complicity in Chile and its relationship with current social and economic injustices is fundamental, due to several

* The authors would like to thank Victoria Basualdo for her commentary on this text's draft. The opinions and conclusions reflected by this chapter belong solely to its authors and in no way to the institutions to which they are affiliated.

[1] N Klein, *The Shock Doctrine: The Rise of Disaster Capitalism* (London, Penguin, 2007).

facts.[2] First, the country was considered for many years the *poster child* of how neoliberalism and authoritarianism together could produce a positive outcome for society. Second, there was rampant corruption present during the dictatorship, and the links between the systematic plundering of the state during the dictatorial government and the deep deficits of state services that have prevailed during the democratic period have been insufficiently studied. Finally, the failure to consider corporate complicity, as well as the way in which the economic policies contributed to social exclusion, generated a narrow view of what human rights entail, marginalising economic and social rights, all of which crystallised in the 1980 Constitution which now a great part of society is attempting to reform.

II. ECONOMIC COMPLICITY AND INEQUALITY

Authoritarian governments suffer from a structural deficit of legitimacy; therefore, their remaining in power is subject to the balanced use of two types of instruments: (1) strategically allocating economic resources, by trying to purchase loyalties and support from key sectors of society; and (2) repressing certain sectors of society or granting civil and political freedoms in an opportunistic way in order to minimise criticism.[3] Buying people's trust and establishing an efficient repressive apparatus both require financial resources. How did this dynamic of rational choices and statistical assumptions operate during the Pinochet dictatorship?[4]

First, Pinochet's government obtained massive external financing thanks to its immediate international geopolitical alignment in the fight against communism. This ensured a continuous and sufficient flow of funds even in a context of low growth, high unemployment, and fiscal deficit.[5]

Domestically, the instruments and channels through which financial resources were allocated strategically, ie in order to gain the support of powerful sectors in Chilean society, included new policies regarding labour, taxation, budget, industry, forestry, mining, banking and finance, urban development, prisons, social security, foreign trade, and the privatisation of state-owned enterprises. The common denominators of said policies were the economic benefits granted to Chilean elites as well as to national and transnational companies, which fostered

[2] N Roht-Arriaza, 'The Belated Centrality of the Economic Dimension in Transitional Justice' in JP Bohoslavsky et al (eds), *Pinochet's Economic Accomplices: An Unequal Country by Force* (London, Lexington, 2020).

[3] B Bueno de Mesquita et al, *The Logic of Political Survival* (Massachusetts, MIT Press, 2003); R Wintrobe, *The Political Economy of Dictatorship* (Cambridge, Cambridge University Press, 1998).

[4] A recently edited book by the authors studies this issue of the role of economic actors during Pinochet's dictatorship in detail. See Bohoslavsky et al (n 2).

[5] JP Bohoslavsky and M Rulli, 'Unraveling the financial assistance to the Pinochet's regime' in Bohoslavsky et al (n 2).

inequality in the country, and were usually reciprocated by a complicit role or at least a condescending attitude towards the regime.[6]

Clearly, the military had its own ideological and political agenda for accessing and remaining in power: utterly defeating the left, re-establishing social order, reconfiguring labour relations, depoliticising the masses and increasing the budget for its own sector. From this perspective, the military appears to have used the economic sector as a tool to stay in power. However, a closer look at that dynamic – which includes, for example, the fact that some of Pinochet's executive officials were the representatives of the very sectors being benefited by the government – will show us how difficult it is to determine the origins of the causative chain: was the government implementing policies that benefited certain economic sectors so that it could remain in power, or were these sectors supporting Pinochet (and they were doing it before the coup) so that he would implement these policies? The answer to this question can lead us to rethink who the accomplices in this situation were.

Economic crimes that greatly benefited military personnel, civilians and businesspeople were another efficient tool for allocating resources and purchasing loyalties. The latter became a reality, for example, in the explicit political support for the government shown by the business chambers or, at the very least, their silence in the face of the crimes against humanity which were being committed. The complicity of journalists, the media, think tanks and academics can be explained as well not only by their clear ideological and political alignment but also by the material benefits they were receiving.

Doubtlessly the radical and rapid transfer of national wealth (after the civic-military coup d'état) in favour of the dominant business groups and to the detriment of the working class, which brought on an abrupt increase of socio-economic inequality, was the result of the imposition of neoliberal economic policies. Discontent was contained with extreme state violence against trade union representatives and with a serious weakening of workers' collective bargaining power, which resulted in a clear deterioration of their working conditions (including their salary). As noted,

> The high levels of inequality in Chile today have their roots in an extremely repressive political context and are the result of a radical transformation of the economic system. In the new institutional framework established by the dictatorship, those who made political decisions did so in a way which entailed a regressive distribution of both the economic benefits and damages that stemmed from circumstantial situations and structural transformations.[7]

[6] The notion of economic accomplices that underlies this text exceeds by far the corruption and illicit enrichment cases from the Riggs Bank scandal. It entails, as explained by the International Commission of Jurists in 2008, the contributions that 'make possible, facilitate or improve the efficacy' of the commission of crimes: International Commission of Jurists, *Corporate Complicity & Legal Accountability* (ICJ, vol I, 2008) 9 ff.

[7] J Rodríguez Weber, 'Promoting and Ensuring Inequality: The Distributive Consequences of the Dictatorship' in Bohoslavsky et al (n 2).

The increase of inequality was not caused by the free operation of supply and demand but by strict economic, social and criminal policies (repression of the trade union movement) the most prominent being the legal obstruction and violent repression of work-related demands and union strikes, the privatisation (and commodification) of key services and companies in the economy with strong social implications (such as health and education), and a monetary, financial and budgetary policy plan with regressive results, particularly during crises.[8]

Growing inequality in Chile caused, among several other damaging effects to society, a rise in unemployment and a drop in real wages. Furthermore, the decrease in social spending caused a slowdown in the improvements of the education and health systems, which had characterised the 1940–1970 period. These structural reforms, implemented during the Pinochet regime, explain the strong resistance that democratic governments and the trade union movement still face in their attempt to prevent Chile from being one of the most unequal countries in the world.

The case of the pension fund administrators (Administradoras de Fondos de Pensiones, AFP) is paradigmatic.[9] An observation of the process and consequences (even today) of the privatisation of the Chilean pension system in 1980, which was carried out without social dialogue or political involvement of workers or trade unions, reveals how this reform directly benefited and strengthened a Chilean economic elite linked with the international financial groups that owned the AFPs. The only sector of the workforce that was not forced to adopt the new system was the Armed Forces. The transition from one system to the other implied a massive rise in fiscal expenditure for the state, higher administrative costs for affiliates, limited and unequal coverage for the general population, a slowdown in the development of capital markets, enormous profits for AFPs and high market concentration in that sector. All of this constitutes one of the costliest legacies passed on by the dictatorship, and accounts for a large part of the current economic and social inequality in the country.

Moreover, the Chilean extractivist model, as it is known today, originated during Pinochet's dictatorship and, in essence, continues to this day.[10] Those economic actors entered the mining business with Pinochet and have become stronger over the last few decades, which explains the close link that still exists between extractivism, state capture and concentrated appropriation of rent in that sector.

[8] Ibid.

[9] M Rulli, 'A Cat with No Bell. The Privatization of the Chilean Pension System during Pinochet's Dictatorship' in Bohoslavsky et al (n 2).

[10] S Smart, 'Extractivism as a Policy: from its Dictatorial Origins to its Democratic Continuity' in Bohoslavsky et al (n 2); J Stillerman, 'Class Conflict and the Ascent of Globalized Business Groups Under Chile's Dictatorship: A Case Study of the Copper Manufacturing Industry' in VA Basualdo et al (eds), *Big Business and Dictatorships in Latin America: A Transnational History of Profits and Repression* (London, Palgrave Macmillan, 2021) 263.

The explanation of how and why Pinochet's dictatorship carried out a broad and unprecedented process of land and state companies' privatisation, operating in a large number of different sectors of the economy, and the social and economic consequences that this process brought forth, makes evident the regression that took place, especially when comparing this with the previous period of greater state participation in the economy, and how the number of state-owned companies went from 596 at the beginning of the dictatorship to only 49 in 1989.[11] Between 1974 and 1978 approximately 350 companies that had been nationalised by the democratic government were restituted to their original owners, between 1976 and 1981 several companies that were controlled by CORFO (Corporación de Fomento de la producción de Chile – Production development corporation) were auctioned, and after the 1982 crisis a process known as *popular capitalism* began, which entailed the sale of shares from the main state-owned companies in order to strengthen the capital market, and the reprivatisation of banks and pension funds. This process of privatisation generated a huge concentration of wealth and income, and an underfinanced state, all of which has contributed to the current inequality rates. These privatisations were plagued by irregularities, gross conflicts of interest and acts of corruption which were detrimental to the national treasury and benefited the concentrated corporate groups that were close to the government, as well as the military and public officers. The violent conquest of the state apparatus and the consequent opacity in the handling of public funds, the lack of freedom of the press and the absence of State counter-powers all made this massive privatisation process possible.

In the same line we should also put a spotlight on the depth, breadth, and social, economic and political implications of the erosion of workers' rights and union activity.[12] Pinochet's regime imposed, in a highly repressive context against the working class, legal changes which consistently attacked union rights, all with the common denominator of undermining workers' collective rights.[13] The so called 'Labour Plan' (Plan Laboral) of 1979 entailed a decentralisation and weakening of collective bargaining in companies, the creation of instruments to guarantee that strikes did not paralyse economic activity, the atomisation and depoliticisation of unions even within a company and a reduction of their reach and negotiating capabilities. The pillars of this (anti)union reform have remained practically intact until today, even after the reform of the 20,940 law of 2016.[14]

The degradation of workers' collective rights was paired with an undermining of those individual rights which determined working conditions, redundancy

[11] S Smart, 'Privatization and Repression: Two Sides of the Same Coin' in Bohoslavsky et al (n 2).

[12] Á Vergara and P Winn, '"The Employers Do What They Want with Us": Unions and Workers under the Pinochet Dictatorship' in Bohoslavsky et al (n 2).

[13] D Marzi, 'Union Law: Anti-Unionism as a Neoliberal Victory' in Bohoslavsky et al (n 2).

[14] Vergara and Winn (n 12).

pay and working hours, among others, and was backed by a fierce and unpunished persecution of union leaders. This form of repression and labour policy correlates and is consistent with the imposition of a neoliberal economic model that resulted in the exclusion of the majority of the population and the enrichment of a few select business groups. The deregulation of the labour market and the weakening of trade union activity, which is reflected in the constantly lowering rates of unionisation in the country, were two of the most entrenched legacies in the transition from dictatorship to democracy.[15]

The Pinochet government's repressive urban policy with regard to the development of Santiago was based on the use of eviction, segregation and violence as tools to increase profits for certain concentrated corporate groups and to ensure that the wealthiest people had exclusive access to the city's most valuable land.[16] Through taxation and public policies which aimed for social control by managing the transformation of the city, and were introduced by force through the state's repressive regime when necessary, repressive city planning became a feature of Santiago. Real-estate was blatantly handed over to the market which generated (and continues to generate) huge income for the developers, at the expense of the violent displacement of thousands of impoverished residents to the periphery of the city who, if they were lucky, ended up with a ramshackle house and access to basic services. All of this further fuelled the socio-economic segregation of the city, in which the horizontal, democratic and humanitarian components have had a marginal effect.

The national mining model imposed by the dictatorship still has deep (negative) social, cultural and natural resources related implications for local communities in northern Chile.[17] The legal and institutional platform forged during the Pinochet administration and reinforced during democracy, which extensively commodifies the extraction of minerals and the use of water, has made it easier for the mining sector to put pressure on the northern communities in order to exploit their water resources both above and below ground. The case of the mining company Sociedad Química y Minera (SQM) in the Atacama Desert is presented in detail, a company that grew its business (and power) during the dictatorship but that was not weakened in democracy, and that for many years was administered by one of Pinochet's sons-in-law.

The counter-reform of the forestry industry brought about by the Pinochet government must also be mentioned, as well as how it still adversely affects the rights of the Mapuche people, the environment, and the socio-economic indicators of the regions involved.[18] The country's large forestry companies supported

[15] P Winn (ed), *Victims of the Chilean Miracle. Workers and Neoliberalism in the Pinochet Era, 1973–2002* (Durham, NC, Duke University Press, 2004).

[16] F Vergara Perucich, 'Pinochet's Repressive Urbanism: The Violent Neoliberalisation of Space in Santiago' in Bohoslavsky et al (n 2).

[17] C Olmos Herrera, 'Autonomy in Times of Economic Complicity: Mining Expansion and Water Practices in Northern Chile' in Bohoslavsky et al (n 2).

[18] J Aylwin, 'Corporate Complicity in Human Rights Violations in Chile: The Case of Forestry Companies and the Mapuche People' in Bohoslavsky et al (n 2).

the coup, and subsequently the dictatorship, with the expectation that Allende's policy regarding this sector, which was geared towards the state management of forestry resources, would be reversed. There were also many high-ranking public officials of the regime that came from the forestry industry. All this support resulted in a substantial expansion of the territories that they owned, many of which were traditionally inhabited by the Mapuche people, and generous financing through state subsidies and exemptions. Large forestry conglomerates also benefited by being able to purchase state businesses at a fraction of their market value. Some of these businesses became involved in criminal repression against their own workers. Despite the fact that the Mapuche people's social protest against the persistence of this industrial forestry model has been growing in the last 20 years, and ghas arnered increasing support from regional and international organisations, crimes and repression against them have intensified.

III. COMPLICITY, ECONOMIC AND SOCIAL RIGHTS, AND THE NEW CONSTITUTION

So far, we have described how the economic complicity that bolstered the dictatorship has deepened and consolidated an extremely unequal country characterised by social exclusion. This has become the reality of many of its inhabitants, who experience a perpetual inequality regarding wealth and income, access to education, health and social security and other economic and social rights, on top of the meagre retirement pensions that most people receive. These circumstances have resulted in a social upheaval led by workers, students and environmentalists as well as an indebted middle class who no longer had any power or influence. These actors are challenging the neoliberal project, and the tension between an unequal economy and an effective democracy is again under the spotlight of the national public debate.[19]

It is not by chance that the sectors of society which have been hit hardest by the social and health crisis[20] that Chile is undergoing are the poorest ones; those who have had to survive under the burden of an unemployment rate which, in combination with the potential workforce, has reached a historic peak of 26 per cent, while the country's corporate groups have seen their wealth increase by 25 per cent on average during the first semester of 2020.[21] This gross income inequality has its roots in the dictatorship's imposition of policies which fostered the concentration of wealth and limited democratic access to

[19] M Ahumada and A Solimano, 'The Chilean Economic Model and Its Subordinate Democracy' in Bohoslavsky et al (n 2).

[20] Instituto Nacional de Derechos Humanos, *Informe Anual 2020: Covid y derechos humanos en Chile* (INDH, 2020) 40–41.

[21] '*Piñera y viuda de Luksic entre ellos: Cinco multimillonarios en Chile aumentaron su fortuna durante la pandemia*' *El Desconcierto*, www.eldesconcierto.cl/economia/2020/12/29/pinera-y-viuda-de-luksic-entre-ellos-cinco-multimillonarios-en-chile-aumentaron-su-fortuna-durante-la-pandemia.html.

resources and their distribution, a trend that grew during the democratic transition governments.

When we speak of inequality, we are not only and exclusively referring to income inequality, but also to an unequal structure which entails advantages for some and disadvantages for others, and which is associated with an intersectional discrimination that, in many cases, is the source of social discontent.[22] An inequality that is evidenced by low wages, job insecurity, unequal access to land depending on one's last name, social violence – mostly related to gender or class – or a justice system that tends to impose punitive measures on those with fewer resources. And regardless of the fact that inequalities have existed throughout all of the country's history, it is possible to establish a clear link of path dependence between Pinochet's dictatorship and the current situation. This forcibly implemented inequality has persisted through every democratically elected government.

One distinctive feature of Chile's inequality is the excessive concentration of wealth in the richest one per cent.[23] Despite the growing amount of evidence, surveys such as the National Socioeconomic Characterization Survey (*Caracterización Socio Económica Nacional – CASEN*) do not often reflect this situation. In order to complement these types of surveys, in November of 2020 Mauricio De Rosa, Ignacio Flores and Marc Morgan presented a few preliminary conclusions from the new series on income inequality in Latin America.[24] These show that inequality is very high in the region, and that official measurements based only on survey data, such as CASEN in Chile, underestimate it. The authors augment the survey's data with information about taxes and national accounts so as to paint a clearer picture of the real level of inequality in Latin America. Thus, they conclude that in the region, those in the top 10 per cent income bracket capture 54 per cent of the national income, which makes it one of the most unequal regions in the world. Chile leads this ranking, its top 10 per cent bracket captures 60 per cent of the average national income (2019).[25] This obviously leads to important consequences in the field of social and economic rights realisation, which are closely dependent on the availability of material resources.

Even though Chile has a long history of wealth concentration in the hands of corporate groups, it was the neoliberal imposition of Pinochet's dictatorship that strengthened this model.[26] In fact, during the 1950s the accumulated wealth

[22] UNDP, *Desiguales. Orígenes, cambios y desafíos de la brecha social en Chile* (UNDP, 2017).
[23] Ibid.
[24] M De Rosa et al, *Inequality in Latin America Revisited: Insights from Distributional National Accounts*, World Inequality Lab – Issue Brief 2020/09, 2020.
[25] Ibid.
[26] C Huneeus and T Undurraga, 'Authoritarian Rule and Economic Groups in Chile: A Case of Winner-Takes-All Politics' in VA Basualdo et al (eds), *Big Business and Dictatorships in Latin America: A Transnational History of Profits and Repression* (London, Palgrave Macmillan, 2021) 263–89.

of the large corporate groups in the country (such as Matte, Edwards, Claude and Yarur) accounted for 7.3 per cent of the Gross Domestic Product (GDP). In 1970 this proportion was 5.3 per cent. However, after the first privatising waves (towards the end of the 1970s) the most important groups in the country accumulated 17.1 per cent of the GDP. Near the end of the dictatorship, the groups Angelini, Matte, CAP, Luksic, Claro, Lecaros and ENERSIS accounted for 18.1 per cent of the GDP. This happened despite the relative infancy of the idea of investment holding companies in the pre-1990 era.[27]

In order to achieve this degree of concentration the previously mentioned legal advantages and privatisations, led by the dictatorship and aimed at helping business groups, were not enough; a criminal alliance between these actors was also required.[28] For example, the Claro group, which was one of the most important ones at the end of the 1970s, controlled Elecmetal, a company that according to the Rettig report provided information to Carabineros (Chile's national law enforcement police) which was used in the forced disappearance of union members.[29] This same Claro group controlled the Compañía Sudamericana de Vapores (a Chilean shipping company which is currently one of largest companies of its type in Latin America) which lent their ships Maipo and Lebu for the transportation of political prisoners during the dictatorship. Agustín Edwards, the owner of Chile's main newspaper, was a key CIA informant and collaborated with the generation of the coup d'etat, as has been declassified in historical files from the US.[30] The relation between the Edwards group and the dictatorship is widely documented, not only the way in which they benefited from major privatisations, but also because Agustín Edwards' direct advisory team at the highest level had direct links with the dictatorship, for example through Enrique Montero Marx, Pinochet's former Interior Minister, Sergio de Castro Spikula, former Economy Minister, or Maurice Poisson Eastman, former vice admiral of the Chilean Navy. It is also not coincidental that the upper echelons of Edwards' current advisory team of executives include seven former ministers and two undersecretaries of Pinochet.[31]

The dictatorship not only fostered path dependence on corporate groups which accumulate wealth, but also put in place an economic system that encourages the concentration of political power. In fact, Chile has historically

[27] A Aguirre Briones, *Los grupos económicos chilenos en perspectiva histórica: entre la industrialización sustitutiva de importaciones y el neoliberalismo 1938–1988* (doctoral thesis, Universitat de Barcelona, 2017).

[28] K Fernández Neira and M Garcés Fuentes, 'Pesquera Arauco and Colonia Dignidad cases' in Bohoslavsky et al (n 2).

[29] Comisión Nacional de Verdad y Reconciliación, *Informe de la Comisión Nacional de Verdad y Reconciliación* (1990) Tomo 1, 143.

[30] CA Moscoso, 'The Media during the Dictatorship' in Bohoslavsky et al (n 2) 184.

[31] M Délano et al, 'La mayoría de los ejecutivos claves del Grupo Edwards perteneció a la dictadura de Pinochet', interferencia.cl/articulos/la-mayoria-de-los-ejecutivos-claves-del-grupo-edwards-pertenecio-la-dictadura-de-pinochet.

experienced an excessively vertical and centralised democratic process, which has benefited mostly the country's elite. This political model, which was enshrined in the country's constitution, can be seen in the excessive powers concentrated by the presidency and the limited political space attributed to civil society,[32] which lacks any sort of mechanism for scrutinising the appointment of diverse authorities that are not democratically elected. This political model appears to please the corporate groups, who have not only become important actors in the political arena, but have also managed to preserve an economic-political model widely known as a form of hierarchical capitalism.[33]

These fraudulent methods have endured through the democratic transition governments and are evidenced by the overrepresentation of the upper class in public office, High Courts, the media and the funding of Chile's politics. In fact, until 2016 anonymous or confidential contributions for the campaigns of individual candidates were allowed, from both natural and legal persons. Moreover, besides these – murky but legal – contributions, a number of companies and business groups created an illegal circuit of political funding. The cases of Penta, SOQUIMICH and Corpesca, among others, have made it easier for socioeconomic inequalities to translate into differences of representation for social groups in decision-making spaces.[34]

Precisely the same corporate groups who benefited from the dictatorship's economic policies are the ones who have supported a political system which denies redistribution. The country's pre-tax inequality rate is 0.49 in the Gini coefficient, and only drops three points after taxes, transfer payments, and social security mechanisms, much below the 14-point average drop for OECD countries, and intermediate in the context of Latin America, where it is higher than Mexico's or Costa Rica's, but lower than countries such as Argentina or Brazil.[35] In addition to this picture of inequality, there exists a completely segmented system of access to economic and social rights. According to a 2017 report by the UNDP:

> [I]n Chile the poorest sector of the population has access to services offered by the State in public institutions and which have quality issues (education) or long waits (health), the middle sectors preferably access private services of better quality, which are co-funded by them and the state (private subsidized education, free choice system – Atención de Libre Elección – at Fonasa) and the high-income sectors acquire private services of higher quality and cost that are not state-funded.[36]

[32] D Carruthers, 'Environmental Politics in Chile: Legacies of Dictatorship and Democracy' (2001) 22(3) *Third World Quarterly* 343.

[33] B Ross Schneider, *Hierarchical Capitalism in Latin America: Business, Labor, and the Challenges of Equitable Development* (Cambridge, Cambridge University Press, 2012).

[34] UNDP, *Desiguales* (n 22) 379.

[35] A Repetto, 'Gini: ¿Estado o mercado?' www.espaciopublico.cl/gini-estado-o-mercado/; UNDP (n 22) 38.

[36] UNDP (n 22) 39.

The causes that led to the constituent process are varied and probably somewhat related to the previously mentioned inequalities. A research team from the United Nations High Commissioner for Human Rights reported socioeconomic inequality and obstacles to the realisation of economic and social rights as the main cause of social discontent.[37]

In that context, 18 October 2019 represents a watershed moment in the history of human rights in Chile. While the corporate groups, represented by SOFOFA,[38] insisted that they 'did not see coming' the number of demonstrations,[39] the government decided to use a degree of force which had not been seen since the dictatorship, and to openly declare that it was 'at war against a powerful enemy'.[40] It is precisely against the backdrop of serious and massive human rights violations that the Agreement for Social Peace and a New Constitution of 15 November 2019 developed. It puts Chile in a historic situation: for the first time in the history of the country the rules under which its democratic life will unfold are going to be written collectively and democratically.

> The agreement to write a new constitution took place in a climate of social unrest due both to the violence that had been carried out by the state as well as to deeply rooted inequalities. This is why the constituent process that Chile is undergoing cannot be separated from the social demands raised during the massive demonstrations, or from the search for truth, justice and reparation in the cases of past and present human rights violations and complicity.

Therefore, those who draft the new constitution should embrace as one of their main goals the acknowledgment and fulfilment of economic and social rights. The first step, we believe, should be to explicitly acknowledge economic and social rights. The current constitution's subsidiary model considers issues such as health, education, social security, water and natural resources, among others, as market goods, with the well-known adverse effects that this has on the enjoyment of human rights. Moreover, the 1980 Constitution does not enshrine key rights, such as the right to adequate housing. Consequently, the priority should be the express recognition of economic and social rights in the new constitution, in accordance with international human rights law standards, which entail, for example, the recognition of the prohibition of discrimination and regression

[37] OHCHR, United Nations Human Rights Office of the High Commissioner, *Report of the Mission to Chile 30 October–22 November 2019*, www.ohchr.org/Documents/Countries/CL/Report_Chile_2019_EN.pdf.

[38] Sociedad de Fomento Fabril is a not-for-profit trade federation that brings together companies and associations linked to the Chilean industrial sector. It brings together nearly 4,000 companies, 47 sectorial associations and 22 regional business associations, available at https://sofofa.cl/.

[39] C Portilla, 'Piñera reconoce que estallido social "no lo vi venir" y acusa "ola de violencia sistemática, profesional, organizada"' *La Tercera* (12 December 2019) www.latercera.com/politica/noticia/pinera-confiesa-no-vio-venir-estallido-social-acusa-ola-violencia-sistematica-profesional-organizada/935757/.

[40] CNN Chile, Piñera: 'Estamos en guerra contra un enemigo poderoso' www.dw.com/es/pi%C3%B1era-estamos-en-guerra-contra-un-enemigo-poderoso/a-50910426.

in any subject related to economic and social rights, the obligation to allocate resources for their progressive fulfilment, and the interdependence and indivisibility of all human rights.

A change in the economic model's focus, to centre on human rights and social improvement rather than the profit of a select few, would mean, for example, a recognition of the social functions of land, housing, water, common goods or natural resources, among others. Regarding city planning and natural resources, for example, it would entail the implementation of active policies of real estate intervention and land-use management. On the subject of water resources, it would mean acknowledging not only the priority of human consumption, but also recognising that it serves other cultural functions too, and the preservation of ecosystems. For pensions, it would involve the establishment of a single model which breaks the ties with the financial market which grants high pensions for a select group of contributors. In the fiscal sphere, it would entail ensuring that the tax system becomes increasingly progressive. In the field of work, it would mean strengthening and guaranteeing the validity of individual and collective workers' rights.

In a nutshell, the elimination of the knots of inequality tied by the dictatorship that we have presented in this chapter should provide the framework for action or the limits that the new constitution should establish for the enshrinement of economic and social rights. However, the recognition of these rights alone would not be enough. There have to be effective ways to realise them. The enshrinement of a catalogue of rights without any way to allow for their implementation would be ineffectual. Therefore, it is fundamental that the new constitution give priority to establishing mechanisms for a more participatory democracy and greater transparency. Such mechanisms will allow a framework for the design of social and economic policies with a direct effect on social and economic rights.

Regardless of the debates around whether, how much, and to what end it is possible to reform the counter-majoritarian institutions – judicial branch – in the country,[41] we can envision the enshrinement of mechanisms which facilitate the people's participation in economic decisions, and in that way limit – or, even better, provide content for – public policies. An example could be mechanisms for participatory budgeting with a focus on human rights, as well as transparent and participatory impact assessments regarding economic policies and rights, in a way that guarantees the democratisation of power and decision-making, which as we have seen are strongly concentrated. Along the same line, mechanisms should be established to ensure that trade unions are able to represent workers in an effective way. These mechanisms would level the playing field for

[41] R Gargarella, 'Diez puntos sobre el cambio constitucional en Chile' *Nueva Sociedad*, No 285, January – February 2020, nuso.org/articulo/diez-puntos-sobre-el-cambio-constitucional-en-chile/.

the unequal actors involved, which would bring about a positive effect on the country's equality rates.[42]

It should be noted that in 2019 the Chilean Government voted in favour of a UN Human Rights Council resolution regarding the 'Guiding principles on human rights impact assessments of economic reforms'.[43] Their realisation and development in the new constitution would signify a giant leap towards their implementation.[44]

Another key issue is the establishment of rules and institutions which prevent, minimise and sanction the abuse of dominant market positions. This would imply taking antitrust initiatives seriously. To achieve this, the dictatorship's economic accomplices who owe their current position to the changes that took place during the period of state terrorism should be held accountable. Furthermore, those companies or businesspeople who are found guilty of complicity with Pinochet's regime should be banned from operating in the country or working with the state. Moreover, a system of background checks should be implemented to ensure that those who were complicit in human rights violations cannot hold public office, particularly in the sectors where their complicit behaviour was registered/proven.[45]

To sum up, the constituent process cannot ignore the inequalities that led to social unrest or the serious human rights violations that Chile has suffered. To untie today's knots of inequality the new constitution must put human rights at the centre of the economic model, which demands that the state should take measures to reduce extreme inequalities, allocate resources to ensure everyone's economic and social rights, and hold accountable the dictatorship's accomplices who still enjoy the privileges of wealth concentration which originated in the policies and measures of the dictatorial regime.

IV. CONCLUSIONS

The architecture of the political, economic and social systems designed and imposed by the dictatorship represents in many ways a heavy burden on Chilean society even today, which clearly shows how past, present and future are inherently connected. Economic inequality in the present, with its political, social, economic and cultural implications, is deeply rooted in the most violent period of the country's history, and looms over its future. The fact that the Chilean 1980

[42] JE Visser et al, 'Trends in Collective Bargaining Coverage: Stability, Erosion or Decline?', *Labour Relations and Collective Bargaining Issues Brief 1* (ILO 2015).

[43] Resolution A/HRC/RES/40/8, voted on 21 March 2019.

[44] UN Independent Expert on Foreign Debt and Human Rights, 'Guiding principles on human rights impact assessments of economic reforms' A/HRC/40/57, 19 December 2018.

[45] A Maye-Rieckh and Pablo de Greiff, *Justice as Prevention: Vetting Public Employees in Transitional Societies* (Social Science Research Council, 2007).

Constitution is one of the most regressive in the region in terms of acknowledgment of economic and social rights is no coincidence.

In 1978, Antonio Cassese was asked by the United Nations to develop a report to study the impact of foreign economic aid and assistance on human rights in Chile. In his 1978 report, he concluded that, on the one hand, most of the international aid and assistance helped to strengthen and keep in power a system that pursued a policy of systematic human rights violations. On the other hand, that in order to obtain economic assistance, the government had to ensure that the economy was 'healthy', which implied a policy of wealth distribution which was detrimental for the vast majority of the population. In other words, economic assistance strengthened the regime and facilitated the perpetration of human rights violations, and in turn, the blood-soaked economic model attracted investments, lured by the resulting high profitability ensured by the so-called social and labour peace.

The concentration of wealth and the progress towards the establishment of a neoliberal market society during the dictatorship are traits that have become deeper entrenched and more widespread after 1990. The democratic period's political economy, which has been subordinated to the economic regime originally established during Pinochet's dictatorship, is now increasingly being challenged by a number of actors that did not benefit from this scheme.[46] On the other side are those who now hold the concentration of economic and political power in the country and that at the same time provide, with the use of market tools, an unequal access to economic and social rights.

Granting the highest legal standing to economic and social rights, strengthening the role of unions in the defence of those rights, as well as making the generation and distribution of resources in the country more democratic in order to ensure the realisation of those rights, are actions which are closely connected with holding the dictatorship's accomplices and beneficiaries accountable. Taking these steps would mean combatting one of the most pernicious consequences of the dictatorship: extreme inequality. All of this should be included in the new constitution.

[46] Ahumada and Solimano (n 19).

3

An Open Constitution to Reverse Chile's Neoliberal Trajectory

FRANCISCA MOYA AND CONSTANZA SALGADO

I. INTRODUCTION

IN THIS CHAPTER we argue that Chile's 1980 Constitution played a paramount role in consolidating the neoliberal model, not only because of its rules but also due to the interpretative culture of the constitutional state. The rejection of this model was the first, as well as the most concrete and 'immediately' achievable demand of the Chilean social outbreak. We argue, then, that to help to reverse the neoliberal trajectory, a new constitution must be open; this would not predetermine the economic and social model but instead leave it to political-democratic discussion and decision. An open constitution would not fix the economic and social model but would have more content than a minimal constitution.

We present this idea in three steps, with three correlative sections. In section II we refer to the concept of economic constitution, looking to its origins and seeking to clarify the different uses for which it has been introduced. On this basis, we review the most characteristic elements of the notion of economic constitution in comparative law and propose a classification based on these elements. Then, in section III, we describe the economic elements embedded in the 1980 constitutional text and explain how the hegemonic doctrine went far beyond the text itself by generating an interpretative culture that viewed it as a neoliberal constitution. We also show how this interpretative culture contributed to protecting the economic model imposed by the dictatorship during the 1980s. Finally, in section IV, we propose an open economic constitution for the new Chilean constitution, which, unlike the 1980 Constitution, would not contain an economic model that restricts the expression of political power. In this regard, we explain the benefits of the open constitution and clarify its differences from minimal constitutions. An additional section of final thoughts can be found at the end of this chapter.

II. ECONOMIC CONSTITUTION

A. Economic Constitutionalism is a Recent Phenomenon

Economic constitutionalism is a relatively recent phenomenon, both in normative and descriptive terms, and is related to the expansion of constitutionalism during the twentieth century, as will be seen in the following sections. This chapter mainly employs the notion of economic constitution in a descriptive sense.

The growth of constitutionalism, Loughlin points out, has implied the expansion of the scope of constitutionalisation,[1] expressed in the economic order through new rights and through the constitutional regulation of new institutions and rules, as we will see subsequently. In this sense, the existence of an economic constitutionalism has been proposed. This concept makes it possible to explain the evolution of the relationship between constitutions and the economic order by distinguishing three periods: 'pure' Constitutionalism, which began in the seventeenth century and lasted until the twentieth century[2] inter-war period; Economic Constitutionalism, which emerged in the twentieth century, mainly after the Second World War; and a third period of New Economic Constitutionalism following the onset of the economic crisis of 2008.

Regarding the first stage, it is argued that constitutions were historically relatively indifferent to the economy and 'did not commit themselves to a specific economic vision of the state';[3] therefore, the state could fit into any kind of economic model. This was because the economy was subsumed within the structure of political power. During the phase known as Economic Constitutionalism, the vast majority of constitutional texts at the comparative level began to incorporate various elements to regulate the economic order. For example, during the last few decades, more than 90 countries have constitutionally regulated the existence of central banks and their function as monetary policy institutions. Rules concerning the market economy, public enterprises, free competition and fiscal policy have also been incorporated. Finally, New Economic Constitutionalism began with the financial crisis of 2008. This period has been characterised by a radical increase in the importance of protecting the functioning of the economy in the drafting and interpretation of national constitutions, to the detriment of the sovereignty of political communities or Member States in the case of the European Union. However, the supposed indifference of the first stage of Constitutionalism concerning the economy is

[1] M Loughlin, 'What is Constitutionalisation?' in P Dobner and M Loughlin (eds), *The Twilight of Constitutionalism?* (Oxford, Oxford University Press, 2010) 47.

[2] G Gerapetritis, *New Economic Constitutionalism in Europe* (London, Bloomsbury Publishing, 2019).

[3] J Couso 'The "Economic Constitutions" of Latin America: between Free Markets and Socioeconomic Rights' in T Ginsburg and R Dixon (eds), *Comparative Constitutional Law in Latin America* (Cheltenham, Edward Elgar Publishing, 2017) 348.

controversial. In this respect, Couso[4] argues that the lack or omission of regulation of the economic structure exhibited by the first constitutions of Europe and the American continent is due to the social, cultural and political hegemony of the market economy during the nineteenth century. Furthermore, the political elites did not feel the need to entrench the free-market capitalist model in the constitution. In contrast, some argue that constitutions and constitutionalism included economic content from the outset, insofar as they protected the notion of legality, the defence of the stability of the legal system and, especially, private property. These ideas, typical of Constitutionalism, have always had a liberal orientation, cementing the distribution of power and functioning as the basis of the new economic and political order in which we live. Referring specifically to rights, Menke and Turner point out that 'without the juridical form of subjective rights, capitalism would not exist',[5] just as it would not exist without its enshrinement in the constitution and protection against state power.[6] Thus, economic content in constitutions is not new if one considers the constitutional regulation of the right to property from this perspective.

B. Normative and Descriptive Uses of the Concept

First, it is relevant to consider that the doctrine employs the concept of economic constitution in different senses. In many cases, the notion of economic constitution is used in a normative way to refer to theoretical developments that propose what the relationship between the constitution and the economic order should be. In general, it is also related to the first notions of the concept, developed in the early 1920s during the discussions on the Weimar Constitution, a process in which the collaboration of Hugo Sinzheimer and his proposal to incorporate a body to promote economic democracy, representing local production councils,[7] was fundamental. Over time, this perspective of economic constitution – as economic democracy – faded, giving way to an understanding of economic constitution based on the postulates of the Ordoliberal school. After World War II, the idea of economic constitution became a critical element of Ordoliberal economic and legal thinking and was very influential in the reconstruction of Germany. Ordoliberal thinking opposed the idea that economic problems are solved spontaneously or over the course of the evolution

[4] Ibid.

[5] C Menke and C Turner, *Critique of Rights* (Cambridge, Polity, 2020).

[6] K Pistor, *The Code of Capital: How the Law Creates Wealth and Inequality* (Princeton, Princeton University Press, 2019).

[7] R Dukes, *The Labour Constitution the Enduring Idea of Labour Law* (Oxford, Oxford University Press, 2014); K Nörr, 'In the Concept of the "Economic Constitution" and the Importance of Franz Böhm from the Viewpoint of Legal History' (1996) 3(4) *European Journal of Law and Economics* 345.

of history. On the contrary, law had a leading role to play.[8] Therefore, the constitution was an instrument of economic policy, envisioned to create conditions in which economic agents could develop their own interests and promote the common interest.[9]

On the other hand, the notion of economic constitution is also used descriptively to account for the way the relationship between the constitution and the economic order has come about and the way the social and political framework that shapes a country's economy has been constructed. In its descriptive use, a country's economic constitution refers to the institutions, rules and interpretative developments of a given constitutional context. In this respect, it is important to keep in mind that while much of this content can be found in the text of the constitution and the legislation that complements it, it can also be the product of interpretations proposed by doctrine or jurisprudence. As described below, some authors in Chile seem to confuse the two ways of using the concept intentionally, pretending to describe content supposedly enshrined in the constitution when in fact they are stating their particular opinion on how a certain matter should be regulated.

C. Elements of Economic Content in Constitutions

Although the constitutional regulation of the economic order of countries is extraordinarily diverse, it is possible to list, in general terms, some elements that can be found in comparative constitutional texts. These are: the form taken by the regulation of private property; the configuration and justiciability of social rights; the constitutional regulation of the relationship between the state and the private sector, through competition and the free market; and the constitutional regulation of monetary and fiscal policy, among others. Incidentally, it is worth noting that these elements generally do not occur together; only some of the issues are expressed. Depending on the form and content of these elements, it is possible to classify the economic content of constitutions, as we will see below.

As stated earlier, constitutional regulation of private property is an element present in almost all constitutions, with relatively similar structures. The constitutional protection of property rights is far from the spontaneous phenomenon that has been argued.[10] In fact, as Allen has pointed out,[11] the inclusion of private property clauses has often been promoted, not merely advised, by various

[8] V Vanberg, *The Constitution of Markets: Essays in Political Economy* (London, Routledge, 2001).

[9] D Gerber, 'Constitutionalizing the Economy: German Neo-Liberalism, Competition Law and the "New" Europe' (1994) 42(1) *The American Journal of Comparative Law* 25.

[10] F Hayek, *Law, Legislation and Liberty* (Taylor & Francis Ltd, 1982).

[11] T Allen, *The Right to Property in Commonwealth Constitutions*, vol 11 (Cambridge, Cambridge University Press, 2000).

international financial organisations. However, the level of relevance or detail that each constitutional text gives to private property rights is not always the same: it differs in its enshrinement and form, in the extent of the owner's power and in the limits it must respect. Limits such as the common good, the protection of the environment, the property of others, or the Chilean 'social function', which works as a justification to limit property, are all examples of this. Finally, the *constitutionalisation* of property, as a statement of commitment to private property and the market economy, influences many of the elements considered below.

A second element that must also be considered in this list is the way social rights are shaped in constitutions, and whether constitutions should consider social rights. Social rights can coexist with various economic models, and their constitutional recognition has proved to be compatible with neoliberal economic and social models. In the latter case, a social rights provision is characterised by private provision, outsourcing or liberalised structures. Subsequently, it is difficult to weigh the extent to which social rights can work to retrench neoliberal trajectories, or the degree to which they do so.

A third group of issues that characterise the economic content of constitutions is the constitutional regulation of the relationship between economic actors, through the promotion of competition and anti-trust regulation, the protection of the free market, and the protection of the consumer rights of public or public services users. Such clauses have been especially prevalent in the constitutions of former Soviet Union countries as a way of reaffirming a commitment to the free market.

Finally, monetary policy and fiscal policy are also elements of the economic content of constitutions. The first is generally expressed by creating public entities specially dedicated to such matters, usually called central banks; these are 'sheltered' from the vagaries of contingent policy.[12] Second, fiscal policy and public debt have also become increasingly important at the constitutional level. The vast majority of the world's constitutions refer to national budgeting, usually a particular form of legislative debate. For several decades now, countries have been incorporating constitutional limits on fiscal spending, known as 'golden rules', to control fiscal indebtedness on the grounds of intergenerational

[12] The protection of the 'independence' of institutions with powers in economic matters has been hotly debated by the doctrine of economics and political science. For an overview see CE Walsh, 'Central Bank Independence' in SN Durlauf and LE Blume (eds), *Monetary Economics* (London, Palgrave Macmillan, 2010); H Berger et al, 'Central Bank Independence: an Update of Theory and Evidence' (2001) 15(1) *Journal of Economic Surveys* 3, and K Mcnamara, 'Rational Fictions: Central Bank Independence and the Social Logic of Delegation' (2002) 25(1) *West European Politics* 47. In Chile, from an economic perspective, see LF Céspedes and R Valdés, 'Autonomía de bancos centrales: La experiencia chilena' (2006) 358(1) *Documentos de Trabajo, Banco Central de Chile*. From a legal perspective, see JC Ferrada, 'La autonomía del Banco Central de Chile: reflexiones acerca de este modelo institucional de gestión de la política monetaria' (2003) 30(1) *Revista Chilena de Derecho* 151.

fairness and protection of international sovereign bond markets with their risky interdependence.

D. Some Categories for Classification

The wide dispersion in the way constitutions include the economic elements mentioned above makes it difficult to classify these constitutions. However, in a recent effort in the context of the European Union, George Gerapetritis has suggested that the constitutions of Member States can be grouped into three categories: free market and competition-oriented constitutions; mixed economy or social market constitutions; and open-ended constitutions.[13]

The first category comprises free market and free competition-oriented constitutions, characterised by explicit and implicit adoption of the language of competition preservation or by the safeguarding of anti-trust practices binding the political options. In other cases, these rules are reinforced by free-market principles, as in the constitutional texts of former socialist states in Eastern Europe such as Romania, Hungary, Croatia, and Lithuania. Here, the constitutions are more emphatic in affirming that the integrity of economic activities will be guaranteed, such as the free movement of goods, services and financial resources and the support of competition and freedom. Other examples of this are the constitutions of Austria and Ireland.

The second category of economic constitutions is the so-called 'mixed' constitution. This category groups together constitutions that combine references to the market economy and the social state. In these cases, the state normally retains significant control over economic planning, control over and monopoly on currency and credit, and the right to intervene in sectoral/geographical sections. The difference between these constitutions and the open-ended constitutions described below is that in mixed constitutions, the margin for governments and political majorities to choose which economic policy to apply is smaller, as the pillars of the free-market economy tend to dominate. Some examples of this are the constitutions of Peru, Spain, and France.

Third, there are open-ended constitutions. These are characterised as constitutions that do not contain specific definitions of the prevailing national economic model, allowing a wide margin for the political government to implement various economic programmes. In this sense, they are the most neutral in terms of serving different possibilities. However, this does not mean that these constitutions are minimal or lack any economic content; they may, for example, contain general orientations. The constitution of Greece is an example.

Considering the proposed conceptualisation and classifications, we will look at the Chilean case and its particularities in the following section.

[13] Gerapetritis (n 2).

III. THE CONSTITUTION OF 1980 AND NEOLIBERAL CONSOLIDATION

The Chilean case is remarkable not only because the current constitution (hereinafter the 1980 Constitution) incorporates several economic elements, but also because it has been interpreted as containing (the protection of) a particular economic model: what we will call *neoliberal capitalism*. This interpretation of the Constitution, in turn, has contributed to generate political practices that consolidate the neoliberal institutional model that the civic-military dictatorship imposed during the 1980s.

Today it is not controversial to state that this model was called into question by the massive protests that broke out in Chile in 2019; these protests triggered the constituent process that is currently underway.

A. The Constitutional Text

Until the 1980 Constitution, Chilean constitutions were silent on economic matters. In contrast, the 1980 Constitution incorporates several of the new economic elements seen above. Thus, it regulates basic aspects of taxation and public charges, and includes, among other things, the prohibition of manifestly unfair or disproportionate taxes (Art 19 N° 20); aspects of monetary policy such as establishing the autonomous nature of the Central Bank at the constitutional level and prohibiting the financing of public spending or loans with direct or indirect credits (Arts 108 and 109); the setting out of the relationship between the state and the private sector by establishing the protection of intermediate groups and their 'adequate' autonomy (Art 1); the principle of non-discrimination in economic matters (Art 19 N° 22); the freedom to acquire all types of property not expressly declared by law to be for public use (Art 19 N° 23); the freedom of entrepreneurship and, as a general rule, the obligation of state-owned companies to submit to market rules (Art 19 N° 21). Additionally, the 1980 Constitution enshrines social rights, such as the right to education, the right to health and the right to social security. At the same time, however, it recognises the freedom to choose between a public and a private provision system as an essential part of social rights, thus ensuring the necessary existence of a market in these areas.

If we use the categories proposed by Gerapetritis[14] (see section II.D) when examining the constitutional *text*, it can be argued that the 1980 Constitution clearly resembles the first category, that is, a constitution oriented towards the free market and free competition. However, if one follows the interpretation that the traditional doctrine created from this set of rules, the Constitution of 1980 goes far beyond this.

[14] See n 2 above.

B. The Interpretative Culture of the Constitution of 1980

The traditional doctrine, ie the doctrine that has always defended the 1980 Constitution and the neoliberal model imposed by the civic-military dictatorship, does not limit itself to describing the aforementioned rules and classifying them according to certain criteria, but deduces from them: (1) a *principle of subsidiarity*, which, understood in the *Chilean way*, consecrates an abstentionist state model in economic-social matters; and (2) an organising order of the economy, the *public economic order*, with a determined content, the axis of which is free market and freedom of entrepreneurship.

C. The Principle of Subsidiarity

The *principle of subsidiarity*, as originally understood, arises from the Catholic intellectual tradition, as a third avenue against laissez-faire capitalism and socialism or communism (statism). According to this principle, between the state and the individual there exist communities of different sizes, and the principle of subsidiarity demands that they should not be absorbed by the state as long as they carry out their activities adequately. This principle is viewed by the European Union as a principle of distribution of competencies between the European Community and its national communities. The principle of subsidiarity operates here as a principle of political-administrative decentralisation, which, as Vallejo rightly points out, means that 'collective decisions [are] taken by institutions located as close as possible to all those potentially affected by them'.[15] In both contexts, as a principle of social organisation and political-administrative decentralisation, the principle of subsidiarity has a negative and a positive component: a mandate of abstention and a mandate of intervention, which are triggered depending on whether the smaller societies or communities are performing their activities or functions satisfactorily.

Although Chile's 1980 Constitution does not expressly refer to the *principle of subsidiarity*, the traditional doctrine has derived it by resorting to an original interpretation of the constitutional economic rules. However, the traditional doctrine has understood the meaning of this principle in terms of the Cold War rather than a third possibility, as opposed to laissez-faire capitalism and socialism, as understood in comparative law. Thus, this principle has been reduced precisely towards one of those extremes: as a mandate of laissez-faire

[15] R Vallejo 'La constitución económica chilena: un ensayo en (de)construcción' (2016) 14 *Estudios Constitucionales* 247, 252–53; M Loo, 'La disciplina constitucional del principio de subsidiariedad en Italia y Chile' in *Revista de Derecho de la Pontificia Universidad Católica de Valparaíso* (2009).

capitalism, or, in more current terms, neoliberal capitalism.[16] This interpretation is rooted in the ideas that guided the dictatorship's re-foundational action in economic and social matters. The dictatorship took this principle as a standard for its economic and social re-foundation, which, based on today's categories, was clearly neoliberal. The principle of subsidiarity was one of the main ideological supports on which the dictatorship consciously built the new Chilean neoliberal model in the early 1980s.[17]

D. The Public Economic Order

The *public economic order* is the second principle that, although not expressly stated, is derived from the economic constitution by the doctrine. As the doctrine states, the principle is not neutral, since, under the 1980 Constitution, the economy 'has a concrete content, whose axis is the entrepreneurial freedom'.[18] Accordingly, the intervention of the state in socio-economic matters should be exceptional, and it does not suffice to invoke reasons of general interest.

What is remarkable is that this *public economic order*, not expressly established in the constitutional text, was used to interpret all the norms of the constitution, blurring the rigorous legal analysis of the content of these norms according to their linguistic meaning.[19] For example, Fermandois and García argued, in a paper published in a prestigious national law journal, that the freedom of labour enshrined in the Constitution should be interpreted in the light of the *public economic order*.[20] Consequently, they claimed that the legal rule establishing that workers who worked and earned on a per-day basis were entitled to proportional pay for the weekly day of rest was contrary to the constitution.[21]

[16] E Soto, 'Consideraciones sobre los fundamentos del principio de subsidiariedad' (1986) 39 *Revista de Derecho Público* 32; R Bertelsen, 'El Estado empresario en la Constitución de 1980' (1987) (2008) 18 *Revista Chilena de Derecho* 115; JL Cea, *Derecho Constitucional Chileno*, vol II (Santiago, Ediciones UC, 2008); E Navarro, 'El Estado empresario a la luz de la Constitución de 1980' (2000) 12 *Revista de Derecho Público* 32; A Fermandois *Derecho Constitucional Económico* (Santiago, Ediciones UC, 2010).

[17] R Cristi and P Ruiz Tagle, *El constitucionalismo del miedo. Propiedad, bien común y poder constituyente* (Santiago, LOM, 2015); A Kowalczyk, 'Transnational Capitalist Classes and the State in Chile' (2019) 25 *New Political Economy* 1; B Alemparte, 'Towards a Theory of Neoliberal Constitutionalism: Addressing Chile's First Constitution-Making Laboratory' (2021) *Global Constitutionalism* 1.

[18] Fermandois (n 16) 29.

[19] JC Ferrada, 'La constitución económica de 1980. Algunas reflexiones críticas' (2000) 11 *Revista de Derecho* 47, 49.

[20] A Fermandois and JF García, 'Compatibilidad entre el derecho a la libre contratación y la fijación de salarios por ley (a propósito de la Ley 20.281 sobre sueldo base)' (2010) 37 *Revista Chilena de Derecho* 343.

[21] Ibid.

The constitution, according to these scholars, protects the will of the parties contained in the employment contract, and this should prevail over the standard set by the legislator in order to protect the workers from the unequal power of their employers.

In the interpretative canon, the *public economic order* protects freedom of enterprise and freedom of contract, the classic freedoms that laissez-faire liberalism invoked to oppose regulatory state intervention. The appeal to this order when interpreting constitutional rules emphasises the economic dimension of constitutional freedoms. Thus, freedom of labour, freedom of association and freedom of education are understood as economic freedoms that oppose social rights and redistributive politics.

E. The Neoliberal Consolidation

As has been documented, the civic-military dictatorship imposed an abstentionist state model in economic matters, in which the state only intervenes in cases where there is no private initiative; therefore, the state does not create value or guide the economic development model, but instead leaves it exclusively in the hands of the market. Regarding social rights, the dictatorship configured a system in which these were understood as rights to targeted benefits that catered mainly to low-income people, while middle and high-income people, in contrast, were able to satisfy their basic needs by acquiring them in the market. In this way, the state ensures the market – which, according to the principle of subsidiarity, has primacy – and offers basic goods and services directly to lower-income sectors that are unable to access these goods and services on their own.

The arrival of democracy in 1990 did not fundamentally change this economic and social institutional base. Although access has expanded, the quality of public services has improved and poverty has decreased, the system remains to this day largely the same as designed during the dictatorship. The 1980 Constitution has played a particularly large role in protecting this model, which, since the 1980s, has comprised the status quo in Chile. There are two reasons for this.

The first is that there arose an interpretative culture on the basis of the Constitution that saw in it both a *principle of subsidiarity* and a *public economic order* of neoliberal content where the constitutional text said nothing.[22] Over the past three decades, the progressive doctrine has assigned democratic

[22] Couso (n 3) 353.

readings to the constitutional text and denounced the distorted way that the principle of subsidiarity has been inferred in Chile.[23] However, this has not broken the model's hegemony: the traditional interpretation, although disputed, has continued to be canon in the matter and has preserved the dictatorship's normative view of the relationship between the constitution and the economy.

The second reason why it can be argued that the 1980 Constitution helped to consolidate the neoliberal model is related to the way it articulates political power. From a sociological perspective, Madariaga has argued that the resilience of the neoliberal trajectory in Chile is partially based on the constitutionalised lock-in network of norms or institutions that have reduced the possibility of governments and political parties to represent alternative policy preferences to the alternative existing neoliberal policies. This kind of institutional lock-in makes certain policy domains more difficult to change by establishing rules that isolate those areas from democratic politics.[24]

The 1980 Constitution imposed limits on the deployment of democratic power through what many have called authoritarian enclaves[25] or traps.[26] The Constitution established a series of rules completely anomalous to democratic constitutionalism, such as: (i) senators appointed by government rather than being directly elected by the citizenry; (ii) an electoral system that over-represented the right-wing heirs of the dictatorship; (iii) super-majority quorums to reform a large number of laws imposed by the dictatorship; and (iv) an ex ante review of legislation by a constitutional court to which the right wing systematically resorted when it did not have the votes to reject transformative bills. Some of these rules have been recently repealed, but several remain entrenched. The operation of these enclaves has contributed to the configuration of a neutralised political power: an eliticised and hierarchically centred power, with no openness to the citizenry, which has seen large consensuses (with the right) as a plus of democracy.[27]

Through authoritarian enclaves and an interpretive culture of the economic constitution, the 1980 Constitution helped to protect the dictatorship's neoliberal model. The Constitution was invoked as a limit whenever efforts endeavoured to modify in a transformative way the rules that configured the system of social rights.

[23] R Vallejo and D Pardow, 'Derribando mitos sobre el Estado empresario' (2008) 35 *Revista Chilena de Derecho* 135; C Viera et al, 'Una aproximación a la idea de "constitución económica2 y sus alcances en la constitución chilena' (2016) 49 *Boletín Mexicano de Derecho Comparado* 1; Vallejo (n 15).

[24] A Madariaga, *Neoliberal Resilience: Lessons in Democracy and Development from Latin America and Eastern Europe* (Princeton, Princeton University Press, 2020).

[25] JM Garreton, 'La redemocratización Política en Chile' (1991) 42 *Centro de Estudios Públicos* 101.

[26] F Atria, *La Constitución Tramposa* (Santiago, LOM, 2015).

[27] F Atria et al, *Democracia y Neutralización* (Santiago, LOM, 2017) 81 ff.

IV. A CONSTITUTION TO REVERSE THE NEOLIBERAL TRAJECTORY

A. An Open, but Not Minimal Constitution

We have seen that the 1980 Constitution not only incorporated economic elements into the text, but was also interpreted as containing a neoliberal model. This reading of the 1980 Constitution and the existence of authoritarian enclaves that neutralised political power – generating legislative inertia and low accountability – contributed to the perpetuation of the neoliberal institutional foundation imposed by the dictatorship. The rejection of this neoliberal institutional model and the deep inequality it allowed was one of the main drivers of the social outburst of 2019. Many of the citizens' hopes for a more dignified life are based on the new constitution, which is seen as a way to dismantle the neoliberal model fixed in the Constitution. Thus, two questions need to be approached in this regard. First, can a new constitution overturn the neoliberal trajectory? Second, how can the new constitution rise to this challenge?

The 1980 Constitution played a huge role in fixing or locking the neoliberal model. However, it is important to note that the resilience of the neoliberal trajectory in Chile is not only based on the Constitution, but also on a neoliberal rationality entrenched in the social culture.[28] This free-market-oriented rationality has operated in Chile for more than four decades and has crept – in some cases involuntarily – into the common sense of most Chilean people, creating an incredible – and undefeatable, as evidenced – faith in the efficiency of markets. Thus, it is important to keep in mind that in order to reverse this neoliberal trajectory, a new constitution is a necessary condition, but not sufficient in and of itself. The issue at hand does not solely concerns the replacement of the neoliberal aspect of the constitution.

Regarding the idea that the new constitution should reverse the neoliberal trajectory, our answer is that it must be an open constitution. Accordingly, guided by the categories presented below, by 'open constitution' we mean a constitution that does not predetermine the economic and social model to be followed, but leaves it up to political-democratic discussion and decision. In contrast to the 1980 Constitution, an open constitution would not decide the economic and social model, but instead articulate political power and provide procedures for further legislative discussion. In an open constitution, Congress, as the representative of the popular will and political forces, would be allowed (in a less restricted way) to discuss the model, its design, and its consequences.

An open constitution, however, does not imply a minimal constitution. A minimal constitution only articulates political power. This is not, however, the way in which the concept of 'minimal constitution' is usually understood in Chile. In Chile it has been very common, in the face of demands for

[28] Madariaga (n 24).

constitutional change, to affirm that a good alternative to the economic constitution of 1980 would be a minimal constitution, minimal being understood as a constitution that would not only articulate power, but also establish and guarantee classic civil and political rights. Thus, for example, García points out that constitutional minimalism seeks to establish 'basic political rules that allow the democratic process to make the bulk of the decisions of social life. And it is precisely because it also seeks to protect rights and freedoms that predate the social pact and the democratic process that certain basic civil and political rights are guaranteed'.[29] According to García, constitutions can withstand few rights, and these are limited only to civil and political rights.

Understood in this sense, a minimal constitution challenges the evolution of social constitutionalism and the social state, appearing neutral and open. Although a minimal constitution can be seen as neutral, in reality it is not. Minimal constitutions have the option of protecting only 'first generation' rights such as property and freedom, to the exclusion of 'third' and even 'fourth' generation rights such as the right to internet access. Thus, protection is given to negative forms of rights such as negative freedoms, which impose a duty of abstention on the state, while ignoring rights, values, or mandates with the function of legitimising and stimulating the realisation of material goals and tasks by the state. A minimal constitution in this sense is, in Böckenförde's terms, a bourgeois constitution.[30] Unlike an open constitution, a minimal constitution does not necessarily open the door for democratic power to reverse the neoliberal trajectory, if desired.

Due to the role the interpretative culture of the constitution has played in Chile, a minimal constitution implies a risk: it could be absorbed by the legal and political system built upon the past constitutional reign, instead of helping to transform it. This risk is driven by inertia. Like almost all constitutions in the modern era, the new Chilean constitution will be developed within an already existing system of norms. The law, jurisprudential decisions and administrative regulation are already in force. All this legal 'habitat' and the interpretative culture that comes with it imposes a tendency towards stability, which would make it possible for the 1980 Constitution, or its 'spirit', to survive. Then, in order to reverse the neoliberal trajectory, the new constitution needs to be a vector of transformation of the system of norms and of the environment in which it will reign. Otherwise, the new constitution may end up tied to the old framework in a kind of inverse version of what Elster noted, reminiscent of the

[29] JF García, 'Minimalismo e incrementalismo constitucional' (2015) 41 *Revista Chilena de Derecho* 267, 274; J Correa, '¿Ha llegado la hora de una Nueva Constitución?' (2013) *Anuario de Derecho Público de la Universidad Diego Portales*; J Correa, *Diálogos constitucionales* (Santiago, CEP 2015).

[30] EW Böckenförde, *Estudios sobre el Estado de Derecho y la democracia* (Madrid, Trotta 2000) 17–47.

dilemma Ulysses faced with the Sirens:[31] a constitution tied to another constitution's pre-commitment. If this were the case, the consequences would be serious: the political community would be lost by eternally returning to Ithaca. Instead of protecting society from its own myopia, as Sunstein would say, such a scenario would entail an imposed blindness.[32]

In the Chilean case, the impact of inertia is even more dangerous than in other contexts. The problem of the inability to transform the system of norms is especially significant, since the legal framework is far from neutral. Mainly built under the 1980 Constitution, the current system of norms has played a decisive role in the implementation of the neoliberal model. Over the last four decades, a substantial amount of legislation and administrative regulation has been enacted in its image and likeness. For instance, the current regulation of the financial markets and the central bank, most of the privatisation of public companies, and the creation of markets for the provision of social rights such as health, education[33] and pensions were all enacted under the umbrella of the 1980 Constitution. It is only in the case of education that some legal reforms have been implemented to reduce the harmful effects of the deregulated inclusion of market rationality. These reforms have promoted the elimination of discrimination against students on socioeconomic grounds and the control or elimination of for-profit schools that receive public resources, among other aspects.

Relevant judicial decisions, both from the Supreme Court and the Constitutional Court, have also been decided by applying a vision of the constitution that promotes the neoliberal model.[34] Beyond some transitory adjustments and reforms aimed at compatibility between the constitution and legislation, the vast majority of legislation and jurisprudence will remain in force even if the constitution is changed. The challenge will then be, should the democratic majorities so desire, to build a new model through the design and implementation of new institutions and public policies that will first materialise in new laws and regulations, and later in the new course of judicial decisions.

To sum up, a new constitution could help to reverse the Chilean neoliberal trajectory, although there are other factors involved in this trajectory resilience that also need to be addressed. Moreover, in order to help this endeavour, the new constitution must be open to give political power a broad capacity for

[31] J Elster, *Ulysses Unbound: Studies in Rationality, Pre-commitment, and Constraints* (Cambridge, Cambridge University Press, 2000).

[32] C Sunstein, 'Constitutionalism and Secession' (1991) 58 *University of Chicago Law Review* 633.

[33] On this topic in Chile, see F Atria, *Derechos sociales y educación: un nuevo paradigma de lo público* (Santiago, LOM, 2014).

[34] For instance, Supreme Court decision N°2396-91 supports the right of private companies to sue the state and demand compensation for regulatory changes, Constitutional Court decisions N° STC 1863-2012 reject the development of state-owned companies, and N° 4317-18-CPR rejects any regulatory conditions giving preferential treatment to state-related institutions such as private universities that receive financial support.

expression, and more than minimal to avoid absorption into the existing system of norms.

B. Why an Open Constitution?

As we have affirmed, an open constitution is one that articulates political power, thus providing a framework for democratic politics to decide, in the light of relevant circumstances, the economic model to follow. Accordingly, the configuration of an effective and responsive power is also fundamental. This is especially relevant in Latin America and particularly in the Chilean case. As Gargarella has noted, Latin American constitutions have devoted themselves to enshrining multiple social rights, principles and social goals, but have neglected the 'engine room', ie the articulation of a responsive political power, capable of transforming social structures.[35] This is particularly true in the case of Chile, whose constitution, as we have seen, incorporates a series of rules that have limited democratic politics.

Nevertheless, the recognition of social rights, principles and goals is also important in an open constitution. In this sense, an open constitution not only recognises civil and political rights, but can also incorporate social rights in order to legitimise state action and use principles and goals to guide democratic deliberation. The recognition of social goals, principles and rights at the constitutional level marks a commitment to the pursuit of citizens' wellbeing, for which democratic politics must be accountable to the citizenry. Such a commitment expresses that the purpose of the state is not only to refrain from intervening in certain spheres, but also to intervene actively in order to ensure the material wellbeing of its citizens. An open constitution is more appropriate for this purpose.

This does not imply that a particular economic model should be defined, or that democratic politics should be limited. Social rights, principles and goals guide and legitimise state action in the pursuit of welfare, but they do not determine the way in which welfare should be shaped in reality, because there is no single way of interpreting this commitment, and no single way of realising it. Different political visions can offer different mechanisms for realising social rights, and it will be up to democratic politics to decide how they are implemented. Thus, an open constitution allows different economic views.

In addition to the arguments already put forward in favour of the open character of constitutions, there is another argument that can be considered pragmatic but no less relevant: an open constitution is more durable and therefore more efficient. Concern about the lifespan of constitutions has only recently

[35] R Gargarella, *Latin American Constitutionalism 1820–2010. The Engine Room of the Constitution* (Oxford, Oxford University Press, 2013).

arisen. The constitution's durability is relevant, since overly frequent constitutional reform may create instability and have negative impacts on citizens, in relation to both the economy (ie impact on growth, inflation, unemployment, recession) and the performance of democracy (ie distrust of authorities, populism, political violence). Regrettably, in many places, constitutions are remarkably ephemeral. This has been shown in relation to the Latin American reality by Negretto,[36] and more globally by Ginsburg, Melton, and Elkins.[37] Looking at the data, rather than the theory, it seems that building a stable and durable constitutional scheme is quite difficult, especially in the countries of the global South and the so-called 'new democracies' of non-Western Europe.

Despite the relevance of durability, we still have very little knowledge of how to create more enduring constitutions. There is no single aspect that guarantees greater stability of a constitution; rather, it arises from a combination of factors. Among them, the nation's political history and the legal and constitutional system in which a constitutional text is inserted are relevant. Nevertheless, again, that is far from all. The institutional design can also tell us about constitutional longevity or stability: the constitutional and institutional design choices matter. As has been reported, the flexible designs of open constitutions have a better capacity to adapt to change and to evolve along with society compared to more rigid or detailed designs.[38]

In this sense, an open constitution is more stable because, since it does not contain a model or 'program', it will not need to be reformed if it becomes necessary to change course or if it does not work. As de Otto says, 'the eventual different order that becomes necessary in the future due to the demands of reality will require the reform of the constitution or will be imposed against it'.[39] An open constitution can help to avoid the costs of reforming a constitution. In contrast, if the model enshrined in the constitution becomes outdated or is rejected by society, the constitution will not only act as a limit but will probably also become the target of criticism and controversy, which could trigger a crisis leading to its replacement.

V. CONCLUSIONS

This chapter has reflected on the possibilities for the Chilean constitutional process to reverse – or help reverse – the neoliberal trajectory that the country has experienced over the last four decades. With this challenge in mind, we began

[36] G Negretto, *Making Constitutions: Presidents, Parties, and Institutional Choice in Latin America* (Cambridge, Cambridge University Press, 2013).

[37] Z Elkins et al, *The Endurance of National Constitutions* (Cambridge, Cambridge University Press, 2009).

[38] Ibid.

[39] I De Otto, *Derecho constitucional* (Madrid, Ariel, 1999).

by explaining the notion of economic constitution and its multiple uses, types, and categories. We then analysed the 1980 Constitution, showing which mechanisms were involved in the entrenchment of the Chilean neoliberal trajectory. This section focused on a 'non-formal' mechanism of entrenchment: the interpretative culture of the constitutional text. We argued that this constitutional culture has played a significant role in securing the neoliberal understanding of the constitutional text, sometimes even expanding the scope of its actual economic content. Finally, we pointed out that a new constitution should take an open form to help reverse the neoliberal trajectory. This means that it should not follow one economic and social model but instead allow for the development of several different models. After defining the notion of an open constitution and distinguishing it from the notion of a minimal constitution, we briefly developed some of the main reasons justifying our chosen option. We argued that an open constitution is more coherent with the democratic principle as well as more durable and therefore more efficient. Additionally, this openness provides a constitution with the capacity to be flexible and adapt over time to societal evolution.

4

Advancing Equal Rights in Constitutions: Insights from 193 Countries

ALETA SPRAGUE, PAM STEK, AMY RAUB AND JODY HEYMANN

I. INTRODUCTION

ALONGSIDE THE LESSONS to be learned from Chile's own rich constitutional history, trends in constitutional drafting globally can offer insights for the country's process of constitutional reform. In this chapter we present global data on constitutional approaches to equal rights to provide context for the citizens, policymakers, and civil society groups who will be shaping Chile's new constitution. In particular, we draw lessons from countries' experiences about why comprehensive equality rights matter; examine trends in constitutional protections over the past half century; and share insights from the global data about the impacts of more detailed equality provisions in key areas. As Chileans set out to make important choices that will shape their country's future, we hope that this contribution provides useful information about the scope and implications of different constitutional approaches to equal rights worldwide.

Over the past 60 years, global movements for the rights of marginalised groups have realised steady gains for equality. Nevertheless, historic and ongoing discrimination continue to put certain groups at increased risk of poverty, educational disadvantage, political marginalisation, and violence. A constitutional approach that would build on past progress and address equal rights comprehensively would include a prohibition of all common forms of discrimination, the flexibility to reach emerging and historically underrecognised forms of discrimination, and guarantees of the social and economic rights critical to equal opportunity and the civil and political rights that enable all voices to be heard.

II. WHOSE RIGHTS? COVERING ALL FORMS OF DISCRIMINATION

A constitution designed to protect universal human rights would explicitly prohibit all types of discrimination, including by guaranteeing equal rights on the basis of sex, gender, sexual orientation, gender identity, race, ethnicity, language, socioeconomic status, disability, migration status, and religion.

A. Sex and Gender

Around the world, women and girls still face significant barriers to realising their fundamental rights. For example, in 2018 girls comprised three-quarters of children worldwide who had never enrolled in school.[1] In nearly every country, women's earnings fall short of men's, and persistent gender gaps reinforce women's overrepresentation in low-wage work and underrepresentation in management positions.[2] Likewise, women occupy just a quarter of parliamentary seats across the 153 countries surveyed by the World Economic Forum.[3] The World Health Organization identifies gender-based violence as a significant global public health problem, which affects women across countries and income groups.[4] Meanwhile, restrictive gender norms undermine men's engagement in caregiving and create barriers to all people pursuing their chosen paths. Both the Convention on the Elimination of All Forms of Discrimination Against Women (CEDAW), ratified by Chile and 188 other countries, and the Sustainable Development Goals (SDGs), adopted unanimously by the UN General Assembly in 2015, commit governments to ensuring gender equality. Addressing discrimination on the basis of sex and gender is foundational to guaranteeing equal rights for all.

B. Sexual Orientation, Gender Identity, and Sex Characteristics (SOGIESC)

Legal discrimination against sexual and gender minorities remains devastatingly common: 68 countries criminalise consensual sexual activity between two adults of the same sex, with penalties in some cases that include lengthy imprisonment

[1] Global Education Monitoring Report Team, *A New Generation: 25 Years of Efforts for Gender Equality in Education* (UNESCO, 2020) 9.

[2] World Economic Forum, *Global Gender Gap Report 2020* (WEF, 16 December 2019) 11, 17; International Labour Organization, *Global Wage Report 2018/19: What Lies Behind Gender Pay Gaps* (ILO, 2018) 68–69.

[3] WEF (n 2) 10.

[4] World Health Organization, *Global and Regional Estimates of Violence Against Women: Prevalence and Health Effects of Intimate Partner Violence and Non-Partner Sexual Violence* (WHO, 2013) 2.

or death.[5] While no SOGIESC-specific treaty exists, UN agencies have affirmed through official guidance that equal rights fully apply to the LGBT+ population. Likewise, regional bodies including the Organization of American States have issued similar decisions and resolutions. Indeed, it was a Chilean case – *Atala Riffo and Daughters v Chile*[6] – that spurred the Inter-American Court of Human Rights to confirm in 2012 that the American Convention on Human Rights prohibits discrimination on the basis of sexual orientation. Given the persistence of SOGIESC discrimination and growing consensus about the need for explicit legal protections, guaranteeing equal rights on the basis of SOGIESC would powerfully support a constitution's ability to fully protect equality.

C. Race and Ethnicity

Discrimination based on race and ethnicity continues to undermine opportunity worldwide. Across countries, children from ethnic minority groups are less likely to complete lower secondary school, and children from linguistic minorities – up to 40 per cent of the world's population – commonly face the difficulties of instruction in a language they neither speak nor understand.[7] In the global workplace, indigenous peoples and other marginalised racial and ethnic groups remain disproportionately employed in low-skilled, low-paid occupations without social protection coverage.[8] Members of marginalised racial and ethnic groups worldwide also face higher risks of violence – in their interactions with state institutions, in workplaces and schools, and in public spaces. Against this backdrop, constitutions are especially important instruments for prohibiting discrimination on the basis of race, ethnicity, and language. Moreover, Chile and 181 other countries have ratified the International Convention on the Elimination of All Forms of Racial Discrimination (ICERD), which condemns all racial discrimination in all aspects of public life.

D. Socioeconomic Status

Discrimination based on socioeconomic status remains commonplace. For example, studies show that employers discriminate in hiring on the basis of

[5] ILGA World: Lucas Ramón Mendos, *State-Sponsored Homophobia 2019*, Global Legislation Overview Update (ILGA, December 2019) 47.

[6] *Atala Riffo and Daughters v Chile*, Merits, Reparations and Costs, Judgment of February 24, 2012, I/A Court HR, Series C No 239 (2012).

[7] United Nations, *Leaving No One Behind – The Imperative of Inclusive Development: Report on the World Social Situation 2016* (UN, 2016) 59.

[8] International Labour Organization, *Implementing the ILO Indigenous and Tribal Peoples Convention No 169: Towards an Inclusive, Sustainable and Just Future* (ILO, 2020) 68.

regional accents, postcodes, dental appearance, and other social class proxies.[9] Meanwhile, in the context of growing privatisation of public goods, financial barriers often limit access to education, healthcare, and even the ability to participate in political processes, jeopardising universally protected rights. Addressing both explicit socioeconomic status discrimination and discriminatory financial barriers would strengthen a constitution's capacity to provide a foundation for equal opportunity.

E. Disability

People with disabilities – a population that includes nearly one billion children and adults worldwide – commonly face both explicit discrimination in employment and education as well as some of the highest rates of implicit bias. Disability discrimination also affects the ability to influence decisionmakers: studies have found that persons with disabilities are less likely to participate in political activities due to factors such as the inaccessibility of polling places.[10] The Convention on the Rights of Persons with Disabilities (CRPD), which has 182 States Parties including Chile and was one of the most rapidly ratified human rights treaties in history, comprehensively guarantees the equal rights and full participation of all people with disabilities, and has provided a foundation for important court decisions and constitutional reforms globally. A constitution that fully guarantees the equal rights of people with disabilities would build on this progress and lay the groundwork for an inclusive society.

F. Migration Status

As of 2020, refugees and other international migrants numbered around 272 million worldwide. Migrants commonly face discrimination that intersects with their ethnicity, nationality and/or religion, alongside restrictions on access to basic healthcare, schools for their children, and safe and fair working conditions. Global agreements protect these rights: the Refugee Convention and the Migrant Workers Convention – both ratified by Chile – guarantee a right to education for all children, regardless of immigration status,[11] prohibit discrimination,[12]

[9] Z Siddique, 'Evidence on Caste Based Discrimination' (2011) 18 *Labour Economics* S146; M Bertrand and S Mullainathan, 'Are Emily and Greg More Employable than Lakisha and Jamal? A Field Experiment on Labor Market Discrimination' (2004) 94 *The American Economic Review* 992; J Moeller et al, 'Assessing the Relationship between Dental Appearance and the Potential for Discrimination in Ontario, Canada' (2015) 1 *SSM-Population Health* 26.

[10] L Schur and M Adya, 'Sidelined or Mainstreamed? Political Participation and Attitudes of People with Disabilities in the United States' (2013) 94 *Social Science Quarterly* 836.

[11] Art 22 of the Convention Relating to the Status of Refugees (Geneva, 28 July 1951); Arts 30 and 45 of the International Convention on the Protection of the Rights of All Migrant Workers and Members of Their Families (New York, 18 December 1990).

[12] Refugee Convention, Art 3; Migrant Workers Convention, Art 7.

and include protections for equal working conditions regardless of citizenship.[13] International treaties also protect the right to health for all.[14] Moreover, when migrants' rights are violated, the consequences affect citizens as well: denying non-citizens' access to preventive healthcare can lead to the spread of infectious diseases, while tolerating unfair work conditions for migrants can undermine labour standards for everyone. Given the large-scale increases in migration compelled and made possible over the past century, addressing non-citizens' rights in constitutions would have important normative and practical impacts.

G. Religion

Across countries, discrimination on the basis of real or presumed religious identity, alongside religious oppression by governments, is responsible for the marginalisation, harassment and human rights abuses of millions. A 2018 Pew Research Center study found that 53 countries – 27 per cent of those surveyed – reported high or very high levels of social hostilities involving religion.[15] Alongside the Universal Declaration of Human Rights, the International Covenant on Civil and Political Rights (ICCPR) – ratified by Chile and 172 other countries – prohibits discrimination on the basis of religion or belief. While protecting equal rights regardless of religion does not justify religious practices that threaten others' rights, constitutionally prohibiting discrimination based on religion, belief, or non-belief would advance foundational democratic principles.

III. WHICH RIGHTS? KEY PROTECTIONS FOR ALL GROUPS

A constitution designed to protect universal human rights would, at a minimum: comprehensively prohibit both direct and indirect discrimination; guarantee fundamental civil and political rights; and enshrine social and economic rights, including health, education, decent working conditions, and income support.

A. Specific and Comprehensive Equal Rights Guarantees

A constitution designed to protect equal rights would provide a comprehensive equality guarantee that bans discrimination on all grounds discussed in the

[13] Refugee Convention, Arts 17, 24; Migrant Workers Convention, Art 25.

[14] Migrant Workers Convention, Arts 28, 43, 45; Art 25 of the Universal Declaration of Human Rights (Paris, 10 December 1948); Art 12 of the International Covenant on Economic, Social and Cultural Rights (New York, 16 December 1966).

[15] S Majumdar and V Villa, 'In 2018, Government Restrictions on Religion Reach Highest Level Globally in More than a Decade' (Pew Research Center, 10 November 2020) 5–12.

previous section. Examples from numerous countries show why specific constitutional protections matter. For example, in Mexico, protections against disability discrimination led to a landmark ruling against a hotel chain that banned people with disabilities from applying for an open job.[16] In South Africa, the constitution's guarantee of equal rights regardless of sexual orientation prompted reform to an immigration law that excluded same-sex couples.[17] Meanwhile, while general equality provisions that do not list the types of discrimination prohibited have nevertheless had important impacts, their coverage is less predictable or consistent, and they do not convey the same normative value as a clear and unequivocal affirmation of a group's equal rights.

B. Indirect Discrimination

To strengthen its prohibitions of discrimination, a constitution designed to advance equality would also prohibit indirect discrimination – policies or practices that are neutral on their face but disproportionately harm certain populations. For example, restricting eligibility for a specific job based on minimum height, while not explicitly discriminating against women, will have the effect of disproportionately excluding female applicants. In some cases, indirect or 'disparate impact' discrimination may be unintentional or the result of implicit rather than explicit biases. In others, however, it is clearly intended to target a particular group while circumventing protections against direct discrimination. An example of the latter is the use of literacy tests as a requirement for voting across the Jim Crow-era southern US, which did not explicitly prohibit voting on the basis of race but was clearly intended to disfranchise Black Americans who had been denied a formal education. Constitutional provisions explicitly barring indirect discrimination have had an impact, including by invalidating a biased employment test in the UK, and ensuring equitable compensation for victims of accidents on public transportation in South Africa. In contrast, in the absence of clear protections against disparate impact, courts have sanctioned grave injustices, such as racial disparities in death penalty sentences in the US.[18]

C. Civil, Political, Social, and Economic Rights

Protections of civil and political rights are foundational for ensuring that everyone can participate in public and private life and influence their governments'

[16] Amparo Directo en Revision 1387/2012 [2012].

[17] *National Coalition for Gay and Lesbian Equality and Others v Minister of Home Affairs and Others* [1999] ZACC 17 (South Africa).

[18] *Essop v Home Office* [2017] UKSC 2; *Mvumvu and Others v Minister of Transport and Another* (CCT 67/10) [2011]; *McKleskey v Kemp*, 481 US 279 [1987].

decisions. Fundamental civil rights include, among others, freedom of expression, association, and belief, the rights to liberty and due process, freedom of movement, and the right to vote free of discrimination or coercion. Likewise, social and economic rights are critical for creating just and inclusive societies in which everyone can meet fundamental needs. While contemporary constitutions recognise a range of social and economic rights, universal guarantees of education, public health and healthcare, decent work, and income security are particularly powerful foundations for advancing equality for all.[19]

IV. THE STATE OF THE WORLD: PROTECTIONS FOR EQUAL RIGHTS IN 193 CONSTITUTIONS

In this section we present data capturing the details of constitutional approaches to equal rights across all 193 UN Member States as of 2017, analysing trends in their adoption over time.[20] While there are some important areas of recent regression, overall, more recently adopted constitutions include far more detailed and comprehensive protections for equal rights than those adopted 50 years ago.

This transformation has been particularly dramatic with respect to constitutional guarantees of equal rights on the basis of sex. Every constitution written since 2000 has addressed sex and/or gender equality, compared to just over half of those adopted before 1970. Altogether, 85% of constitutions worldwide guarantee equal rights or prohibit discrimination on the basis of sex and/or gender.

In contrast to sex discrimination, few countries constitutionally prohibit discrimination based on sexual orientation or gender identity. Encouragingly, however, momentum is building. Since 1996, when South Africa's constitution became the first to explicitly protect equal rights regardless of sexual orientation, 11 more countries have followed, including Fiji in 1997, Ecuador in 1998, and Portugal in 2004. Most recently, Cuba adopted a new constitution in 2019 that prohibits discrimination based on both sexual orientation and gender identity, joining six other countries worldwide with protections on both grounds.

A majority of countries (76 per cent) provide constitutional guarantees on the basis of race and/or ethnicity. In addition, 44 per cent prohibit language discrimination, which is often associated with ethnic discrimination. These

[19] For details on countries' approaches to these rights and their prevalence globally, see J Heymann et al, *Advancing Equality: How Constitutional Rights Can Make a Difference Worldwide* (Oakland, University of California Press, 2020) and A Sprague et al, 'Providing a Foundation for Decent Work and Adequate Income during Health and Economic Crises: Constitutional Approaches in 193 Countries' (2020) 40 *International Journal of Sociology and Social Policy* 1087.

[20] Methods and data source in Sprague et al, ibid, 1092.

protections are more common in newer constitutions: just 49 per cent of constitutions adopted before 1970 address equal rights on the basis of race or ethnicity, compared to at least 73 per cent adopted each decade since.

Over half the world's constitutions (59 per cent) contain provisions that prohibit forms of discrimination on the basis of socioeconomic status. The 1990s was the first decade in which a majority of new constitutions (83 per cent) contained provisions prohibiting discrimination on the basis of socioeconomic status. In the 2000s, this figure dipped to 63 per cent, but rebounded to 83 per cent in the period from 2010–2017.

Globally, just 27 per cent of constitutions guarantee equal rights regardless of disability. Still, data from the past few decades reveals that addressing disability is increasingly becoming a constitutional norm: in the 1990s, only 27 per cent of new constitutions addressed equal rights on the basis of disability, compared to 47 per cent in the 2000s, and 71 per cent in the period 2010–17.

In relation to migration, 22 per cent of constitutions broadly prohibit discrimination based on citizenship, while 60 per cent guarantee equal rights regardless of nationality and 8 per cent prohibit discrimination based on statelessness. Notably, only 25 per cent of constitutions adopted since 2010, and 16 per cent adopted in the 2000s, included explicit guarantees of equal rights for non-citizens, compared to 40 per cent of constitutions written in the 1990s. This shift, though troubling, may primarily reflect geopolitical developments. Following the dissolution of the Soviet Union, almost all constitutions newly drafted in the 1990s protected rights regardless of citizenship. Though countries have been less likely to adopt these constitutional safeguards in the years since, the recent escalation in overt xenophobia across many nations highlights their continuing vital importance.

Nearly four out of five (78 per cent) constitutions prohibit discrimination on the basis of religion, including a full 92 per cent of those adopted between 2010 and 2017. However, as discussed in more detail towards the end of this chapter, far fewer take a comprehensive approach to ensuring equality for all regardless of religion, belief, or non-belief.

While indirect discrimination is a newer concept in equality law, some recently rewritten constitutions provide specific protections against indirect discrimination in their equal rights provisions. Specifically, 5 per cent of constitutions prohibit indirect gender discrimination and indirect racial/ethnic discrimination, respectively. Although these provisions remain relatively uncommon, recent constitutional drafting processes have recognised their importance and the consequences of their omission. South Africa, for example, specifically included indirect discrimination in its 1996 constitution after witnessing the consequences for equality of the US's failure to do so.[21]

[21] AK Wing, 'The South African Constitution as a Role Model for the United States' (2008) 24 *Harvard Blackletter Law Journal* 73.

V. STRENGTHENING EQUAL RIGHTS PROTECTIONS: CONSIDERATIONS FOR SPECIFIC GROUPS

To advance equal rights comprehensively, a constitution would address some of the unique circumstances, barriers to rights, and types of bias commonly experienced by specific groups.

A. Sex and Gender: Addressing Caregiving

In addition to sex and gender, addressing marital status, family status, and pregnancy would provide a stronger foundation for advancing gender equality.

While protections against sex discrimination are now near universal in constitutions, far fewer prohibit discrimination against caregivers. Caregiving discrimination disproportionately affects women but has consequences for workers of all genders. For example, while married women and mothers face discrimination in hiring and promotion due to their perceived status as caregivers, employers also commonly discriminate against men who defy gender stereotypes by prioritising caregiving responsibilities.

To close this gap, some constitutions have begun to explicitly address discrimination on the basis of marital status, family status, and pregnancy – an important development in light of court rulings that protections against sex discrimination do not necessarily encompass discrimination on these related grounds. For example, the US Supreme Court held in 1974 that distinguishing between 'pregnant persons' and 'non-pregnant persons' was not sex discrimination – and therefore not prohibited by its past interpretations of the constitution's equality guarantee.[22] Similarly, in 1981, India's Supreme Court let stand Air India's policy of firing female but not male flight attendants upon marriage, in spite of a constitutional provision barring sex discrimination.[23] Currently, 6 per cent of constitutions offer stronger protections by explicitly prohibiting pregnancy discrimination, while 8 per cent ban discrimination on the basis of marital status. For example, Fiji's constitution provides that '[a] person must not be unfairly discriminated against, directly or indirectly on the grounds of … sex, gender … marital status, or pregnancy'.

B. Sexual Orientation and Gender Identity: Ensuring More Consistent Protections

While courts have advanced SOGIESC rights through a range of constitutional provisions, there is no substitute for an explicit guarantee of equal rights –

[22] *Geduldig v Aiello*, 417 US 484 [1974].

[23] MC Nussbaum, 'India: Implementing Sex Equality Through Law' (2001) 2 *Chicago Journal of International Law* 49.

especially given the demonstrated threat of discriminatory constitutional amendments.

Though few constitutions contain explicit SOGIESC protections, millions of LGBT+ people worldwide have gained rights through court rulings based on other constitutional guarantees. For example, in 2015 the US Supreme Court ruled that the constitution's protections of due process and overall equality guaranteed same-sex couples the right to marry.[24] Similarly, in 2018, the Supreme Court of India overturned a law criminalising same-sex relationships based on both the right to privacy and the constitution's general equality guarantee.[25]

However, while these are important victories, these decisions also demonstrate that, in the absence of clear constitutional language, courts have proven to be unpredictable and unreliable guarantors of equal rights across SOGIESC. In the US marriage equality case, the Court fell short of extending the same level of constitutional protection to the LGBT+ community as provided to other groups, and did not specifically condemn discrimination on the basis of sexual orientation. In India, the 2018 ruling came only after a series of contradictory decisions, including an earlier Supreme Court judgment that broadly dismissed the 'so-called rights of LGBT persons'.[26] As these examples show, without clear constitutional safeguards, court decisions can be overturned and fundamental equal rights questions left unresolved, necessitating further litigation. Additionally, establishing rights in clear language is important for protecting against constitutional amendments to restrict rights: since 2000, 12 countries have adopted constitutional language prohibiting or allowing legislation to prohibit same-sex marriage, illustrating the backlash that often follows gains on equality.

C. Race and Ethnicity: Recognising Intersectionality

Though constitutional protections on the basis of race and ethnicity alone are vital, racial and ethnic discrimination often intersect with discrimination on other grounds, illustrating that both constitutions and courts can strengthen protections by taking a comprehensive and intersectional approach to realising equal rights.

Discrimination often cuts across different aspects of identity. However, the law typically defines each ground of discrimination discretely and courts evaluate each claim sequentially. In her landmark article coining the term 'intersectionality,' Kimberlé Crenshaw describes the case of *DeGraffenreid v General Motors*,[27] in which a US district court dismissed five Black women's

[24] Heymann et al (n 19) 139.
[25] Ibid, 140–41.
[26] Ibid, 140–42.
[27] *DeGraffenreid v General Motors*, 413 F Supp 142, 145 (ED Mo 1976).

discrimination claims against the same employer, finding that 'this lawsuit must be examined to see if it states a cause of action for race discrimination, sex discrimination, or alternatively either, but not a combination of both'.[28] While intersectional discrimination by its nature affects people from all marginalised groups, discrimination based on race or ethnicity is especially likely to be of an intersectional nature, given the historic discrimination across countries that has resulted in racial/ethnic disparities often closely aligning with socioeconomic disparities, the racial, ethnic, and gender segregation of labour markets, and the relationship of race, ethnicity, and migration status.

Although a growing number of countries have begun to legislatively address intersectionality and related concepts like multiple or cumulative discrimination, comparable constitutional provisions remain rare.[29] The UK's Equality Act 2010, which is viewed by some as having constitutional status in the absence of a codified constitution, provides one example, defining 'combined discrimination' as simultaneous discrimination on two grounds, which may include age, disability, gender reassignment, race, religion or belief, sex, or sexual orientation.[30]

In other countries, courts have begun applying their equality clauses using an intersectional lens. For example, in a decision about the rights of aboriginal women, the Supreme Court of Canada affirmed the need to 'recognize that personal characteristics may overlap or intersect (such as race, band membership, and place of residence in this case), and to reflect changing social phenomena or new or different forms of stereotyping or prejudice'.[31] Likewise, in a 2020 decision, the Constitutional Court of South Africa acknowledged that 'Domestic workers experience racism, sexism, gender inequality and class stratification … The application of an intersectional approach helps us to understand the structural and dynamic consequences of the interaction between these multiple forms of discrimination'.[32] Going forward, enshrining acknowledgment of intersectionality in constitutions – or at the very least ensuring that they establish adequate coverage and flexibility to reach intersectional forms of discrimination – would strengthen constitutions' ability to provide sufficient protection.

D. Socioeconomic Status: Eliminating Financial Barriers to Rights

In addition to specific protections against socioeconomic status discrimination, constitutional provisions that remove financial barriers to the fulfilment of

[28] K Crenshaw, 'Demarginalizing the Intersection of Race and Sex: A Black Feminist Critique of Antidiscrimination Doctrine, Feminist Theory and Antiracist Politics' (1989) 1989 *University of Chicago Legal Forum* 131.

[29] S Fredman, *Intersectional Discrimination in EU Gender Equality and Non-Discrimination Law* (European Commission, 2016) 51–53.

[30] Equality Act 2010, s 14. However, at the time of writing s 14 has not yet been brought into force.

[31] *Corbiere v Canada (Minister of Indian and Northern Affairs)* [1999] 2 SCR 203 (Canada).

[32] *Mahlangu and Another v Minister of Labour and Others* (CCT306/19) [2020] ZACC 24.

fundamental rights – including health, education, and voting – can powerfully support their universal realisation.

Members of disadvantaged social classes not only face explicit bias in workplaces, schools, and public spaces, but also commonly confront financial barriers to key resources like health and education, obstacles that effectively discriminate on the basis of socioeconomic status. Conditioning access to healthcare on the ability to pay widens socioeconomic disparities by deterring low-income individuals from seeking care and increasing the risks and costs of preventable diseases and deaths. Likewise, charging tuition for public education leads to the disproportionate exclusion of girls, children with disabilities, and students from low-income families.

In a significant share of countries, constitutions address income barriers directly. Fifty-three per cent of constitutions guarantee the right to free primary school; 30 per cent do so for secondary education. Ten per cent guarantee universally free medical care, while another 6 per cent guarantee low-income children and adults the right to medical care.[33]

These provisions have helped expand access and inclusion. For example, the Kenyan High Court found in 2012 that a maternity hospital's practice of detaining women who could not afford to pay their bills violated the women's rights to health and was a form of unconstitutional discrimination on the basis of socioeconomic status.[34] In 2003, Colombia's Constitutional Court cited the constitution's guarantee of free public education in its ruling that a Bogotá school district should consider social and economic factors when assigning students to schools to prevent excessive transportation costs for families.[35] Together, constitutional prohibitions of discrimination on the basis of socioeconomic status and removal of financial barriers to fundamental rights can advance equality in practice.

E. Disability: Guaranteeing Reasonable Accommodation and Inclusive Education

To ensure equal rights regardless of disability, prohibiting discrimination alone is rarely enough. Guaranteeing reasonable accommodation at work and inclusive education would provide a stronger constitutional foundation for equality.

Beginning in the 1970s, the global disability rights movement helped mainstream the 'social model' of disability, which seeks to ensure substantive equality for persons with disabilities and mandates accommodation and inclusion in addition to formal prohibitions of discrimination. This model posits that

[33] For further data on rights to health and education, see https://www.worldpolicycenter.org/topics/constitutions/policies.

[34] Heymann et al (n 19) 190–91.

[35] Ibid, 190.

persons with disabilities are not excluded from full participation by disability itself but rather by society's failure to adapt to human differences through, for example, accessible infrastructure, information, and political processes. The movement succeeded in the ratification of the CRPD in 2006.

Equality and inclusion remain hollow promises if socially constructed barriers persist. Since the CRPD, countries have made major progress in strengthening laws to ensure equal treatment; however, significant gaps remain in constitutions. Out of 193 constitutions, just two explicitly provide for reasonable accommodations at work, seven address integrated education for children with disabilities, and none include language that clearly mandates full inclusion. However, these provisions have had some impact and can provide an example for other countries seeking to enshrine stronger rights. In Brazil, for instance, the Supreme Court upheld a 2016 law mandating inclusive education in both public and private schools, citing the constitution's provision on integrated education.

F. Migration Status: Ensuring Fundamental Rights Apply Regardless of Citizenship

Framing constitutional rights as belonging to 'citizens' can exclude refugees and other migrants from fundamental protections and undermine standards for all. In contrast, guaranteeing non-citizens' access to basic healthcare, education, and safe working conditions can provide a powerful foundation for upholding universal human rights.

Constitutional equality provisions can offer important support for upholding migrants' rights. When constitutions articulate rights using 'citizenship' language, however, refugees and migrants can face exclusion. Advocates have called attention to this threat. In South Korea, for instance, the National Human Rights Commission called upon the government to replace the word 'citizens' with 'people' throughout the constitution's basic rights provisions.

Beyond inclusive language, however, specific guarantees of equal rights for non-citizens are likely to offer stronger safeguards for equal rights, especially with respect to education, healthcare, and decent work. Globally, 14 per cent of constitutions guarantee non-citizens' right to health, 17 per cent guarantee their right to education, and 21 per cent protect some aspect of equality and non-discrimination in working life, providing an important foundation for upholding these rights regardless of migration status.

G. Religion: Protecting Freedom of Belief While Prohibiting Discriminatory Practices

In addition to prohibiting religious discrimination, constitutions can more fully protect equal rights across religion by protecting freedom of religion, belief, and non-belief, guaranteeing everyone's equal rights without exceptions for religious laws or practices, and avoiding constitutional language that privileges a single religion or religion generally.

A constitution designed to truly support equal rights regardless of belief would ensure that people can observe their faith while nevertheless curbing discriminatory religious practices, and would mandate full state neutrality toward all religions, beliefs, and non-beliefs. International agreements recognise these principles; for example, the ICCPR protects religious freedom, prohibits religious discrimination, and guarantees unqualified freedom of belief but calls for limits on freedom of practice to protect the rights of others.[36]

Alongside the 78 per cent of constitutions that prohibit discrimination on the basis of religion, 95 per cent include protections for freedom of religion. Forty-one per cent of constitutions establish secularism or the separation of church and state, while a quarter explicitly guarantee the freedom to not believe, practise, or disclose one's religion. In addition, 46 per cent of constitutions specify that religious practices may be limited to protect others' fundamental rights. However, some countries' constitutions contain gaps and inconsistencies that threaten the realisation of equal rights regardless of religion or belief. For example, 18 per cent protect freedom of religion but give special recognition to a specific religion. While the practical effects of these provisions may be minimal, they signal a preference for specific religious views, with normative consequences that could prove harmful as patterns of large-scale migration and increasing religious diversity converge with growing nationalist movements worldwide.

Countries have used a number of strategies to safeguard freedom of belief while protecting other rights. Comprehensive guarantees of equal rights on all grounds can help ensure that religious rights do not take precedence over other protected statuses, as can constitutional provisions that specifically address conflicts between religious practices and others' fundamental rights. For example, Nicaragua's constitution guarantees religious freedom but also specifies that '[n]o one may … impede others from exercising their rights … by invoking religious beliefs'.[37] Another strategy to protect the rights of all is to make the constitution the supreme law of the land, without exceptions for customary or religious law. Forty-eight per cent of constitutions worldwide deem constitutional provisions supreme, while an additional 1 per cent make religious laws specifically subordinate to the constitution.

In short, beyond prohibiting religious discrimination, constitution drafters aiming to comprehensively protect equal rights would benefit from examining

[36] Art 18 of the International Covenant on Civil and Political Rights (New York, 16 December 1966); CCPR General Comment No 22: Art 18 (Freedom of Thought, Conscience or Religion) (New York, 30 July 1993); CCPR General Comment 28: Art 3 (The Equality of Rights Between Men and Women) (New York, 29 March 2000).

[37] Heymann et al (n 19) 105.

how references to religion throughout the entire text may influence the rights of people of all beliefs.

H. Emerging, Underrecognised, and Cross-Cutting Forms of Discrimination

While the types of discrimination described throughout this chapter remain troublingly common across countries, they are by no means exhaustive. Moreover, new forms of discrimination emerge as societies evolve. Genetic discrimination, for example, is a new type of discrimination made possible by modern technology. One way that constitutions can reach additional forms of discrimination beyond those specifically prohibited is by including language such as 'or any other status' in their non-discrimination provisions. While no substitute for comprehensively enumerating protected statuses, this 'catch-all' language can provide the flexibility to reach emerging, underrecognised, and cross-cutting forms of discrimination.

VI. ADDRESSING HISTORIC DISCRIMINATION: CONTEXT-SPECIFIC CONSIDERATIONS

Constitutional provisions allowing for affirmative measures to advance equality can help address the consequences of past and continuing discrimination, exclusion, and oppression that limit marginalised groups' present-day opportunities and access to resources.

Across countries, different groups have faced varying degrees of historic discrimination and exclusion, including through laws that limited access to education, employment, and resources. Designing effective affirmative measures is a context-specific undertaking that requires consideration of questions such as which groups to include, how to target these practices, the ideal policy duration, and how to measure policy effectiveness. These design questions can be complex, but well-crafted affirmative measures can help all groups realise the promise of equal rights by mitigating the harms of past injustices and shifting representation and access to institutions.

Across countries, affirmative measures often meet with controversy and have been subject to challenges based on constitutional equal rights guarantees that broadly stipulate equality before the law without providing for affirmative steps to achieve equality in practice. Because affirmative measures are commonly politically contentious, constitutional provisions that specifically allow their implementation provide a strong foundation for these policies and related court decisions. Express constitutional allowances for affirmative measures can protect against narrow readings of equality that mandate identical rather than equitable treatment in all circumstances.

VII. CONCLUSION

Constitutional provisions that have impact for advancing equality in practice encompass a wide range of rights, including: detailed guarantees of equal rights and prohibitions of direct and indirect discrimination; guarantees of civil, political, social, and economic rights; and more targeted approaches to addressing persisting barriers to equal rights for marginalised groups.

In recent decades, constitutional protections have become more prevalent in almost all these areas, reflecting the successes of national and global social movements as well as the influence of stronger and more specific protections in widely ratified human rights treaties. Further, emerging areas of constitutional protection – including guarantees of equality on the basis of caregiving statuses, explicit rights to reasonable accommodations and inclusive education, and explicit protections against discrimination on the basis of sexual orientation and gender identity – signal that continued expansion is both likely and necessary for realising the rights of all.

From a practical perspective, constitutional equal rights guarantees can and have facilitated access to education, jobs, and healthcare and provided individuals the freedom to lead self-directed lives. Equally – and perhaps more – important, however, are constitutions' impacts on shared norms and values, and the expressive power their language holds to affirm the common dignity, humanity, and equal rights of all.

5

Socio-Economic Rights in South Africa's Constitution: Aspirations, Achievements, Disappointments and Lessons

SANDRA LIEBENBERG*

I. INTRODUCTION

SOUTH AFRICA HAS had a history of over 300 years of colonialism and apartheid which dispossessed the Black majority of the population of their indigenous lands and institutionalised a system of racialised oppression and discrimination. With the coming into power of the National Party in 1948, the white minority Parliament, operating under a system of parliamentary sovereignty, enacted a series of laws that brought about widespread impoverishment and systemic discrimination in every sphere of life. Not only were the Black majority deprived of their right to vote and subjected to civil and political oppression, but they were subject to inferior and discriminatory access to economic, social and cultural rights.

The apartheid era was brought to an end by a negotiated transition to democracy. This transition occurred in two stages: the adoption of the 'Interim' Constitution (the 1993 Constitution) which established the institutions, principles and procedures for the adoption of the 'Final' Constitution (the 1996 Constitution). South Africa's first democratic elections were held in April 1994. The adoption of the 'Final' Constitution in 1996 completed the transition from a system of parliament sovereignty to a constitutional democracy with an entrenched and judicially enforceable Bill of Rights.

While the Interim Constitution contained a kernel of socio-economic rights in its Bill of Rights, the 1996 Constitution is famed for its inclusion of a set of economic, social, cultural, land and environmental rights in its Bill of Rights.

* The research assistance of Christiaan Van Schalkwyk and comments of Jackie Dugard on an earlier draft of this chapter are acknowledged with gratitude.

These rights are enforceable by the courts (ie they are justiciable) and subject to the same procedures and judicial remedies as all the other rights in the Bill of Rights (section 38 read with section 176). The 1996 Constitution gives a specific mandate to the South African Human Rights Commission to request information from relevant organs of state 'on the measures that they have taken towards the realisation of the rights in the Bill of Rights concerning housing, healthcare, food, water, social security, education and the environment' (section 184(3)). Another notable feature of the Bill of Rights is the fact that it makes provision for the Bill of Rights to apply directly to private actors (known as horizontal application) (sections 8(2) and 8(3)). The prohibition against unfair discrimination is expressly made binding on private parties in terms of section 9(4) of the Constitution. It also places a duty on courts and tribunals to interpret legislation and to develop the common law and customary law in ways that are consonant with the foundational values of the Constitution, namely, human dignity, equality, and freedom (section 39(2)).

The 1996 Constitution was enacted with the aim of laying the foundations for the construction of a post-apartheid society based on social justice, improving the quality of life of all citizens, and freeing the potential of each person (Preamble to the Constitution). Central to this transformative aspiration was the inclusion of socio-economic rights in the Bill of Rights of the Constitution.

This chapter reflects on the aspirations that accompanied the inclusion of socio-economic rights in the Constitution, their key achievements, as well as key areas of disappointment in their contribution to transformative social change. It concludes with some tentative reflections on what Chile's constitutional project could learn from South Africa's unfinished experiment with justiciable socio-economic rights.

II. ASPIRATIONS

The recognition of socio-economic rights as equal and enforceable rights in the Bill of Rights of the 1996 South African Constitution can be ascribed to a constellation of circumstances.[1] On the one hand, the African National Congress (ANC) was in favour of a constitutional framework that could support and facilitate the massive effort of social and economic redistribution and reconstruction that was needed to redress the brutal legacies of colonialism and apartheid.[2] The inclusion of socio-economic rights in the Constitution was

[1] For an account of this history see S Liebenberg, *Socio-Economic Rights: Adjudication under a Transformative Constitution* (Claremont, Juta, 2010) 14–19.

[2] ANC, *Constitutional Guidelines for a Democratic South Africa* (1989); ANC, *A Bill of Rights for a Democratic South Africa: Working Draft for Consultation* (1990).

seen as a way of promoting a substantive social democracy, and as a counterweight to the traditional negative, formal visions of constitutional rights. As eloquently expressed by former President, Nelson Mandela:

> A simple vote, without food, shelter and health care is to use first generation rights as a smokescreen to obscure the deep underlying forces which dehumanise people. It is to create an appearance of equality and justice, while by implication socio-economic inequality is entrenched. We do not want freedom without bread, nor do we want bread without freedom. We must provide for all the fundamental rights and freedoms associated with a democratic society.[3]

The inclusion of a property clause in the Bill of Rights emerged as a key element in the political compromise for a negotiated transition from apartheid to democracy. The National Party (which governed during the apartheid period, 1948–1994), the liberal Democratic Party, along with predominantly white-owned big business, viewed a property clause as essential to the protection of their interests.[4] Socio-economic rights, including land rights, gave an explicit mandate to the new state to be proactive in adopting legislation and policies aimed at achieving a more equitable distribution of resources and social services.[5] These land rights comprise equitable access to land, tenure security, and property restitution as a result of past racially discriminatory laws and practices. It was thus hoped that they would prevent the Bill of Rights being interpreted in ways that preserved the existing unjust patterns of resource distribution in South Africa.

In addition, an active civil society coalition (consisting of human rights and development NGOs, trade unions, church groups, women's organisations, and academics) campaigned actively for the recognition of socio-economic rights in the Constitution. This alliance was called the *Ad Hoc Campaign for Social and Economic Rights*. They argued that it was both symbolically and strategically important to include socio-economic rights alongside civil and political ones as justiciable rights in the Bill of Rights. The Constitution was described as a mirror, which should reflect the interests of all people, but particularly those disadvantaged by poverty and social exclusion.[6]

The Campaign also argued that recognising socio-economic rights in the Constitution would create political and legal avenues for the poor and

[3] NR Mandela, 'Address: On the occasion of the ANC's Bill of Rights conference' in *A Bill of Rights for a Democratic South Africa: Papers and Report of a Conference Convened by the ANC Constitutional Committee* (1991) 9–14 at 12.

[4] H Klug, *Constituting Democracy: Law, Globalisation and South Africa's Political Reconstruction* (Cambridge, Cambridge University Press, 2000) 124–36.

[5] Section 25(8) of the property clause expressly provides that it should not constitute a barrier to the achievement of land, water and related reforms.

[6] *Petition to the Constitutional Assembly by the Ad Hoc Campaign for Social and Economic Rights* (19 July 1995), extracts published in S Liebenberg and K Pillay (eds), *Socio-Economic Rights in South Africa: A Resource Book* (University of the Western Cape, Community Law Centre, 2000) 19–20.

disadvantaged to protect and advance their material interests. This could be achieved through a combination of policy and legislative advocacy, public interest litigation, and engagement with the national human rights institutions such as the South African Human Rights Commissions and Commission on Gender Equality. These institutions were established in terms of Chapter 9 of the Constitution and described as 'State institutions supporting constitutional democracy'. In these ways, socio-economic rights could be seen as facilitating a form of participatory democracy, particularly in decision-making affecting people's access to the social goods and services needed for a dignified life.

The question of the inclusion of socio-economic rights in the Constitution did not take place without resistance from various sectors, including parts of the legal community that would have preferred to see them not included at all, or recognised in a diluted form as non-enforceable directive principles of state policy.[7]

Ultimately, however, a set of socio-economic rights were recognised as justiciable rights in the Bill of Rights. The formulation of a number of these rights drew inspiration from the International Covenant on Economic, Social and Cultural Rights (ICESCR).[8] Thus, for example, sections 26 and 27 of the South African Constitution impose a duty on the state to take 'reasonable legislative and other measures, within its available resources, to achieve the progressive realisation' of the rights of everyone to have access to adequate housing, health care, food, water and social security. However, as the Constitutional Court has pointed out, the wording is not identical to that contained in the ICESCR.[9] Thus, for example, Art 2 of the ICESCR refers to a State Party taking steps 'to the maximum of its available resources', whereas sections 26(2) and 27(2) refer only to 'within its available resources'.

In contrast, some socio-economic rights – such as children's rights 'to basic nutrition, shelter, basic healthcare services and social services' and the right to 'a basic education', including 'adult basic education' – were included in the Bill of Rights without these qualifying phrases (sections 28(1)(c) and 29(a)). However, like all rights in the Bill of Rights, these so-called 'unqualified' socio-economic rights are subject to limitation in terms of the general limitations clause in the Bill of Rights (section 36). The Bill of Rights also incorporates a right to an environment that is not harmful to health and well-being, and places a duty on the state to protect the environment 'for the benefit of present and future generations, through reasonable legislative and other measures' (section 24).

Ultimately, it was hoped that the recognition of socio-economic and environmental rights as enforceable rights in the highest law of the land would contribute to creating a legal framework that would support the political

[7] Liebenberg (n 1) 11–21.

[8] International Covenant on Economic, Social and Cultural Rights (adopted on 16 December 1966, entered into force, 3 January 1976) 993 UNTS 3.

[9] *Government of the Republic of South Africa v Grootboom* 2001 (1) SA 46 (CC), paras 26–28.

measures needed to achieve wide-ranging economic and social transformation. These rights are amongst the features that have led scholars to describe South Africa's Constitution as a 'transformative constitution'.[10]

III. ACHIEVEMENTS

The socio-economic and environmental rights in the Bill of Rights have informed the drafting of a number of laws, policies and programmes in the spheres of land and housing, healthcare, social security, water, environmental rights, education, and children's rights.[11] They have also been used by civil society and social movements in support of a variety of campaigns, including a child support grant, access to antiretroviral treatment for people living with HIV/AIDS, access to land and housing, education rights, environmental rights, the introduction of a basic income grant, and many more.[12] The South African Human Rights Commission has undertaken a number of inquiries and hearings, and produced reports on various aspects of socio-economic rights realisation in South Africa.[13]

In the sphere of litigation, a rich socio-economic rights jurisprudence has developed. This litigation has resulted in concrete changes to laws, policies and practices, which have benefited disadvantaged groups in South Africa. For present purposes, I highlight four areas in which there have been significant developments in legal doctrines that protect and advance socio-economic rights.

First, the Constitutional Court has developed a nuanced set of legal doctrines and practices for engaging with the tensions between property rights and the right to housing. Access to land and housing for the historically dispossessed Black community are at the heart of the post-apartheid transformation agenda. In a series of progressive judgments, the Constitutional Court has affirmed the importance of the right to housing in the Constitution. In its famous judgment in *Government of the Republic of South Africa v Grootboom* (*Grootboom*),[14] the Constitutional Court elaborated on the implications of the constitutional duty on the state to take 'reasonable legislative and other measures' to realise the right of access to housing in section 26 of the Constitution. It held that

[10] On the transformative, 'post-liberal' nature of the South Africa, see the widely cited article by K Klare, 'Legal Culture and Transformative Constitutionalism,' (1998) 14 *South African Journal on Human Rights* 146.

[11] For example: Restitution of Land Rights Act 22 of 1994; Housing Act 107 of 1997; Social Assistance Act 13 of 2004; National Schools Act 84 of 1996; National Environmental Management Act 107 of 1998; Children's Act 38 of 2006; National Water Act 36 of 1998. South Africa's current development plan is the National Development Plan (2030), www.gov.za/issues/national-development-plan-2030.

[12] See the collection of essays in M Langford et al, *Socio-Economic Rights in South Africa: Symbols or Substance?* (Cambridge, Cambridge University Press, 2014).

[13] Its reports are all available on its website, at www.sahrc.org.za/index.php/publications.

[14] *Government of the Republic of South Africa v Grootboom* 2001 (1) SA 46 (CC).

reasonableness should be interpreted in the light of the values of human dignity, freedom and equality with special attention to the needs of the poor.[15] This required public authorities as a minimum to ensure that emergency housing was available to those who faced homelessness as a result of an eviction.[16]

In a subsequent judgment dealing with the clash between property rights and housing rights in eviction applications, the Constitutional Court held that the role of the courts was not to automatically privilege property rights over housing rights in a 'hierarchical arrangement'.[17] Rather, it should strive to 'balance out and reconcile the opposed claims in as just a manner as possible taking account of all the interests involved and the specific factors relevant in each particular case'.[18] Subsequent jurisprudence has built on these foundations to interpret section 26 and relevant legislation to require that evictions must conform to the principles of fairness and proportionality.[19] In addition, public authorities should ensure that there is 'meaningful engagement' with occupiers prior to eviction applications.[20]

Finally, if an eviction is ordered, alternative accommodation should generally be provided to those who face homelessness, regardless of whether the eviction was initiated by the public authorities or by private parties.[21] This is an extension of the general principle laid down in the *Grootboom* judgment that relief should be provided to those 'who have no access to land, no roof over their heads, and who are living in intolerable conditions or crisis situations'.[22]

The second area of achievement concerns the right of access to healthcare in section 27 of the Constitution. A celebrated judgment of the Constitution Court held that the government's failure to roll out an antiretroviral programme to prevent mother-to-child transmission of HIV during childbirth was unreasonable, and thus a violation of the right of everyone to access healthcare services in section 27 of the Constitution.[23] This litigation formed one part of a wide-ranging campaign by the Treatment Action Campaign (TAC) to promote access to antiretroviral therapy and appropriate medical treatment for people living with HIV/AIDS. This judgment, in combination with a variety of other

[15] Ibid, paras 36, 44 and 83.

[16] Ibid, paras 68–69 and 99.

[17] *Port Elizabeth Municipality v Various Occupiers* 2005 (1) SA 217 (CC).

[18] Ibid, para 23. For a recent judgment upholding the rights of farm dwellers to improve their housing to a more dignified standard despite opposition by the owner of the farm, see *Daniels v Scribante* 2017 (4) SA 431 (CC).

[19] S Wilson, 'Breaking the Tie: Evictions from Private Land, Homelessness and a New Normality' (2009) 126 *South African Law Journal* 270.

[20] *Occupiers of 51 Olivia Road, Berea Township and 197 Main Street, Johannesburg v City of Johannesburg* 2008 (3) 208 (CC); B Ray, *Engaging with Social Rights: Procedure, Participation, and Democracy in South Africa's Second Wave* (Cambridge, Cambridge University Press, 2016).

[21] *City of Johannesburg Metropolitan Municipality v Blue Moonlight Properties 39 (Pty) Ltd* 2012 (2) SA 104 (CC).

[22] *Grootboom* (n 14) para 99.

[23] *Minister of Health v Treatment Action Campaign (No 2)* 2002 (5) SA 721 (CC).

education and advocacy strategies pursued by the TAC, eventually led to South Africa establishing the largest antiretroviral treatment programme in the world.[24]

Third, there have been important gains made in the sphere of education rights campaigns, including those brought by social movements such as Equal Education and other public interest organisations.[25] The Constitutional Court has held that the right to basic education is an 'immediately realisable' right,[26] interpreting the scope of 'basic education' to include the entire phase of primary and secondary schooling in South Africa.[27] It will be recalled that this right is formulated as an unqualified right, unlike the rights in sections 26 and 27. The right to basic education may only be limited in terms of the strict requirements of the general limitations clause (section 36), which include the requirement of a law of general application, a weighty reason and a proportionality inquiry.

The High Courts and Supreme Court of Appeal have also, in a series of cases, developed the substantive content of the right to education. Thus, they have held that it includes school infrastructure, furniture, learner transport, sufficient teachers, and textbooks.[28] In the context of the Covid-19 pandemic, a Provincial High Court held that the failure of the educational authorities to ensure that all learners received a daily school meal in terms of the National School Nutrition Programme during the period of school closures violated both the right to basic education, and children's right to basic nutrition. It ordered the education authorities to ensure that daily school meals were provided to all learners, including those studying at home because their year group had not yet returned to school. The court also imposed reporting obligations on the government, and supervision over the implementation of its orders.[29] One of the socio-economic rights doctrines relied on by the Court in supporting its judgment was the duty of governments to avoid retrogressive measures subject to the strict criteria of justification developed by the UN Committee on Economic, Social and Cultural Rights, and the Committee on the Rights of the Child.[30]

The interrelationship between socio-economic rights and the right to equality is the fourth area to be highlighted.[31] The Constitutional Court has

[24] M Heywood, 'South Africa's Treatment Action Campaign: Combining Law and Social Mobilization to Realize the Right to Health' (2009) 1 *Journal of Human Rights Practice* 14.

[25] F Veriava, *Realising the Right to Basic Education: The Role of the Courts and Civil Society* (Claremont, Juta, 2019).

[26] *Governing Body of the Juma Musjid Primary School v Essay NO* 2011 (8) BCLR 761 (CC).

[27] See *Moko v Acting Principal of Malusi Secondary School and Others* [2020] ZACC 30, 2021 (4) BCLR 420 (CC).

[28] V Faranaaz, *Realising the Right to Basic Education: The Role of the Courts and Civil Society* (Claremont, Juta, 2019) and C McConnachie and S Brener, 'Litigating the Right to Basic Education' in J Brickhill (ed), *Public Interest Litigation in South Africa* (Claremont, Juta, 2018) 281.

[29] *Equal Education v Minister of Basic Education* 2021 (1) SA 198 (GP).

[30] Ibid, paras 43–60.

[31] S Liebenberg and B Goldblatt, 'The Interrelationship between Equality and Socio-economic Rights under South Africa's Transformative Constitution' (2007) 23 *South African Journal on Human Rights* 335.

developed a strong jurisprudence on substantive equality. It has also recognised that legislation that excludes certain groups from social assistance programmes on prohibited grounds amounts to both a breach of the right against unfair discrimination, and the right of everyone to have access to social security.[32] The Bill of Rights recognises both direct and indirect discrimination, and affirmative action measures in favour of disadvantaged groups are regarded as integral to the right to equality. Section 9(2) expressly provides for affirmative action measures.[33] In addition, legislation has been adopted which recognises 'socio-economic status' as a potential prohibited ground of unfair discrimination.[34] 'Socio-economic status' is defined to include 'a social or economic condition or perceived condition of a person who is disadvantaged by poverty, low employment status or lack of or low-level educational qualifications' (section 1).

In a promising judgment, an Equality Court found that the unequal allocation of police human resources to low-income, overwhelmingly Black communities in the Western Cape Province constituted unfair discrimination on the grounds of both poverty and race.[35] However, despite the promising features of the legislation and jurisprudence, the right to equality has not yet played a prominent role in political and legal strategies aimed at challenging systemic socio-economic inequalities in South Africa.[36]

Having identified key achievements of the inclusion of socio-economic rights in the Constitution, the following section identifies some of the disappointments that have been voiced concerning the constitutional promise of socio-economic rights.

IV. DISAPPOINTMENTS

It is more than 25 years since South Africa entered the era of constitutional democracy. Poverty levels are deep, unemployment is very high, and inequality pervasive. Prior to the outbreak of the Covid-19 pandemic, 55 per cent of the population were considered poor in terms of the upper-bound poverty-line of Statistics South Africa, whereas 25 per cent of the population fell below the lower, food-bound poverty line.[37] Poverty disproportionately affects Black

[32] *Khosa and Others v Minister of Social Development, Mahlaule v Minister of Social Development* 2004 (6) SA 505 (CC).

[33] The leading Constitutional Court judgment is *Minister of Finance v Van Heerden* 2004 (6) SA 121 (CC).

[34] Promotion of Equality and Prevention of Unfair Discrimination Act 4 of 2000, s 34.

[35] *Social Justice Coalition v Minister of Police* 2019 (4) SA 82 (WCC).

[36] C Albertyn, 'Contested Substantive Equality in the South African Constitution: Beyond Social Inclusion towards Systemic Justice' (2018) 34 *South African Journal on Human Rights* 441.

[37] Statistics South Africa, *Poverty Trends in South Africa: An Examination of Absolute Poverty between 2006 and 2015* (2017). See also the SA Human Rights Commission, *Equality Report 2017/2018*. www.sahrc.org.za/home/21/files/SAHRC%20Equality%20Report%202017_18.pdf.

people, women, and those living in rural areas. For example, 64 per cent of the Black African population are poor compared to just 1 per cent of the White population group.[38] Furthermore, as noted by the UN Committee on Economic, Social and Cultural Rights, South Africa is amongst the most unequal countries in the world, with a Gini coefficient of 0.63 and a Palma ratio of 7.1.[39] The Covid-19 pandemic and the measures adopted to contain the virus have aggravated the situation, with spiralling levels of poverty, unemployment, hunger, school drop-outs and inequality.[40]

Widespread corruption and state capture have plagued South Africa, particularly during the period of the presidency of Former President Jacob Zuma (2009–2018). President Ramaphosa has said that South Africa has lost close to 1 trillion ZAR through corruption.[41] A high-level Judicial Commission of Inquiry, chaired by the Deputy Chief Justice of South Africa, Justice Raymond Zondo, into allegations of state capture, corruption and fraud in the public sector was established and is in the process of finalising its report.[42]

The delivery of many socio-economic rights such as water and sanitation services, social security grants, land reform, housing, and healthcare services has also been plagued by maladministration and institutional incapacity. This has given rise to regular and widespread so-called 'service delivery' protests and uprisings by impoverished communities.[43] The courts have often had to grapple with the problem of how to get organs of state to comply with their orders in relation to socio-economic rights delivery. In this context, they have formulated a range of innovative remedies such as constitutional damages,[44] and structural interdicts involving expert committees[45] and special masters.[46]

Despite the progressive judgments described in the previous section, the courts have not always interpreted socio-economic rights in ways that advance the underlying values and purposes of these rights. Thus, in the case of *Mazibuko v City of Johannesburg*,[47] the Constitutional Court dismissed a challenge to the sufficiency of the amount of free basic water provided to poor communities

[38] SA Human Rights Commission, ibid, 18.

[39] UN CESCR, *Concluding Observations on the Initial Report of South Africa* UN doc E/C.12/ZAF/CO/1, para 16.

[40] See the outcomes of the National Income Dynamics Study/Coronavirus Rapid Mobile Survey (NIDS-CRAM), https://cramsurvey.org/.

[41] SABC News, 'Corruption has cost SA close to R1 trillion: Ramaphosa' (15 October 2019), www.sabcnews.com/sabcnews/corruption-has-cost-sa-close-to-r1-trillion-ramaphosa/.

[42] For further details of the Commission, see www.statecapture.org.za/.

[43] J Brown, *South African's Insurgent Citizens: On Dissent and the Possibility of Politics* (London, Zed Books, 2015).

[44] *President of the Republic of South Africa v Modderklip Boerdery (Pty) Ltd* 2005 (5) SA 3 (CC).

[45] *Black Sash Trust v Minister of Social Development (Freedom under Law NPC Intervening)* 2017 (3) SA 335 (CC).

[46] *Mwelase v Director-General for the Department of Rural Development and Land Reform* 2019 (6) SA 597 (CC).

[47] 2010 (4) SA 1 (CC).

by the City of Johannesburg. It held that the quantum of 25 litres per person per day provided by the City met the constitutional standard of reasonableness, dismissing the applicants' contention that 50 litres was required to meet the community's basic water needs. It also dismissed the applicant's challenge to the system of prepayment water meters. These meters automatically discontinued the supply of water to households after the free basic water supply was used up unless additional credits were purchased. This judgment was widely criticised,[48] with certain scholars arguing that the Court's judgment implicitly endorsed neoliberal models of service delivery.[49]

Another area in which the Court's jurisprudence has been criticised has been in relation to the application of constitutional rights to private actors. As noted above, the Constitution provides for the horizontal application of the rights in the Bill of Rights. However, more could be done to develop the law to ensure greater human rights accountability by private actors, particularly large corporations.[50]

The entrenched patterns of racially-based poverty and inequality have given rise to criticisms of the compromises that were reached during the political negotiations leading to constitutional democracy in South Africa. These critiques gained traction during the 2015–2016 #FeesMustFall student uprising in the higher-education sector, calling for free, decolonised education in South Africa. Certain scholars have called into question the paradigm of transformative constitutionalism and the role of courts in social change.[51] The property clause in the Bill of Rights, section 25, has been at the centre of these contestations, with critics arguing that the clauses relating to providing compensation for the expropriation of property constitute a barrier to land reform. However, it should be noted that section 25(2) and (3) provides for the calculation of expropriation to take into account a range of factors, including the current use of the property and the history of its acquisition and use. The market value of the property is only one factor to be taken into account in calculating compensation.[52] Political criticisms of the slow pace of land redistribution culminated in the appointment of a joint parliamentary constitutional review committee, which recommended an amendment of section 25 of the Constitution. This amendment would have provided for the possibility of nil compensation where land is expropriated for the purposes of land reform.[53] However, on 7 December 2021

[48] See, for example, LA Williams, 'The Role of Courts in the Quantitative Implementation of Social and Economic Rights: A Comparative Study' (2010) 3 *Constitutional Court Review* 141.

[49] P O'Connell, 'The Death of Socio-economic Rights' (2011) 74 *Modern Law Review* 532, 550–52.

[50] S Liebenberg, 'Socio-Economic Rights beyond the Public-private Divide' in Langford et al (n 12) 63.

[51] See, for example: S Sibanda, 'When Do you Call Time on Compromise? South Africa's Discourse on Transformation and the Future of Transformative Constitutionalism' (2020) 24 *Law Democracy and Development* 384.

[52] Section 25(3)(c).

[53] Constitution, Eighteenth Amendment Bill, https://static.pmg.org.za/191203Draft_advertised.pdf.

the National Assembly failed to pass the Constitutional Amendment Bill due to the requisite two-thirds majority not being obtained. It is more likely that the slow pace of land reform is due to market-orientated state policies, institutional incapacity and maladministration rather than the provisions of section 25 of the Constitution.[54]

The disappointment with socio-economic transformation in South Africa can be attributed to a range of factors. These include the economic policies adopted by successive ANC governments in the post-apartheid period. These have tended to follow orthodox economic theories, which have dismally failed to dislodge entrenched patterns of socio-economic disadvantage and inequality.[55] Moreover, the corruption, maladministration and wastage of state resources referred to above has reduced the resources available for socio-economic rights and undermined ethical and effective governance.[56] The Constitutional Court has recognised that corruption undermines human rights and democracy and that the state has a constitutional duty to establish independent and effective anti-corruption mechanisms to protect human rights.[57] In addition, the delivery of vital social services has been plagued by problems of incapacity in state institutions, especially in the local sphere of government.[58]

The chasm between the constitutional promise of socio-economic rights and the reality of poverty and inequality is indeed deeply disappointing. However, it would be a mistake to conclude that the inclusion of socio-economic rights in the Constitution has been worthless. As described in the previous section, they have created a range of mechanisms for civil society organisations to challenge both the state and private sector conduct impacting on these rights. A number of successful advocacy campaigns (incorporating public interest litigation strategies) have been undertaken. These have advanced the realisation of human rights, including socio-economic rights.[59] The socio-economic deprivations and inequalities in South Africa, which have deepened during the Covid-19 pandemic, are due primarily to the nature of the macro-economic policies adopted, systemic corruption, and governance failures. The struggle to find effective mechanisms to address these systemic issues is an ongoing quest by

[54] J Dugard, 'Unpacking Section 25: What, If Any, Are the Legal Barriers to Transformative Land Reform?' (2019) 9 *Constitutional Court Review* 135.

[55] P Bond, *Elite Transition – From Apartheid to Neoliberalism in South Africa*, 2nd revised edn (University of KwaZulu-Natal Press, 2005); S Johannes (Sampie) Terreblanche, *Lost in Transformation: South Africa's Search for a New Future Since 1986* (KMM Review Publishing, 2012).

[56] This has been documented in reports of the Auditor-General of South Africa, see www.agsa.co.za/. See also K Makwetu, 'Constitutional Accountability for Public Resources: The Role of the Auditor-General' (2019) 30 *Stellenbosch Law Review* 318.

[57] *Glenister v President of the Republic of South Africa* 2011 (3) SA 347 (CC).

[58] A Siddle and TA Koelble, *The Failure of Decentralisation in South African Local Government: Complexity and Unanticipated Consequences* (Cape Town, University of Cape Town Press, 2012).

[59] See, for example, the theory and practice of various campaigns documented in Brickhill (n 28).

civil society organisations and social movements. The socio-economic rights in the Constitution are allies in these struggles.

V. LESSONS

The subject of what lessons Chile can learn from the South African experience of constitutionalising socio-economic rights is a large area, fraught with the complexities of constitutional comparisons and transplants. I restrict myself here to making five general points regarding the lessons to be learnt from the South African experience.

First, it is important to have realistic expectations of what constitutional rights can and cannot do. As may be obvious to many, international and constitutionally entrenched human rights do not automatically produce social change and transformative outcomes. What they can do is help make political institutions, laws, and jurisprudence more responsive to the needs and claims of impoverished and marginalised groups. In so doing, they open political and legal spaces for contesting poverty and inequality by communities and organisations.[60]

The question should not be whether socio-economic rights have 'produced' the desired social change, or whether the Constitution is responsible for persistent poverty and inequality. Rather, we should pose the following question: Do the relevant constitutional provisions facilitate or impede the pursuit of economic and social justice? A constitution that excludes socio-economic rights makes the interests protected by these rights invisible in the country's highest law. It also skews the legal system towards the protection of those who already enjoy economic, social and political power. It is thus important that a country's Bill of Rights contains a holistic framework that protects all dimensions of human well-being and thriving, including socio-economic rights and a healthy environment.

Second, it is vital that the constitutional text clearly establishes that all constitutional rights, including socio-economic rights, apply to private actors. Multinational corporations and the network of laws that govern them have a profound influence on people's ability to access many socio-economic rights, such as healthcare, housing, and social security. This includes through the taxes that they should pay to enable government to deliver socio-economic rights,[61] and in the context of privatisation of public services. Powerful private actors also have a major impact on the health of the environment, including climate change. The Constitution should thus specify that private actors can be held directly accountable for socio-economic rights violations, both within the national territory and extraterritorially. It should also place a specific duty on

[60] S Wilson, *Human Rights and the Transformation of Property* (Claremont, Juta, 2021).

[61] I Saiz, 'Resourcing Rights: Combating Tax Injustice from a Human Rights Perspective' in A Nolan et al (eds), *Human Rights and Public Finance: Budgets and the Promotion of Economic and Social Rights* (London, Bloomsbury, 2014) 77.

the state to regulate these actors appropriately to avoid national and extra-territorial harm to socio-economic and environmental rights.[62] As noted above, the South African Constitution provides for the so-called horizontal application of human rights to non-state actors. However, there remains much work to be done on developing legislation and policy to provide for more effective accountability of private actors, particularly in the sphere of socio-economic rights.

The third point to emphasise is that the ability of socio-economic rights to contribute to meaningful change in a society depends on a well-functioning, integrated network of political, legal and social institutions. In retrospect, I believe that insufficient attention was paid in South Africa's constitution-drafting process to designing mechanisms that could strengthen accountability for socio-economic rights realisation throughout all structures and operational processes of government. As the South African experience has shown, judicial protection has proved valuable in supporting broader campaigns for social and economic justice. However, judicial protection should be complemented by mechanisms that require all institutions of government to consider the impact of their decision-making on human rights, including socio-economic rights. This could include, for example, committees or ombudsmen that check for human rights impacts in policy and legislative processes, particularly in economic policy and budgetary decisions.[63]

Similarly, the public administration should also be required to adopt appropriate procedures and programmes to integrate socio-economic rights into their day-to-day operations. These should include, for example, human rights education, monitoring and evaluation procedures, as well as providing for complaints procedures that are speedy, cheap and accessible to ordinary people.

Fourth, national human rights institutions and ombudspersons should also be given defined roles and responsibilities in relation to socio-economic rights. The role of the South African Human Rights Commission in relation to socio-economic and environmental rights was drafted in rather vague terms. It is accordingly not clear what the Commission must do with the information it has gathered in exercising its mandate under section 184(3) of the Constitution.

Finally, including socio-economic rights in the Constitution in a context in which these rights have received minimal prior recognition in the legal system requires an extensive re-orientation of legal education. If this reorientation does not occur, the lawyers and judges of the future Chile will be hostile to these rights and closed to interpretations that are responsive to the claims of

[62] UN Committee on Economic, Social and Cultural Rights, General Comment No 24 (2017) on *State obligations under the International Covenant on Economic, Social and Cultural Rights in the context of business activities* UN doc E/C.12.GC/24 (10 August 2017).

[63] See, for example: The *Guiding Principles on Human Rights Impact Assessments of Economic Reforms*, 'Report of the Independent Expert on the effects of foreign debt and other related international financial obligations of States on the full enjoyment of human rights, particularly economic, social and cultural rights' UN doc A/HRC/40/57 (19 December 2018).

the poor.[64] Public education campaigns and access to justice are also essential in ensuring that socio-economic rights have real meaning in people's lives.[65]

VI. CONCLUSION

Including socio-economic rights in a constitution does not guarantee the achievement of social and economic justice. However, they provide the fundamental normative commitments against which economic, social and environmental laws and policies can be evaluated, and alternative proposals developed. They also open up a range of avenues for pursuing accountability for these rights, which can be used by ordinary people and their organisations. In the South African context, even social movements that have traditionally been sceptical of the potential of human rights have used the socio-economic rights provisions in the Constitution to win important gains in litigation and advocacy.[66]

Realising the full potential of socio-economic rights depends on a combination of ethical, well-functioning state institutions, a strong and independent judiciary, a range of other accessible accountability mechanisms, along with well-organised trade unions and civil society organisations. It is thus important that sustained attention is paid to building the institutions and organisations that ultimately give these rights their transformative power.

[64] G Quinot, 'Transformative Legal Education' (2012) 129 *South African Law Journal* 411.

[65] TF Hodgson, 'Bridging the Gap between People and the Law: Transformative Constitutionalism and the Right to Constitutional Literacy' in A Price and M Bishop (eds), *Transformative Justice: Essays in Honour of Pius Langa* (Claremont, Juta, 2015) 189.

[66] J Dugard et al, 'Rights-Compromised or Rights-Savvy? The Use of Rights-Based Strategies to Advance Socio-Economic Struggles by Abahlali baseMjondolo, the South African Shack-Dwellers' Movement' in H Alviar García et al (eds), *Social and Economic Rights in Theory and Practice: Critical Inquiries* (London, Routledge, 2015) 23.

6

Publicity and the Rule of Law: Access to Public Information in the Political Constitution of Colombia

VIVIAN NEWMAN

I. INTRODUCTION

UNDER THE RULE of law of any democratic government,[1] the actions of the authorities must be made public. Such publication can be proactively carried out by the state or can be the result of responding to requests by citizens. Access to public information strengthens the legitimacy and governance of democracies, guarantees transparency in the administration of government, and promotes accountability, thereby preventing corruption and authoritarianism.[2] Despite this obvious reality, it was not until 2006 that the Inter-American Court of Human Rights recognised for the first time the existence of the right of access to state-held information as a human right. In the relevant case, Chilean citizen Claude Reyes, along with other citizens, filed a claim for Chile to disclose information about a forestry exploitation project. On this occasion, the Inter-American Court of Human Rights held the view that:

> [i]n relation to the facts of the instant case, the Court finds that, by expressly stipulating the right to 'seek' and 'receive' 'information,' Article 13 of the Convention protects the right of all individuals to request access to State-held information, with the exceptions permitted by the restrictions established in the Convention. Consequently, this article protects the right of the individual to receive such information and the positive obligation of the State to provide it, so that the individual may have access to such information or receive an answer that includes a justification

[1] The General Assembly of the Organization of American States (OAS) recognises the right to access information as a 'requisite for the very exercise of Democracy'. Access to public information: strengthening democracy, OAS AG/RES 1932 (XXXIII-O/03) (adopted at the fourth plenary session, held on 10 June 2003), available at www.oas.org.

[2] Inter-American Commission on Human Rights (IACHR), Office of the Special Rapporteur for Freedom of Expression, 'The Inter-American Legal Framework regarding the Right to Access to Information' OEA Ser L/V/II CIDH/RELE/INF (2012).

> when, for any reason permitted by the Convention, the State is allowed to restrict access to the information in a specific case.[3]

The ruling had a considerable and important impact. In Chile, it accelerated the adoption of access to public information legislation, which was already in the process of adoption. It also catalysed the creation of the Council for Transparency. As a result, other countries in the region started to adopt similar norms. To date, over 22 countries in the Americas have adopted domestic laws which guarantee access to public information, and the Inter-American system has a standardised system in place.[4]

After almost a hundred years of a constitutional framework characterised by a general and unclear vision of human rights, in 1991 Colombia constructed a new Constitution which placed humans and human rights at the centre of the rule of law. The National Constituent Assembly defined and approved the political rules of the community under the rule of law (*estado social de derecho*), which integrated freedom of information into the text of the Constitution, in Arts 20 and 74. These provisions enabled the recognition of the right of access to public information as a fundamental right, which has been supported by the Inter-American System and Colombian constitutional case law.

In this chapter, I will explain, as a contribution to the constitution-drafting process in Chile, the transition from an underdeveloped and unclear understanding of access to documents to an enshrined constitutional right of access to public information. Accordingly, I will describe the Colombian case related to the recognition of this right as a fundamental right in the Political Constitution of 1991. In particular, I will highlight the evolution of the case law that asserted the independence and autonomy of the right to public information, as well as its main contents, which were translated into a transparency statute 20 years later.

Furthermore, based on the dual nature of the right of access to public information – as a right in itself and as an instrumental right used to exercise other rights – I will present two case studies that show the relationship between the right of access to public information and the exercise of economic, social and cultural rights (ESC rights). The first case will emphasise the value of transparency in the criteria used to define the beneficiaries of social assistance programmes in the context of the Covid-19 emergency. In the second case, the value of transparency in monitoring the government's acquisition of Covid-19 vaccines to deal with the emergency and safeguard the right to health will be discussed. These cases will also allow me to demonstrate how, through this right, citizens may challenge the implementation of ESC rights and enforce review and accountability mechanisms over the means and criteria involved. The cases will also evidence the instrumental nature of public information for the exercise of ESC rights.

[3] *Case of Claude Reyes et al v Chile*, Inter-American Court of Human Rights Series C No 151 (19 September 2006).

[4] E Lanza, 'Prólogo' in *A 10 años del fallo Claude Reyes: Impactos y Desafíos* (Ediciones Consejo para la Transparencia, 2016) 9–13, www.consejotransparencia.cl.

II. ORIGIN AND EVOLUTION

A. The National Constituent Assembly: The Origin

Access to information and public documents was recognised as a right of citizens in 1985 through Law 57, which was the first law to recognise the right to request public information in the Latin American region. The Political Constitution of 1991 – perhaps the greatest example of a society-building project undertaken during Colombia's republican history[5] – elevated this right to the rank of an autonomous fundamental right. How did the transit to a constitutional right occur?

In order to analyse the question of the right to public information, the First Commission of the National Constituent Assembly received numerous legislative proposals from both the constituents and political and economic groups. On 10 April 1991, the Commission produced a draft that recognised a right to request disclosure and a right to information, without making any reference to access to public documents. On 26 April 1991, the Commission heard the opinions of several representatives of the press and media, including: former president Juan Manuel Santos, who at the time was still a journalist working for the newspaper *El Tiempo*; Jorge Valencia, from the trade association Asomedios; and Rafael Serrano, from the National College of Journalists. On 22 May 1991, after various talks, liberal constituent Diego Uribe Vargas, who also formed part of the First Commission, presented a new project.

In this new project, which was titled 'Of Information and Communication', Uribe Vargas included a new subsection of the text about freedom of speech, which today is known as Art 20 of the Constitution. He also included subsection 5 about access to public documents, which is now, at least in part, Art 74. This appears to be the text approved by the First Commission, which was subsequently sent to the plenary meeting of the National Constituent Assembly for debate (with minor amendments resulting from subsequent meetings). In the first plenary debate, an article was approved under the title 'Of Our Cultural Patrimony', which encompassed the guarantee of freedom of information and access to public documents, as well as the regulation of the electromagnetic spectrum and other public goods. There were a few disagreements about freedom of information and access to documents, as shown in the vote count of the session report of 18 June 1991.[6]

However, the Coding Commission, which ended up garnering enough power to finish all pending tasks, altered the final order of the constitutional text's

[5] M García-Villegas, *El país de las emociones tristes. Una explicación de los pesares de Colombia desde las emociones, las furias y los odios* (Bogota, Editorial Planeta Colombiana, 2020).

[6] Plenary session report, National Constituent Assembly of Colombia (18 June 1991) 64–66, babel.banrepcultural.org/digital/collection/p17054coll28/id/187/rec/2.

codification without any further explanation. As a consequence, both rights were enshrined in Title II: 'Of Rights, Guarantees and Duties'. While freedom of speech was covered in Art 20 as part of Chapter I: 'Of Fundamental Rights', the right of access to public documents was included in Art 74, as part of Chapter II: 'Of Economic, Social and Cultural Rights'. This final separation became evident in the text presented by the Coding Commission to the Plenary of the Assembly for the second debate. In his report to the Plenary on 30 June 1991, Augusto Ramírez Ocampo, the spokesperson for the Commission, indicated that 'the right of access to public documents is elevated to a constitutional rank, thereby turning public management into a transparent urn'.[7]

On 28 June 1991, the Plenary approved what is now known as constitutional Art 20 (freedom of speech). The following day, it approved constitutional Art 74 (right of access to public documents) without explaining the separation. The Constitutional Court of Colombia would later establish that fundamental rights retain their nature, regardless of the order in which they appear in the Constitution, thereby making their order in the text irrelevant.[8] The Court would also grant autonomy to the right of access to public information, not only with respect to freedom of speech, but also with respect to other rights, such as the right to petition.[9] Specifically, the Court would establish that '[i]n the National Constituent Assembly, the constituents discussed the issue of access to public documents from the perspective of the fundamental right of information and opted for its enshrinement as an independent right from the right to petition (…)'.

B. The Evolution of the Right of Access to Public Information in Constitutional Case Law

As a result of the constitutional constituent process, the right of access to public information is largely derived from Art 74 of the Constitution, which establishes that 'every person has the right of access to public documents, except in the cases established by law'. The right is also connected to, but independent from, the fundamental right to petition, enshrined in Art 23 of the Constitution, which states that '[e]very individual has the right to submit respectful petitions to the authorities on account of general or private interest, and to secure a prompt

[7] A Ramírez Ocampo 'Ponencia para Segundo Debate de la Nueva Constitucion Politica de Colombia' (1991) *Gaceta Constitucional* 112, 7, babel.banrepcultural.org/digital/collection/p17054coll28.

[8] Constitutional Court of Colombia, Judgment T-002 of 1992 (MP Alejandro Martínez Caballero; 8 May 1992).

[9] Constitutional Court of Colombia, Judgment C-274 of 2013 (MS María Victoria Calle Correa; 9 May 2013).

resolution of the same'. Finally, it is intimately linked with the right to freedom of speech, stated in constitutional Art 20, which 'guarantees every person the freedom to express and promote their thinking and opinions, to inform and receive truthful and impartial information, and to establish mass communications media'. The reason for this connection with the right to freedom of speech is related to the fact that the freedom to inform, have an opinion and express oneself includes the freedom to receive information, which is associated with the freedom to promote and divulge ideas.

The right of access to public information and freedom of speech share a common origin and complement each other. They are linked not only by domestic law, but also through international sources of law derived from Art 13 of the American Convention on Human Rights and Art 19 of both the Universal Declaration of Human Rights and the International Convention on Civil and Political Rights. Additionally, they have complementary functions, since the exercise of one right directly contributes to the guarantee of the other. This complementarity goes beyond the classic interdependency of human rights. Information is the raw material in the search for truth, which is produced as the fruit of the contradiction of ideas, such as news, opinion articles, and other forms of knowledge creation and sharing for circulation and consumption. In the same sense, if there is no freedom to express ideas, there will be little space for ideas to become information and knowledge for individuals to form their own personality rights and produce opinions and expressions.[10]

However, despite having a clear link to the rights of petition, freedom of speech and information, the right of access to public information has also been recognised as an autonomous fundamental right.[11] This was not always the case, given that on many occasions the Colombian Constitutional Court oscillated and recognised access to information as a manifestation of the fundamental right to petition or as part of the freedom of information, together with the freedom of speech.[12]

In any case, since its decision C-491 of 2007, the Court has explicitly recognised the autonomy of the right to public information as a fundamental right and has emphasised its importance for guaranteeing transparency of public management in a democracy. The value of this decision lies in the fact that it compiled the requirements necessary for the restriction of this right, as developed by the Inter-American System of Human Rights and by the Constitutional

[10] R Uprimny et al, *Libertad de prensa y derechos fundamentales. Análisis de la jurisprudencia constitucional en Colombia (1992–2005)* (Bogota, Dejusticia, 2006) 6–7.

[11] Constitutional Court of Colombia, Judgment T-473 of 1992 (MP Ciro Angarita Barón; 14 July 1992).

[12] R Uprimny and V Newman, *Subreglas para acceder o rechazar el acceso a la información judicial y de seguridad nacional. Sistematización de la jurisprudencia constitucional en Colombia (2006–2012)* (Bogota, Dejusticia, 2017).

Court. In other words, whoever applies the right of access to information and develops public policy must abide by these principles. The Court said:

> The Court considers that a restriction to the right of access to information is legitimate only when: i) the restriction is authorised by law or by the Constitution; ii) the norm that establishes the limit is precise and clear in its terms so that it does not arbitrarily or disproportionately cover conduct of a public servant; iii) the public servant who decides not to disclose information lists in writing the corresponding decision and offers legal or constitutional support; iv) the law states a temporary limit for the classification of the information; v) there are adequate systems to protect the information; vi) there are administrative and judicial review mechanisms for the classification decisions; vii) documents can be classified but their existence cannot; viii) classification does not affect journalists that access the information and may publish it; ix) the classification is strictly subject to the principles of reasonability and proportionality; x) there are recourses or judiciary actions to challenge the classification decision.[13]

Several of these requirements are materialised in the principle of maximum disclosure or pro-transparency, through which any information held or controlled by public agencies or public servants, fulfilling public functions or delivering public services, must be freely accessible, unless there is an explicit and precise legal or constitutional basis for its restriction. If no such restriction applies, the fundamental right of access to information must prevail. Case law derives three consequences from this principle: (1) the right of access to information must be subject to a limited set of exceptions enshrined in law or in the Constitution itself; (2) the burden of proof for the denial of access to information and the corresponding explanation falls on the obligated public party, and not on the citizen; and (3) when in doubt, access to public information should be granted.

During that same year, in its Judgment T-1025 of 2007,[14] the Constitutional Court reasserted the above-mentioned standards and required the test of strict proportionality whenever the access to public information might clash with other rights or fundamental values. For the Court, 'the refusal to supply the names of members of the public forces may be legitimately based in concerns for the security of the agents or their families if there is a clear and present risk which cannot be avoided by a less restrictive way to rights'. This requirement is particularly important since it is not enough to quote abstract reasons to deny access to public information. Democracy must be under a certain and tangible threat, which would be greater than the harm caused by keeping the information secret and without the possibility of being scrutinised by citizens.

The jurisprudential evolution of this right and its recognition at a legal, statutory level converged in Judgment C-274 of 2013, which reviewed the

[13] Constitutional Court of Colombia, Judgment C-491 of 2007 (MP Jaime Córdoba Triviño; 27 June 2007).

[14] Constitutional Court of Colombia, Judgment T-1025 of 2007 (MP Manuel José Cepeda Espinosa; 3 December 2007).

constitutionality of the Bill that would become Law 1712 of 2014, known as the Transparency and Access to Public Information Law (Transparency Act). I would like to highlight two great advances brought by this decision. First, the Constitutional Court declared that the paragraph that was meant to exclude access to information related to defence, national security, public order, and international relations was unconstitutional because it was a vague and generic exclusion (paragraph 5). Second, the Court affirmed the constitutionality of the shift of the burden of proof when an obligated subject refuses to disclose information, even though the Attorney General's Office had argued for this shift to be declared unconstitutional.

C. Legislative Evolution of the Right of Access to Information: Transparency Act 1712 of 2014

The Transparency Act reflects both the jurisprudential rules derived from the mentioned constitutional case law and the standards of the Inter-American System of Human Rights. Despite the fact that, a few months later, the Congress approved the Right to Petition Act 1755 of 2015 – which included the petition of information and distanced itself from some of the exceptions applicable to the right of access to information – the Transparency Act continues to be the backbone of the access to public information system in Colombia and represents the safeguarding of this right.

The Transparency Act regulates the content of the right to access public information, as well as the principles, obligated entities, exceptions and options for effective judicial redress. Access to public information is defined as the right of every citizen to 'know about the existence of and access public information in possession or under the control of the obligated entities'. Furthermore, this right may only be restricted by limited and proportional exceptions contemplated by law or the Constitution. The obligated entities are the public agencies from all levels of the three branches of government, as well as political parties/movements or any person or legal entity who delivers a public service, performs a public function, or deals with public funds, but only regarding the information directly related to the function, the service or the public funds they engage in. The corresponding effective judicial remedy is a fast constitutional mechanism or writ known as an '*acción de tutela*'. However, if the reservation of information is based on national security or defence, or international relations, cases are processed through another constitutional mechanism, known as '*recurso de insistencia*', which must be resolved within a term of 10 days.

Even though the Transparency Act enshrines multiple guiding principles, both the principle of maximum disclosure and the shift of the burden of proof in the case of refusal to disclose are at the foundation of the interpretation and application of the law. Thus, the obligated entity which seeks to deny access to information is subject to a high burden, which includes: (1) mention of the specific law which enshrines the legitimate objective of the secrecy of the information; (2) application of at least one of the exceptional categories previously established by articles 18 and 19 of the Transparency Act; and (3) a showing of probable and specific present damage that would likely occur. However, these exceptions do not apply to information related to human rights violations or crimes against humanity.

The obligation to inform comprises two aspects: active transparency; and passive transparency. The former, also known as the objective dimension, refers to the obligation of public entities to divulge public information, both proactively and on its own initiative. The latter, also known as the subjective dimension, refers to the obligation to respond to the requests for information made by citizens. In both dimensions, the information must be relevant, complete, accessible and up-to-date, and must include language that is not technical or too complex for the citizen to understand.[15] Information that is overly specialised or that disregards accessibility criteria may be discriminatory, since it would breach the principle of equal opportunity to receive, search and share information.[16]

III. ACCESS TO PUBLIC INFORMATION AS A GUARANTEE OF ESC RIGHTS

A. Access to Public Information: For What Purpose?

Both constitutional case law and the Inter-American standards recognise that access to public information serves three main purposes: (1) it fosters democratic participation and the guarantee of political rights;[17] (2) it ensures the transparency of public activities, which includes demanding accountability, evaluating the functioning of the state and public management, controlling excesses and preventing corruption;[18] and (3) it is instrumental to the exercise of other constitutional rights[19] and to guarantee the exercise of other human rights,[20] including economic, social and cultural rights. The Inter-American Commission on Human Rights has recognised this by mentioning that this right 'imposes on the State the obligation to supply citizens with the maximum amount of information proactively' with regard to 'the information required for the exercise of other rights [and] the availability of services, benefits, subsidies or contracts of any kind'.[21]

[15] Inter-American Legal Committee, *Principles on the Right of Access to Information* CJI/RES. 147 (LXXIII-O/08).

[16] IACHR, 'Declaration of Principles of Freedom of Expression'.

[17] IACHR, 'The Inter-American Legal Framework' (n 2).

[18] *Case of Claude Reyes* (n 3).

[19] Constitutional Court of Colombia, Judgment T-828 of 2014 (MP Gloria Stella Ortiz Delgado; 5 November 2014).

[20] IACHR, 'Informe anual de la Comisión Interamericana de Derechos Humanos 2008. Volumen II: Informe Anual de la Relatoría Especial para la Libertad de Expresión' (25 February 2009).

[21] IACHR, 'The Inter-American Legal Framework' (n 2).

I emphasise this last function. The Inter-American Commission has recognised the value of the right of access to public information as an instrumental right for the 'realisation' of social rights because it allows access to data or documents necessary for the satisfaction of social rights, as well as knowledge of the conditions on how such rights are exercised. This applies, for example, to ensure that the authorities and state agencies publicly explain the decisions adopted and the criteria applied in such decisions. It also applies for the implementation of social programmes, since the citizens have a clear interest to benefit. Without public information, there can be no guarantee of rights, since citizens would not have the possibility of knowing whether the criteria for making decisions involving the distribution of collective funds are adequate and produce fair results, thereby resulting in a minimally acceptable standard of life.[22]

B. The Social Programme Does Not Reach its End Users due to Failures of Access to Public Information

Within the public health emergency brought about by the Covid-19 pandemic, the government of Colombia issued Decree-Law 518 of 2020, which created the Solidarity Income Programme (in Spanish, *Programa Ingreso Solidario* or PIS). This programme aims, among other things, to issue periodic payments from the Emergencies Mitigation Fund to persons and households in a situation of poverty and vulnerability, provided they are not benefiting from other social programmes.[23] The decree establishes that the list of beneficiaries is to be determined by taking into account the persons and households in poverty and vulnerability registered in the System of Selection of Beneficiaries for Social Programmes (SISBEN), together with other information sources that may facilitate the identification and prioritisation of the most vulnerable. However, the authorities in charge of executing the PIS did not publish the selection criteria for PIS beneficiaries selected from SISBEN or other information sources, which resulted in potential beneficiaries not knowing why they were or were not selected.

In this context, Dejusticia assisted 24 women, all heads of household, in exercising their right of access to information regarding the details of the selection mechanism for the programme. These women had not received any help from the PIS, despite being in situations of socio-economic vulnerability and not benefiting from any other social programme. When no reply was received

[22] A Sen, *Economía de bienestar y dos aproximaciones a los derechos* trad E Lamprea Montealegre (Bogota, Universidad Externado de Colombia, 2002).

[23] Decree 518 of 2020 [Presidency of the Republic of Colombia], through which the programme Ingreso Solidario is created to meet the needs of poverty-stricken and vulnerable households throughout the national territory, within the context of the state of financial, social and environmental emergency, 4 April 2020.

in the stipulated time, they presented a constitutional writ or *tutela* in order to gain access to the PIS. The petitioners considered that, apart from the violation of their right of access to information (Political Constitution Arts 20 and 74), their exclusion from the PIS has affected their right to a dignified life (Political Constitution Art 11), an adequate standard of living (Political Constitution Arts 2 and 53), health (Political Constitution Art 49), food security (Political Constitution Arts 2, 44 and 49), housing (Political Constitution Art 51) and equality (Political Constitution Art 13).

Gradually, they began to receive diverging answers to their requests for information and found that the PIS has flaws in its updating and verification mechanisms, and is overly rigid, which adversely affected their chances of becoming beneficiaries. They also confirmed that the problem of transparency regarding the criteria for accessing the social programme persists.

Therefore, the implementation of the PIS has created barriers to the effective guarantee of the economic, social and cultural rights of the 24 women petitioners, while at the same time limiting the required transparency regarding the criteria that shape both the design and implementation of the solidarity income policy. First, information about the specific requirements for the selection of beneficiary households was not duly published. This is a violation of their right of access to information, since it failed to apply the principle of proactive dissemination because the selection criteria were not made public and the information lacked quality. When data is not shared in a timely fashion, citizens are prevented from knowing whether or not they are allowed access to the programme. Second, the methodology for the inclusion or exclusion of beneficiaries of the PIS – which is provided only on the basis of individual requests – violates the right to equality, and with it the rights to housing, food security, and to an adequate standard of living. The programme is implemented following SISBEN criteria which are outdated. These criteria are inadequate to achieve the objectives of the PIS, which are to alleviate the needs of the most vulnerable persons and households, in particular those that arise from the gender dynamics of a country like Colombia.[24]

Citizens do not have access to the criteria used by the administration to include or exclude individuals as beneficiaries of the PIS. Neither is there available information to ascertain how the databases are merged in order to determine the individual beneficiaries. The authorities have the obligation to disseminate and make available to the citizens all of their public information. This is especially important for information regarding a social programme that is fundamental to the exercise of human rights – and even to the survival – of the most vulnerable population in the country. The information provided by the petitioned party must also be understandable, complete, clear and up-to-date, in order to inform citizens of the requirements and particularities of this subsidy.

[24] 'La pandemia no ha permitido al SISBEN encuestar 458.500 ciudadanos' *La Opinión* (Cúcuta, 23 June 2020).

Only when the violations encountered in this case have been remedied will it be possible to guarantee that citizens can: (1) enjoy the economic, social and cultural rights recognised and targeted by this programme; (2) actively take part in the democratic review of the implementation of this state assistance programme and of the correct and transparent allocation of public funds; and (3) assess whether its implementation is adequate, whether it does or does not respect the principle of equality and non-discrimination, and whether or not it is impinging on other fundamental rights. A review by the Constitutional Court of the problem presented would be additional evidence of the materialisation of the right of access to public information in favour of citizens' objectives.

C. Citizens Cannot Participate in their Own Covid-19 Vaccination Programme due to Opacity in Public Procurement

Former US Supreme Court Justice Louis D Brandeis wrote in the 1930s that to fight the opacity in the banking business 'sunlight is said to be the best of disinfectants; electric light the most efficient policeman'.[25] This argument also holds true for the government and its public procurement, not only because it enables the government to be held accountable and creates a barrier for corruption, but also because it allows citizens to participate in public interest issues and provides market information for better negotiations.

In the present case, the public interest at stake is the right to health and the need to achieve immunity from Covid-19 by equitable access to the relevant vaccines at affordable prices. As the UN Committee on Economic, Social and Cultural Rights has stated:

> [e]very person has a right to the enjoyment of the highest attainable standard of physical and mental health, which includes access to 'immunization programs against the major infectious diseases.' Every person also has a right to enjoy the benefits of scientific progress (…) Both rights imply that every person has a right to access a vaccine for COVID-19, which is safe, effective and based on the application of the best scientific developments.[26]

Despite the clear benefit of publicly available information regarding the price per dose or the liability of vaccine manufacturers, there has been extreme opacity on Covid-19 vaccine contracts worldwide,[27] and Colombia is no exception to this. As a result, the Anticorruption Institute filed a FOIA request on 20 January

[25] J Rosen, *Louis D Brandeis, American Prophet* (New Haven, Yale University Press, 2016).

[26] United Nations Committee on Economic, Social and Cultural Rights and Economic and Social Council 'Statement on Universal, Affordable Vaccination against Coronavirus Disease (COVID-19), International Cooperation and Intellectual Property' (23 April 2021) UN doc E_C.12_2021_1.

[27] Transparency International, *For Whose Benefit? Transparency in the Development and Procurement of Covid-19 Vaccines* (Transparency International, 2021).

2021 to access information on Covid-19 vaccine negotiations and contracts, in order to exercise public review of the public resources invested to buy the vaccines, as well as for public interest purposes. The requested information would also give Colombian citizens the possibility of understanding the liabilities of the manufacturers/sellers and the potential to achieve, within the sanitary emergency, the immunisation of the population. The government, through the special unit that had signed the vaccine procurement contracts, timeously answered that this information could not be disclosed as it was protected by confidentiality agreements with Pfizer, AstraZeneca and Janssen, and that the breach would endanger the access to a scarce and inelastic product. The government alleged reserved negotiations and diplomatic instructions, as well as public security and health arguments. The case was then brought to the judiciary by the Anticorruption Institute.

Based on the principle of maximum disclosure derived from the Universal Declaration of Human Rights (Art 19) and the American Convention of Human Rights (Art 13.2), the Administrative Court of Cundinamarca[28] conducted a conventionality test and ruled in favour of disclosing the contracts, since the arguments for reserving the information were not legal, there was no evidence of the necessity to keep the information classified, and the reservation of the information was not proportionate. In other words, in application of the maximum transparency principle, the judgment considered that the government had not demonstrated evidence of the legality of the exception alleged related to why the contracts should be privileged.

The ruling considered that the exception of diplomatic instructions classification is not applicable to corporations, but instead to states or other international public law entities (Vienna Convention 1961), and that negotiations can only be reserved or classified during the negotiations phase and not after the agreement is signed. As for health and security reasons, the court ruled that Covid-19 vaccines and immunisation are global public goods, as considered by Resolution WHA73.1, adopted unanimously by the World Health Organization on 19 May 2020[29] and by Resolution 1, 2021 of the Inter American Commission on Human Rights.[30]

The ruling further mentioned that in the procurement contracts in question, there were no business secrets, and that states have an elevated responsibility to apply the standards of access to information in this context, so that public opinion is informed and citizens can debate ideas, demand accountability and prevent authoritarianism. Moreover, the judgment confirmed that the confidentiality

[28] Administrative Tribunal of Cundinamarca. First Section, Subsection B. Judgment 2021-05-081 RI (Justice Fredy Ibarra; 11 May 2021).

[29] WHO (Draft resolution of the Seventy-third World Health Assembly) 'Covid-19 response' (19 May 2020) A73/CONF./1 Rev.1.

[30] IACHR, 'Covid-19 Vaccines and Inter-American Human Rights Obligations' (6 April 2021) Res 1, 2021.

agreement on the reviewed contracts was limited to the financial and indemnification clauses. However, the confidentiality of such clauses is in violation of Law 1712 of 2014, since the duty of publishing public resources is superior to the contract signed, even when scrutinised under New York law, because it relates to the human right of access to information and freedom of expression. Therefore, the conditions for classifying information were not fulfilled because: (1) the negotiations which preceded the contracts were now concluded; and (2) there was no evidence demonstrating damage to health or public security, nor was there a business secret to protect.

The government's special unit responded with new arguments. First, it filed a clarification petition asking for additional information. The petition also requested an addition to the judgment, which would hold the judiciary responsible *in solidum* for the economic damages resulting from the non-compliance of the confidentiality clauses in the contracts with the pharmaceutical companies. Since the government considered that the Administrative Court of Cundinamarca lacked jurisdiction to assess or decide on the legality or constitutionality of the contracts, it requested for the judiciary to assume the consequences of the ruling that might come from pharmaceutical companies refusing to do business with Colombia, such as a deterioration in the public health and a collapse of the sanitary system. Second, the government asked for the judgment to be nullified, since the Ministry of Health, which was not included in the ruling, had an interest in the process. This interest was related to the fact that it had signed previous non-disclosure agreements with six big corporations (Sinovac, Pfizer, AstraZeneca, Janssen, Cilag and Moderna), and as such, the absence of the Ministry of Health in the litigation constituted a lack of a legitimate plaintiff in the case.

Finally, Janssen Pharmaceutics and Janssen Cilag (Janseen) filed a writ or *tutela* before the State Council (Superior Court of the Tribunal of Cundinamarca), requesting the protection of their rights to due process and access to justice. According to Janssen, it had not been part of the litigation that ordered the disclosure of the contracts which contained highly sensitive and confidential information, including industrial or trade secrets of high commercial and competitive value. Presumably, these secrets were mainly the cost structure, the prices and the commercialisation strategy which, in accordance with a literal and narrow interpretation of Art 260 of Decision 486 of the Andean Community on Intellectual Property, could be considered as secret.

The Administrative Court of Cundinamarca must now decide whether it should nullify the judgment and reconsider whether or not the right of access to information should prevail. The decision would have to take into account the new arguments posited, as well as the provision of the Andean Community, which states that information whose disclosure is the result of a legal provision or court order shall not be considered an industrial secret or public property (Art 261 of Decision 486 of the Common Intellectual Property Regime). The Tribunal must also consider that the Congress authorised the government to declare a general interest in the strategy for immunisation against Covid-19, a decision which also limited liability for vaccine manufacturers to gross negligence, fraud or malpractice. However, the Congress failed to authorise confidentiality agreements or clauses, and as such, transparency and accountability should prevail.

The tension between businesses interests and access to information as a human right should remind us that if Justice Louis Brandeis were in the courtroom today, sunlight would still be the best of disinfectants for any business or government managing the Covid-19 pandemic.

IV. CONCLUSION

The right of access to public information as a fundamental constitutional right has had great value. On the one hand, regarding active transparency, it has helped bring transparency to the criteria that shape both the design and implementation of the solidarity income policy and public procurement. Likewise, it has enabled citizen participation, by allowing them to know, monitor, question and even improve policies and contracts. Only by integrally divulging the elements of policy design and implementation can this constitutional objective be attained.

On the other hand, with respect to passive transparency – or replying to requests for information – information is crucial for the vital subsistence of vulnerable citizens who have been historically ignored and are in need of special constitutional protection, as well as for the accountability of public decisions that can save lives if public finances are properly distributed.

Access to public information contributes to the knowledge needed to assess whether the decisions made, such as in the creation of a social or sanitary programme, are fair and whether they uphold economic, social and cultural rights. It also contributes to the reduction of social inequality and the equitable distribution of collective assets – both principles that inspired the creation of the Colombian Constitution of 1991. These objectives can inform the aspirations of the Chilean Constituent Assembly, which respects Latin American institutionality and strives to reach a more equitable social project.

7

The Path of the Inter-American Court Towards Direct Justiciability of Economic, Social, Cultural and Environmental Rights: Impact on Domestic Legal Systems

JULIETA ROSSI

I. INTRODUCTION

IN RECENT TIMES, the Inter-American Human Rights System (IAHRS) has made great strides in the fields of economic, social, cultural and environmental rights, led by both the Inter-American Court (IACtHR) and the Inter-American Commission on Human Rights (IACHR). These developments are to be commended, as they herald better protection for victims in the Americas (particularly in Latin America) who are severely deprived of the enjoyment of economic, social, cultural and environmental rights and unable to lead autonomous lives in conditions of freedom and equality. Moreover, the region demands a rights-based approach to the issues of poverty, social exclusion and profound discrimination based on sex, gender, gender identity, age, ethnicity, geographic location, socio-economic status, among other factors, phenomena that have been exacerbated by the Covid-19 pandemic which emerged at the beginning of 2020.[1] This unprecedented crisis has exposed the fragility of a world whose operating matrix urgently needs to be restructured, to put people and their fundamental rights at the centre of concerns and actions.

According to the Economic Commission for Latin America and the Caribbean (ECLAC), the outlook for the coming years in developing countries, and in Latin America in particular, is extremely dire,[2] with differential impacts

[1] ECLAC, *Panorama Social de América Latina* (United Nations, 2021).

[2] ECLAC, *América Latina y el Caribe ante la pandemia del COVID-19: efectos económicos y sociales* (United Nations, 2020).

on certain population groups, such as women, children and youth, the elderly, indigenous peoples, African descendants, and people with disabilities. Against this convulsed and uncertain backdrop, we believe that the Court's pivot towards direct justiciability may contribute to the adoption of robust and emancipatory visions of social rights, social democracy and the rule of law in the region, especially through the development of universal public policies on key areas such as health, education and social security, protection for disadvantaged groups, the redistribution of economic resources by progressive fiscal systems, the implementation of limits and restrictions to private property as well as the adoption of policies that promote equal responsibility between men and women in the field of care.

In this context, the main purpose of this chapter is to analyse the IACtHR's path toward the protection of economic, social, cultural and environmental rights up to the adoption of the direct justiciability doctrine. In the analysis of this evolution, it aims also to illuminate how this doctrine could and should be used in the domestic arenas of Latin American countries, particularly in the Chilean context, by different branches of government, in order to give full effect to these rights. First, we will examine what the Court's latest stance and case law mean for the states in the region. Second, we will assess the arguments used by the Court to make these rights enforceable in a direct and autonomous way through the Inter-American legal framework that contemplates them. Third, the chapter will focus on the standards on the right to health, with special reference to older people and people living with HIV and tuberculosis, and on the right to equality and non-discrimination on the basis of gender and the concept of intersectional discrimination. Finally, some challenges that arise in the interpretative path adopted by the Court will be raised, not only in the normative sphere, but also at the socioeconomic level linked to the situation of severe inequality and social exclusion prevalent in the American continent.

II. THE COURT'S CHANGE OF DIRECTION AND ITS IMPACT ON DOMESTIC LEGAL SYSTEMS

The IACtHR's change of direction is of great relevance to the region, as it is in line with, and strengthens, recent developments in constitutional law doctrine and case law that position economic, social, cultural and environmental rights as full and enforceable rights, as well as guidelines for the definition of public policies and development models. In addition, the IACtHR's interpretation of this subject may permeate the domestic sphere and serve as a model for the definition of the content and scope of the social rights protected in the Inter-American legal framework and its corresponding state duties, often in addition to the national constitutional plexus. In particular, the Court's shift is important for countries that are lagging behind in this field, such as Chile, or for those who, having made advances in the past, have regressed in their protection, as is the case in several countries in recent years. In this vein, the Chilean constitutional process represents a unique opportunity to incorporate the new IACtHR jurisprudence as well as to consider the trajectory of many countries of the region in the robust recognition of economic, social, cultural and environmental rights, many of whom have integrated international human rights law frameworks into their constitutions and have included new avenues for its demand by affected people, civil society organisations and national human rights institutions.

The implementation of international human rights law (IHRL) in Latin American countries is a key subject on political and academic agendas and one that poses important challenges. This focus of attention corresponds to the growing weight that IHRL has acquired as a source of law in domestic legal systems in the region, and, therefore, in the progressive harmonisation of case law and the use of international standards by domestic courts.

Indeed, during recent decades, most Latin American states have undertaken constitutional reforms that, to a greater or lesser degree, have reconfigured central aspects of the legal order.[3] In this context, Chile is now, thanks to the persistent struggles of its people, adding a new chapter to its constitutional history, setting aside a constitution with limited or non-existent institutional legitimacy dating from the Pinochet dictatorship.

One of the key transformations in these reform processes has been the inclusion of human rights treaties with a privileged hierarchy (constitutional or supra-legal) which, combined with the recognition of indigenous law in some cases, has led to a broadening of the sources of law applicable to social relations; while some states, such as Argentina, Colombia and Mexico, made reforms to existing legislation, others, such as Bolivia and Ecuador, opted to draft new constitutions. In this way, international human rights law has progressively and with varying intensity begun to play a relevant role in judicial decisions, as well as in the definition and implementation of public policies.[4] In particular, courts in the region have increasingly turned to international law: they apply treaties directly, adopt interpretations of norms established by protection bodies, or monitor the domestic implementation of international decisions or judgments.[5] In turn, this growing weight of IHRL is visible in the creation of public institutions in the legislative and executive spheres to facilitate the process of adaptation and adjustment.

[3] R Uprimny, 'Las Transformaciones Constitucionales recientes en América Latina. Tendencias y Desafíos' in C Rodríguez Garabito (ed), *El Derecho en América Latina. Un Mapa para el Pensamiento Jurídico del Siglo XX* (Mexico, Siglo XXI, 2011).

[4] A Maués and B. Magalhães (eds), *O controle de convencionalidade na América Latina: experiências comparadas* (Lumen Juris, 2018).

[5] J Rossi and L Filippini, 'El derecho internacional en la justiciabilidad de los derechos sociales en Latinoamérica' in P Arcidiácono et al (eds), *Derechos sociales: Justicia, política y economía en América Latina* (Siglo del Hombre, Uniandes, CELS and Universidad Diego Portales, 2010) 195 and 196.

At the same time, the incorporation and application of IHRL in the domestic state sphere has not been linear or peaceful, but rather poses significant challenges. Given that international human rights law, and its interpretations by authorised bodies, must coexist with domestic norms, regulations and practices, its effective entry into the local sphere hinges on a series of issues. Among the most relevant are: the constitutional and legal mechanisms provided for the incorporation of treaties into the domestic constitutional system; the hierarchy and operational or programmatic nature of international provisions; the use of international case law by domestic bodies, and the value assigned to it in the interpretation of treaty norms; the domestic mechanisms provided for the enforcement of international decisions in contentious cases; and the impact of federalism on the application of international covenants.

At this point, it must be emphasised that the value assigned in the domestic sphere to the authentic interpretations of the supervisory bodies is crucial for the proper application and integration of IHRL into the domestic order, especially for a common and harmonious determination of the content and scope of the rights provided for in international instruments. This is fundamental in the field of economic, social, cultural and environmental rights, where their development and clarification has received less attention and where their inclusion as full and enforceable rights, especially by the judicial bodies, is more recent.

In this regard, the IACtHR itself has developed the conventionality control doctrine, which demands that all internal organs of states, in particular the judicial power, as the last instance of control, carry out a *sua sponte* comparison of the internal regulations and other manifestations of the public power with the American Convention on Human Rights (ACHR) (beyond the hierarchy established internally), considering IAHRS case law. And, in light of that comparison, decide whether to enforce those regulations or not and to make other necessary adjustments at different levels, depending on the case.[6]

In sum, the position of the IACtHR in defining the direct application of the Inter-American norms on economic, social, cultural and environmental rights, as well as the process undertaken to clarify their scope and content and order reparations, could influence the domestic bodies of the different branches of government towards adopting a robust and autonomous approach and guaranteeing interpretations that expand the levels of protection in the domestic sphere. In the case of Chile, the constitutional assembly should definitely be influenced by these developments, taking social rights, such as health, education, social security, work, water, food, housing, environment seriously as full and enforceable rights, and guidelines for the design of public policies. It should also consider the need to reduce gaps and possible conflicts between the two

[6] M Carbonell, 'Introducción general al control de convencionalidad' in D Valadés and LR González Pérez (eds), *El constitucionalismo contemporáneo, Homenaje a Jorge Carpizo* (Universidad Nacional Autónoma de México, 2018).

systems, with a view to moving towards a common legal order that integrates domestic and international law, and ultimately towards maximising the extent to which human rights are guaranteed.

III. A BRIEF OVERVIEW: FROM INDIRECT TO DIRECT JUSTICIABILITY

If we had to summarise the Court's actions with respect to the protection of economic, social, cultural and environmental rights since its creation around 40 years ago, it is safe to say that it has been limited, especially if we take into account the direct use of the norms that include these rights in the IAHRS. In general terms, the guarantee of social rights has not been at the centre of the agenda of the system's bodies or in the exercise of its jurisdiction.

In the last 10 years, this process has begun to reverse itself and in a more central way since 2017, since the judgment handed down in *Lagos del Campo*,[7] where for the first time the IACtHR held a state responsible for the violation of Art 26 of the ACHR in an autonomous manner in relation to labour rights and reiterated its jurisdiction to hear and resolve disputes on this matter.[8]

This doctrine was later reaffirmed in subsequent cases where the court addressed violations of various social rights. Thus, it decided *Trabajadores Cesados de Petroperú et al v Peru* (2017) and *San Miguel Sosa v Venezuela* (2018) on labour rights; *Poblete Vilches v* Chile (2018), *Cuscul Pivaral et al v Guatemala* (2018) and *Hernández v Argentina* (2019) on the right to health; *Muelles Flores v Perú* (2019) and *Asociación Nacional de Cesantes y Jubilados de la Superintendencia Nacional de Administración Tributaria (ANCEJUB-SUNAT) v Peru* on the right to social security and *Comunidades Indígenas miembros de la Asociación Lhaka Honhat (Nuestra Tierra) v Argentina* on the rights to the environment, water, adequate food and cultural identity. It also advanced important considerations in this area in Advisory Opinion 23/2017 on Environment and Human Rights.

Until it embarked on the path to autonomous justiciability, the Court opted to examine complaints of violations of social rights through the indirect route of analysing civil and political rights, in many cases making a social, egalitarian and extensive interpretation of these rights. Thus, for example, through the right to private property in Art 21 of the ACHR, it recognised the right to communal property of indigenous peoples and addressed violations of social rights indirectly, through the right to effective judicial protection, equality and non-discrimination, and access to information, or by way of connection with

[7] IACtHR, *Lagos del Campo v Peru*, Judgment of 31 August 2017 (Preliminary Objections, Merits, Reparations and Costs).

[8] E Ferrer Mac-Gregor, M Morales Antoniazzi and R Flores Pantoja, *Inclusión, Ius Commune y justiciabilidad de los DESCA en la jurisprudencia interamericana. El caso Lagos del Campo y los nuevos desafíos* (Instituto de Estudios Constitucionales del Estado de Querétaro, 2018).

the rights to personal integrity and life.[9] Although certain dimensions of social rights have been protected in specific cases, and in some of them vigorously, such as the right to communal land ownership of indigenous peoples, the fact is that this has not been sufficient or satisfactory. In general, social rights remained at an embryonic stage of development, addressed only marginally.

A factor of unquestionable relevance that determined the ambivalence of the organs of the system is the deficient and ambiguous normative panorama set out in the instruments of the IAHRS, in particular the ACHR and the Protocol of San Salvador.

The ACHR contains only one isolated norm, Art 26 (as opposed to Arts 3–25, which protect civil and political rights); as in the International Covenant on Economic, Social and Cultural Rights (ICESCR) at the universal level, this norm provides for broad and, at first glance, vague duties such as the obligation of states to adopt measures progressively and in accordance with the resources available in each state to achieve the full realisation of the rights derived from the economic, social, educational, scientific and cultural standards of the OAS Charter, through international cooperation and assistance. Finally, although the Protocol of San Salvador is more developed in terms of the rights it protects, it has limitations with respect to the petition system, in that it only authorises petitions for two rights (education and trade union rights).

IV. DIRECT AND AUTONOMOUS JUSTICIABILITY OF ECONOMIC, SOCIAL, CULTURAL AND ENVIRONMENTAL RIGHTS THROUGH ARTICLE 26: FROM *LAGOS DEL CAMPO* TO *LHAKA HONHAT ASSOCIATION*

The path taken by the IACtHR towards direct justiciability through the use of specific economic, social, cultural and environmental rights norms has been strongly promoted by academics and activists in the region. In this path, we can identify different stages: a first stage where the IACtHR deploys an erroneous interpretation of Art 26 of the ACHR, which in any case has no concrete effects insofar as it remains hermeneutic at a theoretical level, without practical application; a second stage in which the Court overcomes and rectifies this erroneous interpretation and correctly redirects its hermeneutic line, essentially from its decision in *Acevedo Buendía v Perú* (2009); and a third, recent stage, where the Court finally assumes the path of direct and autonomous justiciability of social rights based on an expansive interpretation of the possibilities of the provision in Art 26.

[9] IACtHR, *Suárez Peralta v Ecuador*, Judgment of 21 May 2013 (Preliminary Objections, Merits, Reparations and Costs); *Gonzáles LLuy et al v Ecuador*, Judgment of 1 September 2015 (Preliminary Objections, Merits, Reparations and Costs) and *IV v Bolivia*, Judgment of 30 November 2016 (Preliminary Objections, Merits, Reparations and Costs).

In the first case of this new doctrine, *Lagos del Campo*, the Court was expected to exhaustively develop its arguments and provide an account of its change in position. However, it offered only an extremely terse motivation.[10]

Thereafter, in a series of subsequent cases, the court reaffirmed its doctrine and refined its reasoning. Thus, in *Cuscul Pivaral*, the court provides a more extensive and solid reasoning and recognises the need to specify its change of direction.[11] The Court takes up arguments that had been raised in concurring votes in previous cases, such as *Gonzáles Lluy* and *Suárez Peralta* as well as in academic works. The Court holds that the main legal issue raised in the case is whether the right to health can be understood as an autonomous right deriving from Art 26 of the American Convention, and whether it has jurisdiction to rule on violations of this right on the basis of Arts 62 and 63 of the Convention.[12]

Here the Court addresses the following three core questions to argue for its pivot: (1) whether Art 26 recognises rights or establishes mere programmatic objectives; (2) whether the generic obligations of Arts 1.1 and 2 of the ACHR apply to ecomonic, social and cultural rights; (3) whether the Court has jurisdiction to analyse violations of the rights established in Art 26 of the ACHR and how the limitation of Art 19.6 of the Protocol of San Salvador on the system of protection is articulated.

In addition, the Court addresses, in the group of cases mentioned, other issues relevant to the direct and autonomous protection of economic, social, cultural and environmental rights, namely: (4) identification of the rights protected by Art 26 of the ACHR and the methodology for deriving them from the OAS Charter; and (5) development of the scope and content of particular rights.

In addressing these issues, especially the first three, the Court uses the methods of interpretation stipulated in Arts 31 and 32 of the Vienna Convention on the Law of Treaties and Art 29 of the ACHR.[13] It appeals to literal, systematic and teleological methods of interpretation, as well as to complementary methods of interpretation. Let us look at how it addresses these issues.

On the first question (1), the Court understands that, according to the literal interpretation (principle of the primacy of the text), the ordinary meaning to be attributed to the provision of Art 26 of the ACHR is that the states undertook to give effect to 'rights' deriving from the economic, social, educational, scientific, and cultural standards contained in the OAS Charter. While the OAS Charter

[10] O Parra-Vera, 'La justiciabilidad de los derechos económicos, sociales y culturales en el Sistema Interamericano a la luz del artículo 26 de la Convención Americana. El sentido y la promesa del caso Lagos del Campo' in Ferrer Mac-Gregor et al (n 8).

[11] IACtHR, *Cuscul Pivaral et al v Guatemala*, Judgment of 23 August 2018 (Preliminary Objections, Merits, Reparations and Costs) paras 73–74.

[12] Ibid, para 73.

[13] Ibid, para 75.

enshrines 'principles' and 'goals' aimed at integral development, it also refers to certain rights, both explicitly and implicitly.[14]

On the other hand, the formulation in Art 26 about the duty of states to 'take steps' to 'achieve progressively the full realization' of the rights derived from the OAS Charter should be understood as a formulation about the nature of the obligation, but not as calling into question the existence of enforceable legal obligations. There are other similar formulas in the ACHR, such as the one established in Art 2, which recognises the programmatic commitment of the States to 'adopt legislative or other measures necessary to give effect to the rights'.[15] Progressivity only modulates the obligation in terms of time and mode of performance, but does not detract from its character as an enforceable legal obligation.[16]

In addition, the Inter-American Court agrees with the Committee on Economic, Social and Cultural Rights' interpretation of Art 2.1 of the ICESCR (in its General Comment 3) in the sense that, although this norm provides for the adoption of progressive measures, it also imposes several obligations with immediate effect. The fact that full effectiveness is envisaged over time does not imply that the obligation is deprived of all meaningful content.[17] This is reinforced by the fact that the goal and purpose of the treaty is precisely 'the protection of the fundamental rights of human beings'. Finally, it appeals to complementary methods of interpretation and analyses the preparatory work of the ACHR in order to reaffirm the meaning arising from the main methods of interpretation.[18]

Regarding whether the general obligations of Arts 1(1) and 2 of the ACHR are applicable to economic, social, cultural and environmental rights, the Court holds that it is. It explains that, although Art 26 is contained in a separate chapter, Chapter III of the ACHR, entitled Economic, Social and Cultural Rights, it is still contained in Part I of the ACHR, 'Duties of States and Protected Duties', and is therefore subject to the general obligations contained in Arts 1(1) and 2 of Chapter I, entitled 'Enumeration of Duties,' as are Arts 3–25 of Chapter II (entitled 'Civil and Political Rights'). This conclusion is also based on the interdependence and reciprocal indivisibility of all rights, which must be understood integrally and universally as human rights without hierarchies between them and as being equally enforceable.[19]

In relation to the third question raised, the Court affirms its jurisdiction to hear violations of all the rights of the ACHR, including Art 26, in accordance with Arts 62 and 63 of the ACHR,[20] even though the Protocol of San Salvador

[14] Ibid, para 78.
[15] The Court cited the cases *The Last Temptation of Christ v Chile* (2001), para 90, and *Tarazona Arrieta et al v Peru* (2014), para 169.
[16] IACtHR (n 11) para 79 and 80.
[17] Ibid, para 81.
[18] Ibid, paras 95 and 96, and paras 90 and 93.
[19] Ibid, paras 83, 84 and 85.
[20] Ibid, paras 86–89.

limits it to trade union rights and to the right to education. A systematic and good faith interpretation leads to the conclusion that in the absence of an express restriction in the Protocol limiting its jurisdiction to hear violations of the Convention, this limitation should not be assumed by the Court. No subsequent express act of the states implies a modification of the ACHR and the interpretation must be the most favourable and least restrictive.

With regard to the rights protected by Art 26 of the ACHR, the Court has developed a certain methodology for their identification. We will take the *Poblete Vilches* and *Cuscul Pivaral* cases on the right to health as an example of the Court's analysis to determine that this right is indeed protected by Art 26 of the Convention.[21] Thus, first, it considers that the right to health can in fact be derived from the norms of the OAS Charter, although there is no specific reference to this right contained in it.[22] It analyses Arts 34.i and 34.l, in particular the provision in Art 45.h of the Charter which reads: 'States agree to strive for the development of an efficient social security policy'. The Court notes the existence of a close relationship between the commitment of states to guarantee an efficient social security policy and their duty to ensure healthcare, even more so in the context of endemic diseases. The court concludes that there is a sufficiently specific reference to derive the existence of the right to health from the OAS Charter. Thus, an important criterion is established that even when a social right is not explicitly recognised in the text of the OAS Charter, this does not prevent it from being derived from formulations that indirectly or implicitly refer to it.

Second, it refers to the American Declaration of the Rights and Duties of Man, Art XI of which expressly guarantees the right to health. It puts forth two arguments. On the one hand, it appeals to its doctrine on the integration of the Declaration to interpret the OAS Charter in the area of human rights, established in its Advisory Opinion OC-10/89. This provision is relevant in defining the scope of Art 26, given that 'the American Declaration constitutes, as relevant and in relation to the Charter of the Organization, a source of international obligations'. It then refers to Art 29(d) of the American Convention insofar as it determines that no provision of the ACHR may be interpreted as excluding or limiting the effect that this Declaration and other international acts of the same nature may produce.[23]

With similar arguments, the Court derives from the OAS Charter the protection of the rights to work, to social security, to a healthy environment, to adequate food, to water and to participate in the life of the OAS Charter and considers them protected by Art 26 of the Convention.[24]

[21] Ibid, para 110.

[22] Ibid, para 98.

[23] Ibid, paras 107, 108 and 109.

[24] IACtHR, *Lagos del Campos* (n 7); *Muelles Flores*, Judgment of 6 March 2019 (Preliminary Objections, Merits, Reparations); *Lhaka Honhat*, Judgment of 6 February 2020 (Preliminary Objections, Merits, Reparations).

In order to determine the scope of the social rights protected in Art 26 of the ACHR and of the State's duties, the Court has resorted to the international and national body of law on the matter, in accordance with a systematic, teleological and evolutionary interpretation of the ACHR.[25] In this regard, Courtis points out that the methodology used by the Court to identify the content and concrete obligations arising from the rights at stake has not been entirely consistent. Here, the Court has moved forward rather by taking ad hoc steps, without clearly projecting a theory or a model that would allow us to envision what analysis it suggests for future cases.[26]

In this context, Art 29 of the ACHR provides for the *pro persona* principle, which expressly refers to the norms of general international law for the interpretation and application of the ACHR. Thus, in determining the international responsibility of a state on the basis of the ACHR or other Inter-American treaties, and as has been its consistent practice, the Court may interpret the obligations and rights contained therein in light of other relevant treaties and norms.[27]

In the same vein, the Court has affirmed that human rights treaties are living instruments, the interpretation of which must keep pace with changing times and current living conditions. It has also held that a progressive interpretation is consistent with the general rules of interpretation established in Art 29 of the American Convention and in the Vienna Convention on the Law of Treaties in its Art 31, third paragraph.[28] Moreover, in this hermeneutic exercise, the Court gives special emphasis to the American Declaration, in accordance with the doctrine on its integration to the OAS Charter on human rights already cited.[29]

V. SCOPE OF THE RIGHT TO HEALTH: ELDER PEOPLE, HIV/AIDS, TUBERCULOSIS, AND INTERSECTIONAL DISCRIMINATION

In this section we will take right to health cases as a reference to give an account of the way in which the Court formulates its relevant standards. In them, the court takes into account both the body of international law in force and

[25] IACtHR, *Poblete Vilches*, Judgment of 18 March 2018 (Preliminary Objections, Merits, Reparations and Costs), para 103; *Cuscul Pivaral* (n 11) para 73 and *Muelles Flores* (n 24) 73.

[26] C Courtis, 'Prologue' in M Antoniazzi et al, *Interamericanización de los DESCA, El caso Cuscul Pivaral de la Corte IDH* (Instituto Max Planck de Derecho Público Comparado y Derecho Internacional Público, Instituto de Estudios Constitucionales del Estado de Querétaro e Instituto de Investigaciones Jurídicas Universidad Nacional Autónoma de México, 2020).

[27] IACtHR, *Lhaka Honhat* (n 24) para 196. In turn, the Court cites the precedents in *Muelles Flores* and *Hernández*.

[28] This chapter authorises the use of interpretative means such as agreements or relevant rules or practice of international law which states have expressed on the subject matter of the treaty: ibid, para 197.

[29] IACtHR, *Lhaka Honhat* (n 24) para 188.

domestic legislation to determine its scope and content, based on the aforementioned provision in Art 29(b) of the ACHR.[30]

In the *Poblete Vilches* case, the Court considered the provision of the Chilean Constitution that protects the right to health and the domestic regulation in this regard. It also mentions the broad regional consensus on the right to health, insofar as it is explicitly recognised in various constitutions and domestic laws of the states of the region.[31] The Court appeals to international law standards on the right to health: Art 25(1) of the Universal Declaration of Human Rights, Art 12 of the ICESCR and Art 10 of the San Salvador Protocol.[32]

In order to specify the content of the right, the Court relies heavily on the standards already developed by the Committee on ESC rights. It uses General Comment 14 on the Right to Health and other relevant General Comments.[33] Based on these sources, it mentions several essential and interrelated elements that must be met in the area of health, namely availability, accessibility, acceptability and quality, and in the area of emergency medical care. With respect to acceptability, health facilities and services should, as far as is relevant here, include a gender perspective and a consideration of the patient's life span. The patients must be informed about their diagnosis and treatment possibilities, and their will must be respected, through free, prior and informed consent.[34]

It refers to standards linked to basic and immediate benefits in urgent or emergency medical situations for the elderly.[35] The Court considers then that there are aspects of the right to health that must be guaranteed immediately, without any conditions; that is to say, that they are not subject to progressive realisation.[36] At the same time, it makes explicit the constant duty to regulate and provide for mechanisms of supervision and oversight of health institutions, both public and private, especially with respect to emergency services.[37]

Regarding the accessibility component, it argues that the State is obligated to guarantee equal and non-discriminatory treatment to all persons who have access to health services, according to Art 1(1) of the ACHR. It points out that 'Other status' allows age to be included as a category prohibited by the norm. It thus explicitly prohibits age discrimination in access to health services.[38]

[30] IACtHR, *Poblete Vilches* (n 25) para 111.

[31] Ibid, para 113. Among them are Argentina, Barbados, Bolivia, Brazil, Colombia, Costa Rica, Dominican Republic, Ecuador, El Salvador, Guatemala, Haiti, Honduras, Mexico, Nicaragua, Panama, Paraguay, Peru, Suriname, Uruguay and Venezuela.

[32] IACtHR, *Poblete Vilches* (n 25) para 114.

[33] UN CESCR, General Comments 3, 4, 5, 6, 15, 16, 18, 19 and 20 cited by IACtHR (para 115).

[34] IACtHR, *Poblete Vilches* (n 25) paras 121, 125–132, 161–162 and 166.

[35] Ibid, paras 104 and 134.

[36] M Aldao and L Clérico, 'El derecho social autónomo a la salud y sus contenidos. El caso Poblete Vilches y el examen de (in)cumplimiento de las obligaciones impostergables y no ponderables' in M Morales Antoniazzi and L Clérico (eds), *Interamericanización del derecho a la salud. Perspectivas a la luz del caso Poblete de la Corte IDH* (Instituto de Estudios Comparados del Estado de Querétaro, 2019) 344.

[37] IACtHR, *Poblete Vilches* (n 25) paras 119 and 124.

[38] Ibid, para 122.

Here the IACtHR alludes to two conceptions of the right to equality, on which it had already ruled in previous cases and advisory opinions: a negative one related to the prohibition on arbitrary differences in treatment and a positive one related to the obligation of states to create conditions of real equality for groups that have been historically excluded or that are at greater risk of being discriminated against.[39] In this sense, the duty to adopt positive measures is underscored with respect to persons in vulnerable situations or at risk, such as the elderly. This population group is entitled to enhanced protection and therefore requires the adoption of differentiated measures.[40]

In this case, the Court for the first time hands down a decision on the scope and specificities of the right to health of the elderly based on the important development and consolidation of universal and regional standards. It mentions the Inter-American Convention on the Protection of the Human Rights of Older Persons, General Comment 6 of the Committee on ESC rights and the case law of the European Court of Human Rights.[41]

In short, the Inter-American Court establishes a clear and powerful standard, of particular importance if we consider the demographic changes in the region and the ageing of the population: the elderly must be considered as subjects of rights of special protection and therefore subjects of comprehensive care, with due respect for their autonomy and independence. This special protection translates into reinforced obligations to respect and guarantee their right to health, which implies providing them with the health services necessary for their condition in an efficient and continuous manner.[42] At the same time, it should be noted that the application of these standards to the specific case has been criticised, since the Court did not take into account the structural limitations of the Chilean health system, which would have ultimately caused the death of Mr Poblete Vilches.[43]

In addition, in the *Cuscul Pivaral* case, the court reiterated standards already outlined in the *Gonzáles Lluy* case on comprehensive care for people living with HIV/AIDS. In particular, in determining the different components of this care, it

[39] See among the most recent developments, IACtHR, Advisory Opinion 24/17, 'Identidad de Género e Igualdad y no discriminación a parejas del mismo sexo'. On the evolution of the concept of structural inequality in the Inter-American system, see V Abramovich, 'De las violaciones masivas a los patrones estructurales: nuevos enfoques y clásicas tensiones en el Sistema Interamericano de Derechos Humanos' *Revista Derecho PUCP*, No 63.

[40] IACtHR, *Poblete Vilches* (n 25) para 127.

[41] Ibid, paras 125–132.

[42] Ibid, para 132.

[43] A Martin and L Clerico, 'El derecho social autónomo a la salud y sus contenidos. El caso Poblete Vilches y el examen de (in)cumplimiento de las obligaciones impostergables y no ponderables' in M Morales Antoniazzi and L Clérico (eds), *Interamericanización del derecho a la salud. Perspectivas a la luz del caso Poblete de la Corte IDH* (Instituto de Estudios Comparados del Estado de Querétaro, 2019).

took into account the specific international guidelines on HIV/AIDS.[44] Similarly, in the *Hérnández* case, where the medical care of a person who had contracted tuberculosis in the context of confinement was at stake, the court took into account the International Standards for Tuberculosis Care, which constitute an authoritative reference for determining the specific scope of the right to health in these cases.[45] These guidelines, which in principle are not binding, were integrated by the Court into the content of the right to health when it comes to people living with HIV and tuberculosis, and thus become enforceable.

In the *Cuscul Pivaral* case, the Court also made progress in conceptualising and applying the notion of intersectional discrimination in order to take an integral and comprehensive view of the violations of the right to health and the differentiated and more harmful impacts caused to the group of women victims of the case, living with HIV/AIDS, who were also pregnant and had low incomes.[46]

In this regard, the Court pointed out that intersectional discrimination is the result of the confluence of different factors of vulnerability or sources of discrimination associated with certain conditions of a person; and discrimination against women on grounds of sex and gender is indivisibly linked to other factors that affect them. Thus, states must recognise and prohibit in their legal instruments these intersecting forms of discrimination and their combined negative impact on the women concerned. They must also adopt and implement policies and programmes to eliminate these situations.[47]

The Inter-American Court had already referred to the concept of intersectional discrimination in *Gonzales Lluy* where it recognised that certain groups of women suffer discrimination throughout their lives based on more than one factor combined with their sex, which increases their risk of suffering acts of violence and other violations of their human rights.[48] In the case of *IV v Bolivia*, the IACtHR was also asked to determine whether in the case of the victim of the facts denounced there was multiple discrimination or whether the different criteria alleged converged in an intersectional manner in the configuration of a particular and specific situation of discrimination.[49] On this point, the

[44] Office of the United Nations High Commissioner for Human Rights and Joint United Nations Programme on HIV/AIDS, International Guidelines on HIV/AIDS and Human Rights. Consolidated version 2006.

[45] IACtHR, *Hernández v Argentina*, judgment of 19 November 2019 (Preliminary Objections, Merits, Reparations), para 79.

[46] IACtHR, *Cuscul Pivaral* (n 11) para 138. In this regard, see M Góngora Mera, 'Discriminación en clave interseccional: tendencias recientes en la jurisprudencia de la Corte Interamericana de Derechos Humanos' in M Antoniazzi et al, *Interamericanización de los DESCA, El caso Cuscul Pivaral de la Corte IDH* (Instituto Max Planck de Derecho Público Comparado y Derecho Internacional Público, Instituto de Estudios Constitucionales del Estado de Querétaro e Instituto de Investigaciones Jurídicas Universidad Nacional Autónoma de México, 2020).

[47] IACtHR, *Cuscul Pivaral* (n 11) para 138.

[48] IACtHR, *Gonzáles Lluy* (n 9) para 288.

[49] IACtHR, *IV v Bolivia* (n 9) para 247.

Court emphasised that sterilisation without consent was a phenomenon that in various contexts and places has had a stronger impact on women who are part of groups with a greater vulnerability to suffer this human rights violation, either because of their socioeconomic status, race, disability or because they live with HIV.[50]

VI. CONCLUSION

To sum up, it is worth mentioning that direct justiciability promises to contribute to a greater extent to the protection of social rights. Among other reasons, this approach allows for greater precision in identifying the social rights affected, as well as clarifying and amplifying their specific content and the State's obligations in this area. As a result, it can contribute to the determination of the reparations due to victims in a more appropriate manner, based on a greater development and specificity of the violations of these rights. These advantages can be seen by comparing the cases in which the Court has indirectly addressed the impacts of economic, social, cultural and environmental rights with more recent cases in which the Court has resolved them directly. Likewise, the fact that the Court has also made important contributions by way of connection, especially on the state's responsibility in the stewardship of the health system, should not be overlooked.[51]

As noted, the IACtHR's change in approach is of great relevance for the constitutional reform process in Chile, as it positions economic, social, cultural and environmental rights as full and enforceable rights as well as guidelines for the definition of public policies and development models. In addition, the jurisprudence of the IACtHR on this subject may serve as a reference for the definition of the content and scope of the social rights to be incorporated in the new Chilean constitution.

Finally, the IACtHR should advance and clarify its initial interpretations. In this vein, it may be useful that the Court deepen and specify the regime of obligations established by the ACHR, particularly with respect to the articulation and relationship between the obligations of 'respect' and 'guarantee', 'adopt measures' and 'progressivity and non-regression'. This precision is of the utmost importance for the determination of the type and scope of reparation measures in specific cases. It is also relevant for the consolidation of a common scheme of obligations aimed towards unification and not separation, reinforcing a holistic and integral vision of all human rights.

[50] UN Special Rapporteur on violence against women, its causes and consequences, 'Multiple and intersectional forms of discrimination and violence against women', A/HRC/17/26 (2011).

[51] Courtis (n 26).

In turn, although the Court advanced some criteria by which to determine compliance with the obligations of progressivity and non-regression,[52] it must intensify the development of clear parameters and do so in a way that is linked with the state's duty to use the maximum available resources. This assessment should include fiscal policy, both in terms of expenditure allocation and the tax system. In this regard, the imposition of higher tax burdens on higher-income social sectors should be promoted, especially in times of crisis and resource constraints. This clause still deserves due attention and an analysis of its redistributive potential. Similarly, the organs of the system should develop the scope of the obligation of non-regression in the context of adjustment and austerity programmes and measures such as those that many countries in the region have experienced in the past and are still suffering today.

Another crucial development which the Court and the bodies of the IAHRS should examine in more detail is the special protection of vulnerable groups. Latin America continues to be the most inequitable continent on the globe and reparations in this regard should involve positive measures, differentiated and redistributive public policies to address inequalities based on sex and gender, gender identity, race and ethnicity, age, disability, socioeconomic status, and territorial location. The focus should be on the consequences of identifying a situation of structural inequality, in order to achieve in-depth, substantive transformations of the causes that generate such visible and sharp disparities that characterise the region.

[52] J Rossi, 'Obligación de progresividad, no regresividad y máximo de los recursos disponibles. Puntos de encuentro y desencuentro entre la Corte Interamericana y el Comité de Derechos Económicos, Sociales y Culturales de las Naciones Unidas' in M Antoniazzi et al, *Interamericanización de los DESCA, El caso Cuscul Pivaral de la Corte IDH* (Instituto Max Planck de Derecho Público Comparado y Derecho Internacional Público, Instituto de Estudios Constitucionales del Estado de Querétaro e Instituto de Investigaciones Jurídicas Universidad Nacional Autónoma de México, 2020).

8

Constitutional Provisions on Disability Rights: National Approaches and International Context

GONZALO MORENO, MICHAEL ASHLEY STEIN AND JODY HEYMANN

I. INTRODUCTION

ACCORDING TO THE World Health Organization (WHO), over one billion people – or around 15 per cent of the global population – have some form of disability.[1] Persons with disabilities have been called 'the world's largest minority',[2] and experience discrimination and bias worldwide. In the past two decades, the disability rights movement has made significant progress in advancing recognition of the human rights and fundamental freedoms of persons with disabilities, culminating in the 2006 Convention on the Rights of Persons with Disabilities (CRPD). As statements of national values, blueprints for subsequent legislation, and crucial factors for court decisions and legal reform, constitutions have become tools of significant importance to both tear down existing barriers and implement the comprehensive and holistic obligations created by the CRPD.

This chapter draws on globally comparative data on constitutional provisions, along with landmark court decisions based on those provisions, to highlight the extent to which the world's constitutions protect the fundamental rights of persons with disabilities. The data we present is part of a quantitative database of constitutional rights in all 193 UN member states, current as of 2017

[1] World Health Organization, 'Disability and Health' www.who.int/en/news-room/fact-sheets/detail/disability-and-health.

[2] 'Fact Sheet on Persons with Disabilities' United Nations Enable, www.un.org/disabilities/documents/toolaction/pwdfs.pdf.

and created by the WORLD Policy Analysis Center (WORLD) at the University of California, Los Angeles.[3]

Our data show that, over the past few decades, constitutions have become increasingly (and specifically) protective of the rights and freedoms of persons with disabilities. Even if these protections are still relatively infrequent across all countries, this should not obscure recent progress since the adoption of the CRPD. Our data also show that enacting new constitutions – as opposed to amending them – may offer the best path for both incorporating the provisions of the CRPD and more generally expanding the constitutional protection of persons with disabilities. This latter finding highlights the importance of the relatively infrequent incidences of new constitution-drafting opportunities, such as Chile's in 2021–22.

In the following sections, we discuss the evolution of the international human rights framework for the rights of persons with disabilities, culminating in the CRPD, as well as their linkages to the creation and enforcement of constitutional protections at national levels. We then present data on the nature and prevalence of constitutional approaches to the definition of disability, as well as approaches to the rights of persons with disabilities to equality and non-discrimination; accessibility and reasonable accommodation; social and economic rights such as education, work, and health; and civil and political rights such as liberty, freedom of movement, and political participation. We also present data on the specific approaches of countries that have enacted a new constitution after having ratified the CRPD. We conclude by discussing the accelerating trends in constitutional protections.

II. THE INTERNATIONAL CONTEXT OF DISABILITY RIGHTS

Across the world, persons with disabilities face significant barriers to education, employment, and healthcare. In low- and middle-income countries, the school enrolment rates of children with disabilities are commonly 30–50 percentage points lower than those of children without disabilities;[4] and those children

[3] In addition to data on constitutional rights for persons with disabilities, this open-access database includes global information on constitutional approaches to equality and non-discrimination across race/ethnicity, sex/gender, migration status, religion, sexual orientation and gender identity, and socioeconomic status, as well as constitutional provisions on education, health, family, religion, labour, and a range of civil and political rights. To learn more about WORLD's methodology, refer to the relevant section of the WORLD website (WORLD Constitutional Rights Database – Methods) and the appendix 'Methods' in J Heymann et al, *Advancing Equality* (University of California Press, 2020). All WORLD data can be accessed at www.worldpolicycenter.org. For a longer analysis on the role of courts after the passage of the CRPD, see A Lawson and L Waddington (eds), *The UN Convention on the Rights of Persons with Disabilities in Practice* (Oxford, Oxford University Press, 2018).

[4] D Filmer, 'Disability, Poverty, and Schooling in Developing Countries: Results from 14 Household Surveys' (2008) 22 *World Bank Economic Review* 141.

with disabilities who do enrol in education often face discrimination or receive poor-quality education.[5]

Disparities in participation also exist when persons with disabilities enter the labour market. In 27 countries in the Organisation for Economic Co-operation and Development, the aggregate employment rate of working-age persons with disabilities in the late 2000s was 44 per cent, compared to 75 per cent for working-age persons without disabilities.[6] Even when employed, persons with disabilities are more likely to be in part-time positions,[7] earn lower wages,[8] and encounter greater barriers to career advancement.[9]

Persons with disabilities also encounter barriers to accessing quality healthcare.[10] In a WHO study, persons with disabilities reported a greater need for inpatient and outpatient care, as well as a greater likelihood of not receiving that care, than persons without disabilities.[11] This same study summarises disparities in access to healthcare in areas as diverse as cancer screening, sexual and reproductive health, and dental care.[12]

Persons with disabilities are also more likely to experience violations or restrictions of their civil and political rights, including the rights to vote, marry or have children, and generally exercise their legal capacity.[13] Legal environments

[5] P Harpur and MA Stein, 'Children with Disabilities, Human Rights, and Sustainable Development' in C Fenton-Glynn (ed), *Children's Rights and Sustainable Development* (Cambridge, Cambridge University Press, 2019); J Heymann and K McNeill, *Children's Chances: How Countries Can Move from Surviving to Thriving* (Cambridge, MA, Harvard University Press, 2013); United Nations Educational, Scientific and Cultural Organization, *Education for All Monitoring Report 2013/2014* (UNESCO Publishing, 2014).

[6] Organisation for Economic Co-operation and Development, *Sickness, Disability and Work: Breaking the Barriers. A Synthesis of Findings Across OECD Countries* (OECD Publishing, 2010) 21.

[7] MK Jones, 'Does Part-Time Employment Provide a Way of Accommodating a Disability?' (2007) 75 *The Manchester School* 695; OECD (n 6) 52; L Schur, 'Dead End Jobs or a Path to Economic Well Being? The Consequences of Non-Standard Work for People with Disabilities' (2002) 20 *Behavioral Sciences and the Law* 601.

[8] S Maldonado, *Trabajo y Discapacidad en el Perú: Mercado Laboral, Políticas Públicas e Inclusión Social* (Lima, Fondo Editorial del Congreso del Perú and Programa de Naciones Unidas para el Desarrollo, 2006); S Mitra and U Sambamoorthi, 'Wage Differential by Disability Status in an Agrarian Labor Market in India' (2009) 16 *Applied Economic Letters* 1393; OECD (n 6) 53–54.

[9] D Wilson-Kovacs et al, '"Just Because You Can Get a Wheelchair in the Building Doesn't Necessarily Mean That You Can Still Participate": Barriers to the Career Advancement of Disabled Professionals' (2008) 23 *Disability & Society* 705.

[10] N Drew et al, 'Human Rights Violations of People With Mental and Psychosocial Disabilities: An Unresolved Global Crisis' (2011) 378 *The Lancet* 1664; E Evans et al, 'Service Development for Intellectual Disability Mental Health: A Human Rights Approach' (2012) 56 *Journal of Intellectual Disability Research* 1098; H Mannan et al, 'Core Concepts of Human Rights and Inclusion of Vulnerable Groups in the Disability and Rehabilitation Policies of Malawi, Namibia, Sudan, and South Africa' (2012) 23 *Journal of Disability Policy Studies* 67; MA Stein et al, 'Health Care and the UN Disability Rights Convention' (2009) 374 *The Lancet* 1796.

[11] World Health Organization & World Bank. *World Report on Disability* (WHO, 2011) 60.

[12] Ibid, 61–62.

[13] See eg Drew et al (n 10); M Redley et al, 'The Voting Rights of Adults with Intellectual Disabilities: Reflections on the Arguments, and Situation in Kenya and England and Wales' (2012) 56 *Journal of Intellectual Disability Research* 1026.

that deny persons with disabilities the right to participate in political life, 'one of the key avenues through which marginalised groups most effectively seek equality',[14] severely constrict their chances to advocate for recognition of their rights. This includes social and environmental barriers such as inaccessible voting booths or retrogressive practices employed by election commissions.[15] Persons with disabilities also face an especially higher risk of involuntary confinement. For example, children with disabilities in Central and Eastern Europe are estimated to be nearly 17 times as likely to be institutionalised as children without disabilities.[16]

Global recognition of the rights of persons with disabilities has advanced markedly over the past half century. The International Bill of Human Rights – which comprises the Universal Declaration of Human Rights (1948), the International Covenant on Economic, Social and Cultural Rights (1966), and the International Covenant on Civil and Political Rights (1966) – put forward a set of broadly applied fundamental rights and freedoms. Over the following decades, claims by advocates for women, children, persons of colour, migrants and others led to the promulgation of additional UN instruments that focused on identity-specific rights. A growing global disability rights movement, led by disabled peoples' organisations (DPOs), drew attention to the inadequacy of the broad language in the International Bill of Rights, which failed 'to address the specific needs and obstacles that a person with disabilities faces'.[17] Efforts to articulate specific protections for persons with disabilities include the 1975 Declaration on the Rights of Disabled Persons; World Programme of Action Concerning Disabled Persons, adopted in 1982; International Labour Organization (ILO) Convention No 159 on Vocational Rehabilitation and Employment (Disabled Persons), adopted in 1983; and UN Standard Rules on the Equalization of Opportunities for Persons with Disabilities, adopted in 1993. Each of these advanced disability rights but, crucially, lacked enforcement mechanisms.

The global disability rights movement's efforts culminated in the adoption of the CRPD, which became the first disability-specific UN human rights treaty. The CRPD advances a human rights-oriented model of disability focused on dismantling socially constructed barriers in order to achieve the 'full and effective

[14] J Fiala-Butora et al, 'The Democratic Life of the Union: Toward Equal Voting Participation for Europeans with Disabilities' (2014) 55 *Harvard International Law Journal* 71, 83.

[15] See JE Lord et al, 'Facilitating an Equal Right to Vote for Persons with Disabilities' (2014) 6 *Journal of Human Rights Practice* 115.

[16] UNICEF 'Children and Young People with Disabilities Fact Sheet' 24, www.unicef.org/disabilities/files/Factsheet_A5__Web_REVISED.pdf.

[17] E van Weele, 'The UN Convention on the Rights of Persons with Disabilities in the Context of Human Rights Law' in J Anderson and J Phillips (eds), *Disability and Universal Human Rights: Legal, Ethical, and Conceptual Implications of the Convention on the Rights of Persons with Disabilities* (Netherlands Institute of Human Rights, 2012) 9.

participation and inclusion in society' of persons with disabilities (Art 3). It presents a holistic framework for ensuring the fundamental rights of persons with disabilities, including the rights to equality and non-discrimination (Art 5), accessibility (Art 9), reasonable accommodation (Art 2), education (Art 24), work and employment (Art 27), health (Art 25), liberty and security of person (Art 14), liberty of movement (Art 18), and participation in political and public life (Art 29).[18]

The CRPD is increasingly influencing the way that constitutions, and the courts that interpret them, view the rights and freedoms of persons with disabilities. For example, in India's first court ruling recognising reasonable accommodation at work,[19] the Bombay High Court borrowed from the CRPD's definition of reasonable accommodation to enforce the constitutional rights to equality, equal opportunity in employment, and life and personal liberty.[20] Additionally, disability rights' advocates involved in constitutional reform processes have used the CRPD as a point of reference and a model for disability-specific rights protections: during the drafting of Zambia's 2011 constitution, a local coalition of disability rights advocates pushed for the inclusion of equal recognition before the law for persons with disabilities, as well as for changes in provisions related to legal capacity and decision-making.[21]

Some national constitutions also formally domesticate international treaties, including the CRPD, thereby effecting concrete changes in the lives of persons with disabilities even in the absence of disability-specific provisions in the text of the constitution proper. For example, the Czech Republic's constitution states that treaties ratified by the country, which include the CRPD, 'form a part of the legal order; if a treaty provides something other than that which a statute provides, the treaty shall apply'.[22] In a 2016 decision, the Vyškov District Court recognised the right to inclusive education for children with disabilities, citing Art 24 of the CRPD alongside this constitutional provision.[23]

III. PROTECTION OF DISABILITY RIGHTS IN CONSTITUTIONS WORLDWIDE

Despite the increasing saliency of specific constitutional protections for persons with disabilities in the world as a whole, these protections remain relatively infrequent in the areas highlighted by the provisions of the CRPD.

[18] Convention on the Rights of Persons with Disabilities (New York, 13 December 2006).

[19] *Ranjit Kumar Rajak v State Bank of India* [2009] 5 Bom CR 227.

[20] Constitution of India 1949, amended to 2016, Arts 14, 16, 21.

[21] J Lord and MA Stein, 'Prospects and Practices for CRPD Implementation in Africa' (2013) *African Disability Rights Yearbook* 109.

[22] Constitution of the Czech Republic 1993, amended to 2013, Art 10.

[23] *Judgment No 10 C 250/2014-124* [2016].

A. Disability Definitions and Terminology

Terms that are commonly used to refer to persons with disabilities 'may both reflect and influence attitudes towards them'.[24] Article 1 of the CRPD states: 'Persons with disabilities include those who have long-term physical, mental, intellectual or sensory impairments which in interaction with various barriers may hinder their full and effective participation in society on an equal basis with others'. Out of 193 national constitutions, only three track the CRPD's approach of defining disability with reference to exogenous factors as determinants of disability. For example, Zambia's constitution states that '"disability" means a permanent physical, mental, intellectual or sensory impairment that alone, or in combination with social or environmental barriers, hinders the ability of a person to fully or effectively participate in an activity or perform a function as specified in this Constitution or as prescribed'.[25]

Even when constitutions have not yet adopted language consistent with the CRPD, they can play a role in at least curtailing the use of derogatory, biased and discriminatory language in national laws. For example, in 2015 the Constitutional Court of Uganda assessed the wording of section 130 of the country's Penal Code Act, which referred to persons with mental disabilities as 'idiots' and 'imbeciles'. Calling this language 'dehumanising' and 'derogatory', the Court held that it contravened Art 24 of the Constitution, on 'respect for human dignity and protection from inhuman treatment',[26] and submitted revised wording.[27]

B. Equality and Non-Discrimination

Globally, 27 per cent of constitutions explicitly prohibit discrimination or guarantee equal rights on the basis of disability (for example, the constitution of Ecuador provides: 'All persons are equal and shall enjoy the same rights, duties and opportunities. No one shall be discriminated against for reasons of … disability …'[28]). This is a relatively small proportion when compared to the number of constitutions that explicitly guarantee equality or non-discrimination for other protected groups: for example, 85 per cent of constitutions provide

[24] GK Auslander and N Gold, 'Disability Terminology in the Media: A Comparison of Newspaper Reports in Canada and Israel' (1999) 48 *Social Science & Medicine* 1395.

[25] Constitution of Zambia 1991, amended to 2016, Art 266.

[26] Constitution of the Republic of Uganda 1995, amended to 2017, Art 24.

[27] *Centre for Health, Human Rights and Development, et al v The Attorney General* [2015] Constitutional Appeal 1 of 2013.

[28] Constitución de la República del Ecuador 2008, amended to 2015, Art 11(2).

comparable guarantees on the basis of sex/gender, as do 76 per cent on the basis of race/ethnicity.[29]

Despite these comparatively small percentages overall, the past few decades have seen a steady increase in the proportion of constitutions that guarantee equal rights for persons with disabilities. Whereas 11 per cent of current constitutions adopted before 1990 explicitly guarantee equal rights or non-discrimination to persons with disabilities, 71 per cent of constitutions adopted in 2010–2017 do so. Despite this positive development, five countries' constitutions continue to guarantee equal rights only to the extent that persons with disabilities are deemed capable of exercising them. For example, the constitution of Timor-Leste states: 'A disabled citizen shall enjoy the same rights and shall be subject to the same duties as all other citizens, except for the rights and duties which he or she is unable to exercise or fulfil due to his or her disability'.[30] Provisions such as Timor-Leste's open the door to discriminatory treatment by focusing on the perceived limitations of persons with disabilities, instead of focusing on equality and the environmental barriers whose removal can help maximise inclusion.

Disability-specific constitutional guarantees of equality are invaluable tools for courts to enforce the rights of persons with disabilities. In 2014, the Supreme Court of Justice of Mexico ruled that a job posting that specified that persons with disabilities need not apply was unconstitutional under Arts 1 and 5 of the Constitution,[31] which prohibit discrimination on the basis on disability and guarantee the right to work, respectively.[32] Constitutional guarantees can also serve as a stepping stone for legal reform. When Ecuador introduced a comprehensive disability law in 2012, its preamble cited the provisions in Art 11(2) of the Constitution, quoted above, as one of its bases.[33]

Nonetheless, general constitutional equality guarantees, which lack language specific to disability, can in some contexts be effective tools for advancing equal rights on the basis of disability.[34] For example, citing the general guarantee of equality in Art 14 of the Constitution,[35] the Delhi High Court ruled that deaf individuals should be eligible to take a driving test.[36] However, courts do not always interpret general equality guarantees to specifically protect persons with disabilities. Infamously, in 1927 the United States Supreme Court dismissed a constitutional equal protection claim and upheld a statute permitting involuntary eugenic sterilisation.[37]

[29] Heymann et al (n 3) 22, 49.
[30] Constitution of the Democratic Republic of Timor-Leste 2002, s 21.
[31] *Amparo Directo En Revisión 1387/2012* [2014].
[32] Constitución de los Estados Unidos Mexicanos 1917, amended to 2017.
[33] Ley Orgánica de Discapacidades 2012.
[34] See B-O Bryde and MA Stein, '*General Provisions Dealing with Equality*' in M Tushnet et al (eds), *Routledge Handbook of Constitutional Law* (London, Routledge, 2012).
[35] Constitution of India 1949.
[36] *National Association of the Deaf v Union of India* [2011] WP(C) 10849/2009.
[37] *Buck v Bell* [1927] 274 US 200.

C. Accessibility and Reasonable Accommodation

CRPD Art 9 calls on states parties to 'ensure to persons with disabilities access, on an equal basis with others, to the physical environment, to transportation, to information and communications ...' Globally, only 6 per cent of constitutions include guaranteed or aspirational protections (ie protections phrased in non-authoritative language) of the right to accessibility of public places for persons with disabilities. Four of 193 constitutions include provisions to ensure accessibility of transportation. Three constitutions guarantee the right to use Braille as an alternative form of communication, as do five for sign language. An additional 4 per cent of constitutions commit to promoting the use of sign language.

Providing reasonable accommodation is essential for countering barriers to the exercise of fundamental rights, including equality. Article 2 of the CRPD, for instance, defines reasonable accommodation as 'necessary and appropriate modification and adjustments not imposing a disproportionate or undue burden, where needed in a particular case, to ensure to persons with disabilities the enjoyment or exercise on an equal basis with others of all human rights and fundamental freedoms'.[38] Only two of 193 constitutions directly address reasonable accommodation.

Although courts can extend explicit constitutional guarantees of equality for persons with disabilities to provide the right to accessibility and reasonable accommodation – as in the Supreme Court of Canada citing section 15 of the Canadian Charter of Rights and Freedoms in holding that hospitals should provide interpreters for the deaf[39] – accessibility and reasonable accommodation remain, in the majority of cases, the next frontier for the formulation of disability rights in constitutional frameworks.[40]

D. Social and Economic Rights

i. Education

Globally, 28 per cent of constitutions guarantee educational rights to children with disabilities; 19 per cent do so by providing this guarantee specifically to children with disabilities, while another 9 per cent protect the right to education generally and at the same time guarantee the right to equality to, or prohibit discrimination against, persons with disabilities. Fourteen per cent of

[38] Convention on the Rights of Persons with Disabilities.

[39] *Eldridge v British Columbia (Attorney General)* [1997] 3 SCR 624.

[40] This is particularly important in an increasingly interconnected environment, where equitable access to the virtual world is both a real concern and a promising avenue for social inclusion. See J Lazar and MA Stein (eds), *Disability, Human Rights, and Information Technology* (Philadelphia, University of Pennsylvania Press, 2017).

constitutions guarantee specialised education or general educational support for children with disabilities, and 2 per cent specifically require schools to be accessible to children with disabilities.

Constitutional mandates for the integration of children with disabilities in general school systems remain, however, infrequent: Only 3 per cent of constitutions explicitly guarantee the educational integration of children with disabilities. For example, the constitution of Bolivia provides: 'The State shall promote and guarantee the continuing education of children and adolescents with disabilities ... under the same structure, principles and values of the educational system'.[41]

These provisions, however, can have profound effects within a country's education system. To illustrate, the Brazilian Supreme Federal Court dismissed a challenge from a consortium of private schools asserting that a law requiring private schools to provide inclusive education was unconstitutional; the court cited Art 208 of the constitution, which tasks the state with implementing the right to education through 'special educational assistance for the handicapped, preferably within the regular school system',[42] and affirmed that all schools, whether public or private, had a constitutional duty to promote inclusive education.[43]

ii. Work

Twenty-two per cent of the world's constitutions guarantee the right to work for persons with disabilities; 12 per cent do so by making this guarantee explicit to workers with disabilities, and an additional 10 per cent guarantee work rights to everyone and prohibit discrimination in employment on the basis of disability at the same time. For example, the constitution of Malawi states: 'Every person shall be entitled to fair wages and equal remuneration for work of equal value without distinction or discrimination of any kind, in particular on basis of gender, disability or race'.[44] An additional 10 per cent of constitutions generally guarantee the right to work or non-discrimination at work, and at the same time guarantee equality for, or prohibit discrimination against, persons with disabilities. However, two constitutions out of 193 – Denmark and Saudi Arabia – continue to limit the right to work to 'able-bodied' citizens, potentially opening the door to employment discrimination against adults with physical disabilities. Section 75(1) of the Constitutional Act of Denmark states that '[i]n order to advance the public interest, efforts should be made to afford work to every able-bodied citizen on terms that will secure his existence'.[45]

[41] Constitución Política del Estado Plurinacional de Bolivia 2009, Art 85.
[42] Constituição da República Federativa do Brasil 1988, amended to 2017.
[43] *Ação Direta de Inconstitucionalidade* [2016] 5357/2015.
[44] Constitution of the Republic of Malawi 1994, amended to 2017, s 31.
[45] Constitutional Act 1953.

iii. Health

Twenty-one per cent of constitutions guarantee the health rights of persons with disabilities; 13 per cent do so by explicitly providing this guarantee. For example, the constitution of Spain states: 'The public authorities shall carry out a policy of preventive care, treatment, rehabilitation and integration of the physically, sensorially and mentally handicapped by giving them the specialised care they require'.[46] An additional 8 per cent of constitutions guarantee the health rights of all, and at the same time guarantee equality or explicitly prohibit discrimination on the basis of disability. In addition, 7 per cent of constitutions broadly guarantee free medical services – a provision that, even if it does not refer explicitly to persons with disabilities, may nevertheless play a strong role, given the well-documented links between disability and poverty.[47]

E. Civil and Political Rights

Persons with disabilities still encounter explicit, legally-imposed restrictions that have been largely eliminated for other socially marginalised groups, often based on presumptions about the overall group, or about particular types of disabilities, without accounting for the diversity of individuals' circumstances and experiences.

i. Liberty and Freedom of Movement

Twenty-five per cent of the world's constitutions explicitly protect the right to liberty for persons with disabilities; 10 per cent guarantee this right explicitly, and a further 15 per cent guarantee the right to liberty generally and at the same time protect equal rights for persons with disabilities. However, five of the constitutions that explicitly guarantee the right to liberty to persons with disabilities also include potentially broad restrictions to this right, such as guarantees of equal rights only to the extent that persons with disabilities are perceived to be able to enjoy them, and nine of these constitutions explicitly protect the right to liberty for persons with disabilities but make specific exceptions for mental health conditions. This type of provision has been historically used to justify the involuntary commitment of persons with disabilities in psychiatric facilities or congregate care settings. Overall, 19 per cent of all constitutions, 36 in total, explicitly state that the right to liberty can be denied to persons with mental health conditions; of the 36, 29 allow this denial for the protection of the community and the treatment of the individual concerned, a further three allow the denial for the protection of both the community and the

[46] Constitución española 1978, amended to 2011, Art 49.
[47] *World Report on Disability* (n 11) 39–40.

individual concerned, one allows the denial for the protection of the community only, and the last three require no reason for the denial. Four constitutions also deny freedom of movement to persons who are not 'of sound mind' and only 8 per cent of the world's constitutions guarantee access to medical treatment when the right to liberty is infringed.

ii. Voting and Eligibility for Legislative Office

The realisation of fundamental rights depends on countries designing inclusive approaches. Physically inaccessible voting venues or materials and procedures that only work for sighted persons are just two of many examples that frequently severely restrict the rights of persons with disabilities in practice even if such limitations are not prescribed by law. Only five constitutions contain provisions designed to facilitate voting for persons with disabilities, and some are phrased in more detail than others. For example, while Uganda's constitution provides that 'Parliament shall make laws to provide for the facilitation of citizens with disabilities to register and vote',[48] a similar provision in the constitution of Malta mentions only those voters who are blind.[49]

Moreover, 23 per cent and 32 per cent of constitutions worldwide potentially deny persons with mental health conditions the right to vote and hold legislative office, respectively. For physical health conditions, the numbers are much lower, only three and four constitutions respectively. For example, the constitution of Uruguay states that '[c]itizenship is suspended: 1. By physical or mental ineptitude which prevents free and reflective action,' but does not specify how physical disabilities could prevent reflective action.[50] These provisions are not necessarily interpreted with caution, nor are they inconsequential. In Hungary, blanket voting restrictions on persons under guardianship resulted in the disenfranchisement of over 71,000 people, and yet only 8,000 to 12,000 of those were considered to have 'severe' or 'profound' disabilities that could plausibly impair voting capacity.[51]

IV. NEW CONSTITUTIONS FOLLOWING THE CRPD'S ADOPTION

The data we have presented include the constitutions of all 193 UN member states, regardless of if, when or how they were amended. Constitutions can, of course, be amended quite frequently. As of the time of writing, Colombia's constitution has been in force for 29 years and has been amended at least once in 20 of those years; in Brazil, this figure is 27 out of 32 years, and in

[48] Constitution of the Republic of Uganda 1995.
[49] Constitution of Malta 1964, amended to 2016, Art 56(10).
[50] Constitución de la República 1966, amended to 2005, Art 80.
[51] Fiala-Butora et al (n 14) 92.

Mexico it is 76 out of 103 years.[52] Amendments can and sometimes do introduce new rights for persons with disabilities; for example, Guyana added 'disability' as a protected ground against discrimination in a 2003 amendment to its constitution.[53]

And yet, according to the data we have collected over almost 15 years, newly drafted constitutions have so far been a more common avenue to implement and expand the rights of persons with disabilities. In between the initial (2007) and latest version (2017) of our database 17 countries added specific and guaranteed prohibitions of discrimination on the basis of disability where they had none before. Of the 17, 14 did so by including these protections in newly drafted constitutions, while only two introduced this protection via amendments.[54]

Given that new constitutions are far less frequent than amendments to existing ones, it is comparatively rare that circumstances align for a country to pass a new constitution that can take into account newly acquired international commitments and contexts. As of 2017, only nine countries that had ratified the CRPD had also passed a new constitution after their CRPD ratification. Nonetheless, in this small group, the presence of crucial constitutional protections for persons with disabilities is, for all practical purposes, universal. All nine countries specifically prohibit discrimination on the basis of disability. All nine countries guarantee the right to work for adults with disabilities, or guarantee the right to work to all citizens and prohibit discrimination on the basis of disability at the same time. All nine countries also guarantee the right to education for children with disabilities, or guarantee the right to education to all children and prohibit discrimination on the basis of disability at the same time. All nine guarantee the health rights of persons with disabilities, or guarantee the health rights of all and prohibit discrimination on the basis of disability at the same time. All nine guarantee the right to freedom directly or by granting this right to all and prohibiting discrimination on the basis of disability, and eight of the nine do the same for the right to liberty.

Even constitutional provisions that are far more infrequent, such as those around accessibility and reasonable accommodation, are more likely to be taken up during the drafting of a new constitution. Of the only four countries worldwide that constitutionally mandate accessible schools, two introduced their constitution after ratifying the CRPD. Of the only seven countries worldwide that guarantee or aspire to the integration of students with disabilities in education, two included this provision in a new, post-CRPD constitution, as did four of the nine countries that constitutionally guarantee accessibility

[52] See Constitute Project, www.constituteproject.org/search?lang=en.

[53] Constitution (Amendment) (No 2) Act 2003.

[54] The seventeenth country is the UK, which has, of course, no codified constitution but introduced this protection in the Equality Act 2010; while we include the Equality Act 2010 as part of the UK's constitutional order for reasons related to our sourcing methodology, we acknowledge that opinions about its constitutionality are not unanimous.

in public transportation and/or public spaces. In addition, the three constitutions worldwide that guarantee the right to hold legislative office to persons with disabilities were written by countries after their ratification of the CRPD, as were two of the three constitutions worldwide that guarantee the right to vote. These figures all show an increasing consideration of constitutional frameworks as the appropriate venue to both implement the international obligations created by the CRPD and generally expand the rights and freedoms of persons with disabilities.

V. CONCLUSION

Overall, the data presented in this chapter reveal that, across the four types of fundamental rights and freedoms examined, the share of national constitutions guaranteeing protections for persons with disabilities remains a clear global minority. This is especially true when comparing this figure to the share of global constitutions that protect from discrimination on the basis of sex/gender, or race/ethnicity, or religion.

However, this overall figure obscures recent and accelerating progress. While 11 per cent of all current constitutions that were adopted before 1990 explicitly guarantee equality or non-discrimination on the basis of disability, 71 per cent of those adopted between 2010 and 2017 do so; similar trends can be observed in constitutional access to social and economic rights for persons with disabilities, including those related to employment, education and healthcare. This trajectory reflects the impact that the disability rights movement has had on human rights discourse and on the subsequent revamping of legal frameworks, and is especially noticeable in those countries that enacted a new constitution after they had signed the CRPD.

We know that constitutional advancements in a specific country can have ripple effects outside of that country's borders. Legal norms, cultures, and forms of reasoning frequently cross-pollinate across the world. For example, an equality amendment proposal by the disability rights coalition Initiativkreis Gleichstellung Behinderter [Initiative for Equality of the Disabled], publicly read before the German Constitutional Commission in 1992, drew strong influences from the then relatively recent Canadian Charter of Rights and Freedoms, which grants equal protection of the law to those with physical or mental disabilities.[55] Two years later, Art 3 of Germany's Basic Law was amended to include the phrase: 'No person shall be disfavoured because of disability'.[56]

[55] Canadian Charter of Rights and Freedoms 1982, amended to 1993, s 15(2); KC Heyer, 'The ADA on the Road: Disability Rights in Germany' (2002) 27 *Law & Social Inquiry* 723.

[56] Basic Law of the Federal Republic of Germany 1949, amended to 1994.

Enacting a new constitution is an uncommon occurrence when compared to the relatively higher frequency of constitutional amendments. However, the amendment process is often constrained by procedural and political barriers that limit strong disability protections from coming into effect. In contrast, the drafting of a new constitution is a much more favourable context for transformative progress. Chile, one of the original signatories of the CRPD, faces a unique opportunity to ensure that the rights of Chileans with disabilities measure up to current best constitutional practices as well as to the highest standards in international human rights law.

This is all the more so with the engagement of citizens with disabilities in the drafting. During the electoral process to select the drafters of its 2022 constitution, for instance, Chile reserved a candidate quota of 5 per cent for persons with disabilities.[57] Constitutional reform processes can beget changes in public discourse and attitudes, which create the political environment for the introduction of further reforms. As Mahomed, Lord, and Stein write, '[t]he very processes by which constitution-building takes place are significant for their visibility-enhancing and constituency-broadening potential'.[58] Describing constitutional reform in Uganda, the authors note that the efforts of DPOs led to the constitution's recognition in 1995 of the rights of persons with disabilities, and 'strengthen[ed] their constituency as a potent political force'.[59]

While the CRPD is most obviously a binding international instrument, it is also the end product of decades of advocacy by DPOs. This advocacy has led to a growing codification, both within the CRPD and in the constitutions that have been newly enacted since its entry into force, of what a just and equitable framework of rights and freedoms looks like for persons with disabilities in the twenty-first century. As both the cornerstone of a country's legal system and a declaration of its collective values, new constitutions such as Chile's can play a key role in expanding disability rights worldwide.

[57] Ley 21298 of 23 December 2020, Artículo único referring to disposición Cuadragésima Séptima.

[58] F Mahomed et al, 'Transposing the Convention on the Rights of Persons with Disabilities in Africa: The Role of Disabled Peoples' Organisations' (2019) 27 *African Journal of International and Comparative Law* 335, 338.

[59] Ibid.

9

Persons with Disabilities in the Chilean Constitution-Making Process

PABLO MARSHALL, VIVIANA PONCE DE LEÓN AND EDUARDO MARCHANT

I. INTRODUCTION

CHILEAN SOCIETY IS organised in a particularly hostile way for persons with disabilities: a way that harms them systematically through a set of structures that result in barriers to the exercise of their rights.[1] A society which discriminates, not always consciously and deliberately, against persons with disabilities, also renders invisible their needs and interests and tends to ignore their voices. Consequentially, persons with disabilities have traditionally been marginalised from political decision-making and participation in a broader sense and it is usual for them to see that their interests are displaced from the debates and adopted decisions. This is particularly problematic from a democratic perspective, with their democratic participation being marked by circumstances such as a lack of accessibility at polling stations or the deliberate exclusion from the electoral roll of those declared judicially interdicted.

The necessary social transformation to reverse the exclusion to which persons with disabilities are subjected requires a process of reflection that must be followed by measures to make visible and empower persons with disabilities. The aim of this chapter is to analyse the potential of the current constitutional process in Chile to reflect on the position that persons with disabilities occupy in society. Particularly, it focuses on how an effective political participation of persons with disabilities in the constitution-making process can serve this objective. It considers the concrete measures that have been taken to allow such participation, including both potentialities and difficulties. For this, the

[1] This chapter was partly funded by the research grant Fondecyt 1190343, ANID-Chile. The first part of the chapter is based on Pablo Marshall, Viviana Ponce de León and Eduardo Marchant, 'Las personas con discapacidad en el proceso constituyente chileno' (2020) 16 *Anuario de Derechos Humanos* 235. The authors thank the research assistance of Beatriz Ruiz.

first section of the chapter introduces a conceptual and normative framework that first identifies the challenge of a constitutional transformation that both benefits and allows the participation of persons with disabilities and then describes a normative framework for the political participation of persons with disabilities based on the Convention on the Rights of Persons with Disabilities. The second section describes and analyses the operation of the mechanism of electoral quotas incorporated into the Chilean constitution-making process to strengthen the participation of persons with disabilities in the constitution-making body.

II. PERSONS WITH DISABILITIES IN THE CONSTITUTION-MAKING PROCESS

A. A Constitution for Persons with Disabilities

Constitutions are texts that fundamentally define the organisation and operation of state offices and their relationship with citizens. A constitution-making process consists of creating those definitions and including them in a normative text. It is important to start by illuminating the objectives of a constitution-making process that seeks to improve the lives of persons with disabilities.

A study published in 2016 shows the frequency of constitutional norms specifically aimed at guaranteeing the rights of persons with disabilities in 193 jurisdictions. The specific rights that are most found constitutionally entrenched in comparative constitutional law are social rights: education (28 per cent), health (26 per cent) and labour rights (18 per cent). Also, there are a significant number of constitutions that entrench disability-specific regulation of the right to equality and non-discrimination (24 per cent) and the rights of political participation (22 per cent). Finally, in a much more limited number the study found the regulation of freedom of movement and expression (9 per cent) and the right of association (7 per cent).[2] The specific mention of persons with disabilities in the regulation of constitutional rights is not a definitive solution to overcoming the barriers that affect them. It is, however, a first step. Complementary legislation, strategic litigation and social mobilisation is required to ensure that constitutional rights are fulfilled in practice. Constitutional provisions not only have a regulatory effect that can be important for persons with disabilities, through legislative and judicial channels, but they also have an important symbolic effect, that can contribute to promoting

[2] A Raub et al, 'Constitutional Rights of Persons with Disabilities: An Analysis of 193 National Constitutions' (2016) 29 *Harvard Human Rights Journal* 203, 235–36.

respect for the rights of persons with disabilities as well as the construction of a more inclusive society.

Specific regulations for persons with disabilities, however, does not exhaust the potential content of a new constitution in this area. There are two additional paths that can be taken when drafting a new constitution. First, an inclusive institutional design, that is, thinking not only about rights, but also about the composition of the state offices and their powers, in a way that makes them accessible to persons with disabilities. Second, clauses, articles or paragraphs specifically aimed at the protection of persons with disabilities, for example, including the principle of accessibility or the principle of universal access, where appropriate, and the rights to reasonable accommodation and support for persons with disabilities. This is the case with Arts 70–72 of the Bolivian Constitution, which guarantee specific rights of persons with disabilities: the prohibition of discrimination, abuse and violence, and the commitment of the state to positive actions, among others.[3]

B. What Contribution Can Persons with Disabilities Make to the Constitutional Process?

Beyond the incorporation in the new constitution of norms that allow the improvement of the lives of persons with disabilities, it is unquestionably important that such persons participate in the process of creating a new constitution. As we shall see, persons with disabilities are entitled to participate and that right must be respected by considerations of principle. However, their participation can be defended for more than simply those reasons. It also can be welcomed from the point of view of the specific contributions only they can offer: only persons with disabilities, through knowledge acquired by their own life experiences, can outline in detail measures to devise a constitution that allows the construction of a more inclusive society. This means both recognising the epistemic authority of persons with disabilities in matters that involve understanding their own experiences, and requiring that people without disabilities deploy a certain degree of humility.

However, the contributions made by persons with disabilities do not come solely from their personal experiences. Their contributions will be much richer and will surely include new, critical, and challenging views for people without disabilities. Further, despite all the barriers that have made their organisation difficult, persons with disabilities have organised into collaborative and supportive networks that allow them to articulate their demands collectively. An example of this collective capacity is the letter sent in June 2020 by a group

[3] Other constitutions that entrench special regulations for persons with disabilities are, notably, Ecuador (Arts 47–49), Zimbabwe (Art 22), Kenya (Art 54) and Uganda (Art 35).

of leaders of organisations of and for persons with disabilities to the National Congress, requesting that the issue of disability and the right to participate of persons with disabilities be raised as critical points that needed to be integrated into the constitution-making process.[4]

The active participation of persons with disabilities in the constitution-making debate may also contribute to the development of better social arrangement for those who do not have any disability, to the extent that it can contribute to making visible the inherent vulnerability of all human beings and the care that we all require at some point in our adult lives. To understand this, it must be recalled that disability is a widespread phenomenon. According to the latest national survey on disability, around 2.9 million people – or roughly 16.7 per cent of the Chilean population – have a disability.[5] The prevalence of disability tends to increase. The ageing of the population will make disabilities more common; there is consequently an urgent need for accessible environments and services. The ideas of vulnerability, interdependence and solidarity that have formed part of the traditional struggles of persons with disabilities, can form a valuable contribution to the Chilean constitution-making process.

C. The Requirements of International Law and its Implementation

The right of participation is guaranteed to all people in a series of international human rights instruments. However, for the purposes of the political participation of persons with disabilities, the most relevant is the Convention on the Rights of Persons with Disabilities (CRPD). The CRPD establishes a series of general principles that it is important to consider when drafting a new constitution. Two articles of the CRPD, complemented by general comments of the Committee on the Rights of Persons with Disabilities, provide important guidance regarding the inclusion of persons with disabilities in the constitutional process itself.[6]

The first is Art 4 (para 3), which imposes on States parties the duty to consult and actively collaborate with persons with disabilities for the preparation and application of legislation and policies to make the CRPD effective, in addition to other processes for the adoption of decisions on issues related to persons with disabilities. Issues indirectly 'affecting persons with disabilities might concern constitutional law, electoral rights, access to justice, the appointment of the administrative authorities governing disability-specific policies or public

[4] P Selles, 'Carta de organizaciones sociales' *El Mostrador* (Santiago, 31 July 2020).

[5] Senadis, *Segundo Estudio Nacional de la Discapacidad* (Senadis, 2015).

[6] However, the emphasis in the two articles that will be analysed does not imply that there are no other provisions of the CRPD whose normative content impacts the exercise of political rights by people with disabilities, for example: the right to equality and non-discrimination (Art 5), accessibility (Art 9), equal recognition as a person before the law (Art 12) and independent living and inclusion in the community (Art 19).

policies in the field of education, health, work and employment'.[7] Furthermore, 'States parties should also consider consultations with and the involvement of persons with disabilities as a mandatory step prior to the approval of laws, regulations and policies, whether mainstream or disability specific'.[8] The duty to consult should be considered an essential step in the constitution-making process, given that various issues will arise in the process that directly or indirectly affect people with disabilities. Such consultation should take place early in the decision-making processes and contribute to their results. The opinions gathered in the consultation phase should be duly considered, which means that persons with disabilities must be listened to not as a mere formality or symbolic gesture but with their comments and demands being considered in a way that ensures they are reflected in the decisions taken.[9] Organisations of persons with disabilities must be informed about the results of these processes and provided with a clear explanation of how their views were considered.[10]

The second relevant article is Art 29 of the CRPD, which provides that persons with disabilities must be granted political rights and the possibility of enjoying them on equal terms with others. It must be guaranteed that they can participate fully and effectively in political and public life, directly or through freely chosen representatives, including the right and opportunity to vote and be elected. It also provides for the obligation to actively promote an environment to allow full and effective participation. The full participation of persons with disabilities implies their regular presence at high-level meetings and negotiations. Their effective participation implies that their contributions must be reflected in any final decision that is adopted.[11] Although there are a number of guidelines to meeting these demands, there are still considerable gaps in their implementation.[12] Among the criteria that could contribute to reducing these gaps are transparency, participation in decision-making processes right from the initial stages, broad collaboration of all relevant actors, the deployment of educational campaigns to raise awareness, among others.[13]

Both the duty to consult and the right to political participation are recognised, no doubt, in respect of individual persons with disabilities. However, both

[7] CRPD, 'General comment No 7 (2018) on the participation of persons with disabilities, including children with disabilities, through their representative organizations, in the implementation and monitoring of the Convention' (2018) UN doc CRPD/C/GC/7, para 20.

[8] Ibid, para 15.

[9] Ibid, para 48.

[10] Ibid, para 23.

[11] M Birtha, 'Nothing About CRPD Monitoring without Us: A Case Study on the Involvement of the Disability Movement in Policy-Making in Zambia' (2013) 1 *The African Disability Rights Yearbook* 115.

[12] A Waldschmit et al, 'Implementing the UN CRPD in European Countries: A Comparative Study on the Involvement of Organisations Representing Persons with Disabilities' in R Halvorsen et al (eds), *The Changing Disability Policy System: Active Citizenship and Disability in Europe* (New York, Routledge, 2017) 177.

[13] Birtha (n 11) 133.

these rights are also extended to organisations created in order to act, express, promote, pursue or defend the rights of persons with disabilities. Ensuring the meaningful participation of these organisations often faces a number of challenges, including a lack of resources and technical capacity and the absence of a uniform voice and balanced participation of the organisations.[14] To address these difficulties, States parties must provide the support and funding necessary to guarantee the broadest participation in the consultation processes. On the other hand, it is important to ensure the participation of organisations that reflect diversity within disability, as well as a variety of organisational forms, social segments, age groups, and persons with disabilities who experience multiple and intersectional forms of discrimination.[15]

D. Towards an Inclusive Constitution-Making Process

A fundamental part of the political participation of persons with disabilities is that they are able to integrate a constitution-making body. In this sense, Art 29 of the CRPD establishes the right of persons with disabilities to effectively stand as candidates in electoral processes, hold office and perform any public function at all levels of government, including the integration of a constitution-making body. Although it is not common for persons with disabilities to be prohibited from accessing elected office,[16] such persons do experience significant barriers in accessing instances of relevant political participation. Various studies have highlighted that the political participation of persons with disabilities is an issue that must extend beyond the formal consecration of rights in positive law texts: it requires exploring the extent to which states prepare plans and allocate resources to ensure that spaces for political participation are accessible to persons with disabilities.[17] The inclusion of persons with disabilities in political participation must be expressed in the adoption of affirmative measures. In the comparative literature, in which the CRPD resonates, two types of measures have been considered.

First, the establishment of participation quotas for persons with disabilities has been suggested. They may take the form of reserved seats, as in the elections to the National Assembly of Uganda,[18] or quotas on electoral lists, as in the municipal elections in Tunisia.[19] Although this strategy may contribute to

[14] Birtha (n 11) 133–36.

[15] S Rattray and E Lako, *Disability Inclusive Development in UNDP: Guidance and Entry Points* (New York, UNDP, 2018).

[16] Raub et al (n 2) 233–35.

[17] L Schur et al, *People with Disabilities: Sidelined or Mainstreamed?* (Cambridge, Cambridge Unversity Press, 2013) 107–109.

[18] UNDESA/DSPD, *Report of the United Nations Consultative Expert Group Meeting on International Norms and Standards Relating to Disability* (New York, UNDESA/DSPD, 1998).

[19] A Zobairi et al, *Political Participation of Women and Men with Disabilities in Tunisia: An IFES Assessment* (Arlington, IFES, 2018).

generating a critical minority of persons with disabilities capable of exerting some decisive influence on the contents of the new constitutional text, it has the potential drawback of generating the phenomenon of the single-issue label,[20] ie the practice of assuming that only representatives with disabilities will address issues related to disability.

Second, and responding to the single-issue label objection, consultation with persons with disabilities, through their organisations, is seen critical for the legitimacy of the process from a disability perspective. On this point, it should be remembered that consultations must be based on transparency, mutual respect, genuine dialogue and sincere will to reach collective agreements and should be developed in accordance with procedures that respond to the diversity of persons with disabilities.[21] Additionally, in order to ensure that no one is left behind in relation to consultation processes, States parties should designate persons in charge of monitoring assistance, detecting under-represented groups and ensuring that they are addressed. accessibility requirements and reasonable accommodation.[22]

III. THE ELECTORAL QUOTA FOR PERSONS WITH DISABILITIES IN THE CONSTITUTION-MAKING PROCESS

A. The Constitutional Reform on Quotas for Persons with Disabilities

Immediately after the agreement of 15 November 2019, which laid the foundations for the creation of a new Chilean constitution, many voices were raised to demand an inclusive constitution-making body. The current structures of representation in the National Congress are so delegitimised that it could not guarantee that the constitution would express the demands that had mobilised a large part of the population. Three ideas monopolised the discussion for greater inclusivity: gender parity; reserved seats for indigenous peoples; and the easing of the rules for filing independent candidates and lists. The inclusive constitution-making body priorities did not consider persons with disabilities. This situation, however, changed surprisingly when, during the parliamentary discussion that established complementary rules to the agreement for a new constitution, a new provision was incorporated, specifically designed to encourage the participation of persons with disabilities.

In late 2019, the Chamber of Deputies approved a provision establishing that electoral lists for the constitutional convention should be formed, with a least 10 per cent of their candidates being persons with disabilities. However,

[20] OSCE/ODIHR, *Guidelines on Promoting the Political Participation of Persons with Disabilities* (Warsaw, OSCE/ODIHR, 2019).

[21] CRPD (n 7) para 47.

[22] CRPD (n 7) para 54.

that percentage was rejected in the Senate, amidst fears that a large number of the lists would be challenged for breach of the quota. In return, it was proposed to lower the quota requirement to 1 per cent, although this proposal was also rejected. After an extensive parliamentary discussion of almost a year, the rules regarding the reserved seats for indigenous peoples and the participation of persons with disabilities were approved through a constitutional reform (Law 21.298). Regarding persons with disabilities, the reform incorporated a transitory amendment 47, according to which, in the elections of the members of the constitutional convention, electoral lists of one or more political parties should reserve at least 5 per cent of the electoral places for candidates with disabilities. It was decided that the disability status of a candidate could be accredited by legal certification or by demonstrating that they were in receipt of a disability benefit or pension. Finally, it was decided that a failure to comply with these requirements would lead to the rejection of all candidates on the list. However, procedures to correct the infringement of this requirement were provided.

The adoption of this electoral quota marks a milestone in terms of the political participation of persons with disabilities in Chile, not only because it reinforces the idea that the points of view of persons with disabilities represent a valuable input for the elaboration of the new constitution, but also because it permits the anticipation of a greater concern and promotion of the rights of persons with disabilities in the constitution-making process.

B. Reform Problems

Despite the generally positive effect of the reform, certain problematic issues could be noted both during the parliamentary discussion and in the implementation process. It is disappointing to note the limited participation of persons with disabilities during the discussions on reform. The records and reports of both the Chamber of Deputies and the Senate show that organisations of persons with disabilities were not invited to express their views on a regulation that affect them directly. The voice and perspective of persons with disabilities was only represented by María Soledad Cisternas, who was invited in her capacity as Special Envoy of the UN Secretary-General on Disability and Accessibility. The absence of both persons with disabilities and their organisations becomes more obvious if contrasted with the high levels of participation from representatives of indigenous peoples during the parliamentary debates. In relation to implementation problems, it seems that the mere incorporation of electoral quotas is insufficient to guarantee that persons with disabilities can effectively participate on equal terms and later, if elected, exercise their offices. Regarding this point, studies have documented the experiences of persons with disabilities in access to public office, showing barriers arising from the lack of accessibility. These are expressed in different ways, such as participation in campaign rallies, discussion and deliberation within the collective body in which they participate, and distribution of relevant information for decision-making.[23] From this perspective, two points are critical and should be addressed with a view to the future participation of persons with disabilities in the constitution-making process.

In the first place, it is necessary to develop an accessibility strategy that comprehensively covers the different instances or moments of participation within the constitution-making discussion. A strategy of this type will enable elected persons with disabilities and those who are involved in the discussions to be provided with the accommodating measures that are needed to permit their participation under equal conditions (for example, accessible buildings and accesses, adapted or preferential seating, Braille materials, sign language translation, written information in easy-to-read format, personal assistance arrangements, etc). An accessibility strategy should also allow persons with disabilities and their associations to be heard in the constitution-making process in the context of the consultations that, as we have seen, are required by the CRPD so that persons with disabilities can express their opinion about the decisions that affect them.

Second, it is necessary to bring the existing diversity of persons with disabilities in society into the constitution-making debate. This diversity is linked to the issue of the *hierarchy of impairments*.[24] This expression has been used in disability studies to convey the idea that perceptions and attitudes towards persons with disabilities vary and usually depend on the type and origin of their impairments. Some have addressed this problem in relation to appointment or election to public office, indicating that there are differences in public perceptions of a person with a disability depending on the origin or type of impairment.[25] In this regard, a study on persons with disabilities as candidates in the 2013 provincial elections in British Columbia (Canada) found that all the people who stood as candidates for the elections had physical disabilities (wheelchair users) and that, therefore, their experiences did not reflect the variety of experiences of people with other types of disabilities.[26] Taking seriously the inclusion of persons with disabilities in the constitution-making process should mean being aware of this diversity and, consequently, ensuring that different realities and experiences of disability are represented in the debate.

[23] E Evans and S Reher, 'Disability and Political Representation: Analyzing the Obstacles to Elected Office in the UK' (2020) *International Political Science Review* 1; M Waltz and A Schippers, 'Politically Disabled: Barriers and Facilitating Factors Affecting People with Disabilities in Political Life Within the European Union' (2020) 35 *Disability & Society* 1290.

[24] M Deal, 'Disabled People's Attitudes Toward other Impairment Groups: A Hierarchy of Impairments' (2003) 18 *Disability & Society* 897.

[25] Waltz and Schippers (n 23) 9–10.

[26] B Langford and M Levesque, 'Symbolic and Substantive Relevance of Politicians with Disabilities: A British Columbia Case Study' (2017) 40 *Canadian Parliamentary Review* 8, 11.

C. A Look at the Implementation of the Quota

Complying with the disability quota, political parties registered 41 candidates with disabilities, constituting a 3.3 per cent of the total competing candidates, which totalled 1,373 nationwide. However, it should be noted that the candidates registered in compliance with the quota do not exhaust the universe of persons with disabilities who were running for the constitutional convention. This is explained by the fact that candidates with disabilities were also registered in lists of independent candidates, to which the quota requirement did not apply.

For the election of the constitutional convention, the national territory was divided into 28 districts. Within these 28 districts, the 41 candidates with disabilities were distributed as follows: 4 districts had 3 candidates; 10 districts had 2 candidates; 9 districts had only 1 candidate with disability; and, finally, in 5 districts there was no participation of candidates with disabilities. In general terms, in 23 of the 28 districts, there was at least one person with a disability running for office due to the application of the electoral quota. From this point of view, the candidates with disabilities were distributed in the various electoral districts, without being concentrated in one or more specific districts. However, in almost a third of the electoral districts there was only one candidate with a disability running due the application of the quota. This fact should alert us to whether the 5 per cent rate as a compulsory quota was sufficient to significantly promote the participation of persons with disabilities in this election.

Table 1 Candidates corresponding to persons with disabilities presented by each electoral list or pact subject to compliance with the quota of Law 21.298. Constitutional Convention (2021)

Party List	Percentage (%)	No of candidatures
Apruebo Dignidad	6.15	9
Ciudadanos Cristianos	6.45	2
Lista del Apruebo	6.45	10
Partido de Trabajadores Revolucionarios	5.55	2
Partido Ecologista Verde	5.06	4
Partido Humanista	8.33	1
Partido Unión Patriótica	5.36	3
Vamos por Chile	5.38	10

Source: Own elaboration based on data provided by Chile's Electoral Service (SERVEL)

Table 1 shows that party lists subject to the requirement of the quota supported a number of candidates with disabilities at a rate just above the minimum required by the law. The highest percentage is exhibited by the *Partido Humanista* (8.33 per cent), but this percentage translated into only one candidate with a disability. Table 1 allows us to observe that the participation of persons with disabilities as candidates for the constitutional convention was mainly concentrated in the three most important coalitions of the Chilean political scene (represented in the electoral list *Apruebo Dignidad* [left], *Lista del Apruebo* [centre-left] and *Vamos por Chile* [right]).

In addition to the quantitative aspect, it is interesting to specify certain attributes that describe and characterise, at least generically, the profile of the 41 persons with disabilities who participated as candidates under the quota. Considering factors such as sex, type of disability, political party affiliation and participation in organisations, our question is: who were these people?[27]

Table 2 Profiles of the candidates with disabilities. Constitutional convention (2021)

Criteria	Majority	Minority
Sex	21 men	20 women
Type of disability	24 physical disabilities	5 sensory disabilities
Affiliation to a party	23 affiliated	18 not affiliated
Organisations of PD	32 not affiliated	9 affiliated
Civil society organisations	30 do not participate	11 participate
Previous political experience	40 had no experience	1 has previous experience
Campaign advertising	28 self-identified as PD	13 not self-identified as PD
	28 advance disability policies	13 not advance disability policies

Source: Own elaboration based on data provided by Chile's Electoral Service (SERVEL) and extracted from the campaign advertising, social networks and other open sources

Table 2 summarises the profiles of the candidates with disabilities to the constitutional convention. The set of candidates maintained a balance between men (21) and women (20), an issue which is consistent with the gender parity rule that operated in the formulation of the electoral lists. Regarding the type of disability of the candidate, there was a clear predominance of people with physical disabilities. In those instances where this information could be obtained (29), 24 candidates were people with physical disabilities, while only five were candidates with sensory disabilities (three cases of visual impairment and two of hearing impairment). Another relevant variable is the previous affiliation to a political party of candidates with a disability. This is important to the extent

[27] In addition to the information provided by the Electoral Service, the data presented in Table 2 were extracted from the electoral propaganda of the candidates, social networks and other open sources on the Internet.

that Law 21.298 established that the electoral quota was only compulsory for lists of political parties. In this regard, it is interesting to note that, of the 41 candidacies, 18 of them were persons with disabilities who were not members of a political party. This indicates that in a considerable number of cases, political parties (whether by necessity or by choice) met the electoral quota recruiting persons with disabilities outside their own membership.

As noted above, an important degree of political participation of persons with disabilities is embodied in the work of groups or Organisations of Persons with Disabilities (OPDs). From this perspective, the affiliation to OPDs in the group of candidates with disabilities is remarkably low: only 9 out of the 41 candidates declared an affiliation to an OPD. This number increases slightly if you consider the level of participation of candidates with disabilities in civil society organisations or social movements: 11 candidates declared that they participate in some social movement or in some type of civil society organisation. Finally, another interesting characteristic is a marked tendency towards the participation of persons with disabilities who had no previous experience in formal politics (holding elected or unelected public offices, previously running for office, political party chairperson). Only 1 candidate declared that they had previous experience in politics, which consisted of having served as regional head of a political party.

Finally, before addressing the electoral results, it is interesting to analyse what role disability played in the campaign advertisements and materials of the 41 candidates. In most cases (28), candidates openly self-identified as persons with disabilities. This proportion is consistent with the number of candidates (28) who included the reference to legal initiatives and the adoption of disability policies as a relevant element of their electoral campaigns. Along these lines, the most recurrent topics were constitutional recognition and protection of persons with disabilities, equality and non-discrimination against people with disabilities, accessibility, labour inclusion and inclusive education.

D. Far Away from the Constitutional Convention: The Results of Candidates with Disabilities

The number of chosen representatives in relation to the number of candidates with disabilities is disappointing. Contrasting the results obtained by these 41 candidates in relation to those of the candidates who were elected, the numbers are the following: 25 candidates did not reach 1 per cent of the votes (only 5 of the 155 elected candidates obtained less than 1 per cent and all of them were elected due to highly voted partner in their list); 15 candidates achieved a result within the range of 1–4 per cent (62 of the elected candidates were within this range); and only 1 candidate obtain more than 5 per cent of the votes (88 of the elected candidates obtained a more than 5 per cent of the votes).

Of the 41 candidates with disabilities in standing for election, only one candidate was elected to participate as a member of the constitutional convention, drafting the new Constitution. What is distinct in this case is that the election of this candidate was produced by application of the gender parity rule, which guaranteed equal results in the allocation of seats among genders. Despite having a partner with more votes (3.18 per cent), Adriana Cancino (secretary of the Nancagua Disability Association, hearing impairment and reduced mobility) (2.64 per cent) was elected as a following most voted for female candidate. However, the gender parity rule also worked against candidates with disabilities. This occurred in the case of Pamela Vargas (a teacher of special education, with a physical disability) who, despite having obtained the third majority within her electoral district (7.75 per cent), was not elected since the first and a second majority were also obtained by women (in a district with four seats). Another notable case is that of María Soledad Cisternas (former president of the Committee on the Rights of Persons with Disabilities, blind), who despite having obtained enough votes to be elected in her district (3.42 per cent) was also excluded by the application of the gender parity rule, although outside the quota requirement because she was standing as an independent candidate.

The operation of the correction mechanism in these last two cases to ensure gender parity in integration of the constitutional convention suggests that there is a need to adopt an intersectional approach in the design of affirmative action measures. Greater attention to representing intersectional identities would reflect better the diversity within each group and strengthen protection to individuals who, by belonging to more than one disadvantaged group, face multiple barriers. Therefore, it would have been desirable to incorporate a mechanism to prevent the parity rule from neutralising the disability quota in order to avoid achieving gender equality at the expense of persons with disabilities.

E. The Failure of the Quota: A Restricted Quota for a Politically Invisible Group

Analysed from the point of view of its aims, the electoral quota did not achieve the desired effect of promoting the participation of persons with disabilities in the constitutional convention. What reasons can be offered to explain this? A first group of reasons relates to the design of the electoral quota itself. First, setting the quota at 5 per cent, as a consensus formula between the original proposal of 10 per cent and the subsequent indication of 1 per cent, resulted in a reduced number of candidates with disabilities. This low overall number of candidates resulted, in turn, in a low rate of candidates with disabilities competing in each electoral district. It should be recalled that five electoral districts (which represents a number close to 20 per cent of the districts) had no candidates with disabilities competing for the respective seats. Second, another important reason for the limited impact of the quota is associated with who was obliged to comply with it. Placing the compulsory quota only on the lists of political parties, and excluding the lists of independent candidates, meant that, from the outset, the possibilities for participation of candidates with disabilities were restricted. In a national political scene where citizens are disenchanted with traditional political parties, the quota was designed to promote the political participation of persons with disabilities precisely under the umbrella of those discredited actors. That may help to explain its low impact on the result. It is interesting to note that the initial design of the quota (different from the one that was finally approved by the National Congress), which established a higher quota (10 per cent) and a greater scope in relation to the lists subject to compliance, including independent lists, would have probably resulted in a more favourable scenario for the success of candidates with disabilities.

However, the failure of the electoral quota may also be explained by reasons related to the 'profile' of the candidates with disabilities. The fact that most the candidates with disabilities were people without political experience speaks to the invisibility of disability in the political sphere. Given this fact, one may question whether the quota is an adequate and effective policy to achieve the aim of greater participation of persons with disabilities in bodies of popular representation. If this were the aim, would not a policy of reserved seats have been more effective, as indeed it was in the case of indigenous people?

The answer to this question is undoubtedly yes. Although quotas on electoral lists have proliferated around the world to increase the political participation of certain historically underrepresented groups, their effectiveness is the subject of intense debate. In practice, the implementation of quotas systematically reveals the extensive gaps between their stated aims and their impact in terms of descriptive and substantive representation. These gaps are due, among other factors, to the fact that the design of quotas does not always consider adequate incentives for parties to seek highly competitive candidates and allocate corresponding resources to them. Precisely for these reasons, electoral quotas were discarded as suitable measures to ensure by themselves the effective presence of women and indigenous peoples in the Convention.

It is yet to be seen to what extent the quota has helped to empower persons with disabilities to exercise their rights, make visible their interests and demands, raise awareness among the public about the need for inclusion or to overcome stereotypes about competence in the public sphere. To be sure, more research is required regarding the symbolic benefits that this measure may have generated. For now, the results of the election to the constitutional convention show the long and arduous road that remains to be travelled in Chile towards the political inclusion of persons with disabilities.

IV. CONCLUSIONS

The Chilean constitution-making process faces the challenge of giving persons with disabilities a voice so that they can defend their interests and rights and present their views on matters that affect them. International human rights law has developed the right of participation with regard to persons with disabilities. First, they have a right not to be excluded from the electoral roll, and to have accessible voting mechanisms. Second, they have a right to participate politically through their own associations. The latter are the main means by which states can fulfil their duty to consult persons with disabilities. In addition to those well-established rights and duties, political participation in the constitution-making process requires the adoption of plans to give accessibility before, during and after each electoral event, as well as during the operation of the constitution-making body.

Notwithstanding the foregoing, for a constitution-making process to be classified as truly inclusive, it is not enough for persons with disabilities to be able to participate in plebiscites and elections. A fundamental aspect of participation implies being part of the constitution-making body itself and having one's opinions seriously consulted on matters of concern. In the framework of the current constitution-making process in Chile, this aspect has taken the form of electoral quotas for persons with disabilities. Although that policy moves in the right direction, attempting to make the constitution-making body more inclusive, it did not achieve its goal.

There are several reasons for the failure of the quota. Some of them point to aspects of design, such as the absence of an intersectional approach in the design of affirmative action measures, the reduced requirement of 5 per cent of candidates with disabilities or the fact that the requirement only applied to political parties' lists. Others, on the other hand, are related to the profiles of the persons with disabilities chosen as candidates and their lack of political experience. In any case, the results of the implementation of the quota in Chile show the limited scope offered by these kinds of policies: although they may increase participation, they are not capable of guarantee the effective inclusion of traditionally underrepresented social groups, such as persons with disabilities.

10

The Right to Education in Chile: Evolution, Critical Issues and Perspectives of Change

ALFONSO HENRIQUEZ R.

I. INTRODUCTION

AS PART OF the broader process of economic, political, and social transformations it imposed, the civic-military dictatorship (1973–1989) implemented an education reform that substantially modified the two defining features that had characterised the development of the Chilean private education system during most of the nineteenth and twentieth centuries: the preeminence of public education and the administration's direct role in providing that education. This reform introduced market dynamics to regulate the supply of education, thus favouring its privatisation and fostering increased inequality and the exclusion of lower-income students from the possibility to access better quality education. The first governments of the Coalition of Parties for Democracy maintained many of these elements, but significant change began to occur after 2006 that justifiably sought to put an end to many of these disparities. Understanding this evolution is key to the emerging constitutional debate, as it will help us understand the origins and flaws of the current educational system and the reasons why the criticism it has received is justified.

Thus, this chapter offers a general perspective of the main transformations that Chilean educational law has undergone in recent decades. For this, I focus on three significant milestones: first, the changes established during the dictatorship, emphasising the structural transformations relevant to the subsequent discussion. Second, I mention the elements of continuity that characterised the governments of the Coalition of Parties for Democracy in the 1990s. Third, I reflect on the scope of the modifications introduced during President Michelle Bachelet's two administrations. To conclude, I present some proposals to strengthen the state's role as the main duty-bearer of the right to education. This means that the new Constitution must recognise the social function of freedom of education, the role of public education, the different dimensions of the formative process, a series of principles that serve as a guide for legislators to make these aspirations a reality and establish mechanisms to legally safeguard this right.

II. EDUCATION AND THE MARKET: ORIGINS AND CONTINUITY

Under the 1980 Constitution, the state's provision of the right to education is inserted within a broader context, established in the idea of a welfare state. In accordance with this model, rights are understood as constraints on public authorities, meaning that the administration has no other choice but to play a passive role and not intervene in each person's area of freedom. This conceptualisation of the state had several consequences for social rights, particularly in the case of the right to education.

In effect, as of 1973 the authorities assigned the private sector a more central role in education and reduced the participation of the state as a provider of educational services. For that purpose, they created a new financing system that consisted of a universal school voucher system. In practice, this meant that the state would provide the school organising bodies, hereafter the patrons (the person or legal entity that owns an educational institution), with a certain monthly sum of money for each student who effectively attended classes, regardless of whether they were publicly subsidised or privately funded. The idea was to promote private investment in new schools and to foster competition among educational institutions. Since funds were not secured, educational institutions would have to mobilise their resources to attract more students to receive the corresponding subsidy. This strategy forced the patrons, even from public schools, to commercialise their educational services in a more market-driven way.[1]

To create this coverage model, the authorities expanded the scope of freedom of education, expanded curriculum adaptability, as well as employment and labour laws for teachers and created a universal and mandatory system to measure learning outcomes that would serve as a parameter to assess the quality of education in educational institutions.[2] The objective was clear: to end

[1] C Salgado, 'El derecho a la educación' in J Bassa et al (eds), *La Constitución chilena* (Santiago, LOM Publishing, 2015) 79.

[2] C Bellei, 'Evolución y contexto de las políticas educacionales sobre la educación pública en Chile' in C Bellei (ed), *Nueva educación pública, Contextos, contenidos y perspectivas de la desmunicipalización* (Santiago, Center for Advanced Research in Education, 2018) 24.

the public-school monopoly over education and to encourage the corresponding expansion of the private sector.

In this context, the idea of a state-run education system was contradictory. The function of the state in the previous period was linked to the idea that the government was the main party responsible for education and, therefore, it was its duty to create the supply of public schooling. However, under the new model the subsidy was granted indiscriminately, without considering whether the patron was from a public or private school, and expansion of public education would infringe upon the objectives the dictatorship pursued when establishing this system.[3]

Because of this, and to avoid distortions in the new market, the government decided to move the administration of public educational institutions from the Ministry of Education to the municipalities. This would allegedly allow more efficient resource management, removing the bureaucracy surrounding centralised administration of education and bringing it closer to local needs and realities. This created a hybrid system in which the Ministry was responsible of providing advisory services and assessing the educational-curricular orientation of institutions, while municipalities oversaw the system's administration.[4]

Ultimately, all these changes undermined public education to the point that, towards the end of the period, student enrolment in state schooling was significantly reduced, while it had doubled in private institutions.[5] Lastly, these regulations lead to a devaluation of teacher training and their exclusion as relevant social and educational actors. A good example of this was that teacher education ceased to be at the university level and the fact that many educators now had to abide by the regulations established in the Employment Code, which resulted in the loss of previously acquired rights.

All these transformations were announced in a series of documents, such as the Presidential Directive on national education and in a public letter that Augusto Pinochet sent the Ministry of Education at the time. In both cases, the need to replace state-run education with state-subsidised education was highlighted, together with the need to move towards a more commercial regulation and to foster freedom of education and parents' freedom of choice.[6] Thus, under this model, said freedom was understood as an instance that sought to ensure to patrons a wide range of action in the configuration of their educational programme and the definition of the requirements and conditions of student access, which are aspects required by the Organic Constitutional Law

[3] Salgado (n 1) 80.
[4] Bellei (n 2) 26.
[5] Ibid, 27.
[6] A Falabella, 'School Markets in Chile and the Emergence of the New Public Management: The Fabric of Policies between a Neoliberal Dictatorship Regime and Center-Left Democratic Governments (1979–2009)' (2015) 36 *Educação e Sociedade* 699, 703.

on Education (LOCE).[7] This conceptualisation gave parents and students no alternative but to accept or reject the conditions imposed by the establishment to which they had freely decided to apply. This was justified, since freedom of education was based on the broader concept of free enterprise or economic freedom, recognised and guaranteed in Art 19, No 21 of the current Constitution, and that it was rooted in the general guarantee of freedom that the 1980 Charter inspired. According to these ideas, patrons could unilaterally establish the admission conditions and requirements, select the students, and reject those who did not meet their requirements.[8]

As for the first governments of the Coalition of Parties for Democracy, they kept this system in place and only introduced minor changes aimed at correcting deficiencies, without questioning the underlying voucher system. In this respect, the authorities tried to improve the equity of the system and reduce inequality and access problems through the development of certain programmes targeting the most vulnerable sectors. Among them, Chile's 900 Schools Programme for the Underprivileged is worth mentioning, as this programme focused on the 10 per cent worst-performing schools in terms of learning outcomes. The aim of the programme was to renovate the facilities of these establishments, increase the number of libraries, carry out training workshops for teachers and conduct educational interventions with students, among others.[9] Examples include the programme for Improvement of the Quality and Equity of Elementary Education, or MECE-Básica in Spanish (1992–1997), which sought to improve the working conditions in schools and to introduce significant innovations to the learning process; the Elementary Education in Rural Chile programme, which was focused on overcoming the isolation many teachers work in, providing documents, books and study guides as well as supporting student learning; the Educational Improvement Projects (PME) that sought to decentralise the educational work and to provide schools with better tools so they could, in turn, develop more autonomous work; and the Enlaces project, an initiative that aimed to encourage information technology and computer-based development of educational establishments.

Over the course of this period, the amounts and types of subsidies were also increased, to increase the funds targeting the most vulnerable sectors, as their conformation was unattractive from a market-oriented perspective. This is worth noting because it meant that the Governments of the Coalition had come to accept the financing system imposed by the dictatorship, thus consolidating the idea that competition among educational institutions was the best incentive to improve quality education.[10]

[7] F Atria, *Derechos sociales y educación: un nuevo paradigma de lo público* (Santiago, LOM Publishing, 2014) 139.

[8] Salgado (n 1) 87.

[9] MI Picazo, *Las políticas escolares de la Concertación durante la transición democrática* (Santiago, University Diego Portales, 2013) 285.

[10] Ibid, 298.

Finally, two relevant changes were also introduced during this period: the extension of the school day and the shared financing system. The full school day was created with the objective of extending and restructuring the use of time in schools, improving teaching practices, the quality of learning and equity of access.[11] The shared financing system represented a mechanism that allowed private-subsidised and municipal schools to charge the students' families a supplementary fee for the educational service.[12] As will be discussed later, even though this formula allowed diverse social sectors to access an education that the state could not offer them, at the same time it generated a complex process of segmentation and inequality.

III. STRUCTURAL TRANSFORMATIONS

In 2006, secondary education students led a series of protests under the battle standard of abolishing the LOCE, the end of municipalisation and the introduction of changes to the higher education access process, among other objectives. This movement consolidated the need to eliminate the voucher system and the privatisation model, typical of the dictatorship, in the public agenda, demanding structural changes that would allow a model in which the state would play more prominent role.[13] For this, students organised marches, protests, and the occupation of educational institutions in different cities and regions across the country, which lasted for several months and had an impact on a scale that authorities did not foresee. The Michele Bachelet administration pushed through certain relevant transformations in response to this crisis.

The most significant of these transformations was, without a doubt, the enactment of the General Education Law (LGE), which replaced the LOCE. This law defined education in quite a broad manner by indicating that education is an activity that should be framed in the respect for and advocacy of human rights and fundamental freedoms (Art 2). In addition, it established that students held certain rights and that it was the state's duty to safeguard equal of opportunities and educational inclusion as well as to promote the reduction of inequalities that exist between the students and which arise from their economic, social, or ethnic circumstances, among others (Art 10). Furthermore, it limited the practice of freedom of education by banning discriminatory access requirements (Art 13), for example, and the imposition of sanctions based on the breaching of financing obligations with the respective educational

[11] S Martinic et al, 'Jornada escolar completa en Chile. Representaciones de los profesores sobre sus efectos en los aprendizajes' (2008) 1 *Iberoamerican Journal of Educational Evaluation* 125, 126.

[12] F Atria, *Veinte años después, Neoliberalismo con rostro humano* (Santiago, Catalonia Publishing, 2013) 40.

[13] M Rifo, 'Student Movement, Education System and Current Political Crisis in Chile' (2013) 12 *Polis* 223, 226.

institutions (Art 11 subsection 4). Along the same lines, the LGE established that patrons had to be organised as a legal entity governed by public or private law and solely dedicated to work in the education field, would have to conform to the curricular bases of the Ministry of Education of Chile (MINEDUC), meet national learning standards and have an internal regulation that would oversee relations between the establishment and the different members of the school community (Art 46).[14]

Another change was the transformation of the Chilean National Council of Education (CNED), whose main function became safeguarding and promoting the quality of primary, secondary, and tertiary education within the framework of equity assurance systems for school and higher education. This system was completed with the creation of two new institutions: the National Quality Agency, in charge of assessing and guiding the quality of education; and the Department of Education, the body tasked with overseeing compliance with the regulations and rights and duties of educational agents. This regulatory framework founded a reform system based on standards, which is characterised by the state's creation of certain quality requirements directed at education service providers –which are evaluated, in many cases, by standardised tests – and non-compliance woth which can lead to a series of consequences for educational centres (including closure).[15]

However, and despite these changes, the regulation did not substantially modify the Chilean educational model as it kept in place the subsidiary principle, the voucher system, co-payment, and the possibility of establishing student selection mechanisms. In addition, they did not take responsibility for the need to make progress towards strengthening the public school system and dealing with the teachers' and administrators' demands for improved working and training conditions.[16]

Thus, in 2011, in the middle of President Sebastián Piñera's administration, students and teachers placed the issues related to education at the heart of public debate once again. Due to this, the 2013 presidential campaign was marked by educational issues. The urgency of a reform that would take care of these transformations became one of the central concepts of President Michelle Bachelet's second administration, which established the objective of guaranteeing the right to education and ending its commercialisation. On this matter, one of its most emblematic projects was the so-called inclusion law, which introduced significant changes. The most relevant were the prohibition against selection processes in private schools that received public funding, the gradual elimination of the shared financing system and the establishment of a series of requirements that patrons would have to meet to be able to request a subsidy, such as solely

[14] A Henríquez, *El principio de protección del alumno en el contexto de la relación educacional* (Santiago, Thomson Reuters Publishing 2018) 322.

[15] Bellei (n 2) 33.

[16] Ibid, 34.

allocating the resources they received to the improvement of education, thus avoiding for-profit education.

These changes elicited intense debate that even reached the Constitutional Court. In fact, for some political sectors, these measures unfairly restricted freedom of education, which made sense as student selection and co-payment had been traditionally understood as being part of the area protected by said freedom. However, these mechanisms were problematic, since they allowed patrons to choose the type of students they wanted to teach, serving as a mechanism for exclusion and discrimination. At the same time, this tended to increase inequality and segregation regarding access to education, which constituted an almost insurmountable obstacle for less fortunate families.[17] In addition, as student selection and co-payment favoured socioeconomic segregation of the educational supply, the most disadvantaged students ended up concentrating in establishments that were less attractive for the more affluent families, which in the long run restricted their learning possibilities as well as their future development (known as the peer effect).[18] As shall be seen, in this system, freedom of choice did not exist for everybody but only for families that were in a condition to meet the selection and enrolment requirements that the respective patrons decided unilaterally.

For the above reasons, the Constitutional Court, based on the idea that the state was obliged to avoid all discrimination in the access to education, decided there was a need to ensure that the exercise of freedom of education would not result in extreme disparity among social groups.[19] On this basis, it was understood that the measures the legislation had established were legitimate and that student selection and co-payment were incompatible with the equal opportunity principle and the inclusive development of a democratic society.[20] The Court also noted that the school voucher system did not seek to protect freedom of education but to assure education free of charge, so that the allocation of funds in terms of the purposes specified by the Constitution could not be omitted by the legislation.[21] Lastly, it reiterated that, if the establishment chose to receive public financing, it would have to comply with the requirements that the law establishes, especially if it sought to guarantee access to education on equal footing.[22]

In addition to this project, the government also introduced new regulations for teachers. The reform included all teachers in the education system financed

[17] G Elacqua et al, 'Evidencias para eliminar -gradualmente- el Financiamiento Compartido' (2013) 14 *Claves de Políticas Públicas* 1, 7.

[18] C Bellei, 'Study of Socioeconomic and Academic Segregation in Chilean Education' (2013) 39 *Estudios Pedagógicos* 325, 331.

[19] Constitutional Court of Chile (2015) Rol Number 2.787, 30.

[20] Ibid, 31.

[21] Ibid, 52.

[22] Henríquez (n 14) 236.

by the state (whether they were in public or private schools), in a model that sought to improve their work performance and academic and economic situation. In this regard, the law granted the teaching profession a university-level rank, established new requirements for those who opted to study education, created a professional development system based on the different education levels where the educator could work (primary, secondary and tertiary education), set up an induction and mentoring mechanism at the beginning of the professional career, significantly improved basic wages for classroom teachers and reduced the maximum number of teaching hours, among other modifications.[23]

At the end of this period, the law creating the New Public Education System (NEP) was enacted, introducing one of the most important transformations Chilean educational law has experienced in recent years. This new law had an ambitious goal: to lay the foundations for renovating and strengthening Chilean public schools.[24] To this end, the regulation provided for the creation of three entities: the Directorate of Public Education (DEP), in charge of coordinating the Local Public Education Services (SLE); the SLE, which are intermediate bodies that replaced municipalities as patrons and took over the task of optimising administration of education as well as of defining the best strategies to secure the supply of public education in the areas under their supervision;[25] and the Local School Boards, units whose function is to represent the interests of educational communities.[26] This reform is characterised by the fact that instead of establishing a centralised administrative system with all functions concentrated in the Ministry of Education, it creates a set of intermediate levels of education governance. These levels would play a mediating role between the schools' requirements and the different forms of central government by orienting their actions towards the construction of a real public education system.[27] Ultimately, this law allowed the first step towards a gradual de-municipalisation of education, leaving behind one of the dictatorship's main legacies.

IV. PROBLEMS AND CHALLENGES

A series of measures taken during the Chilean dictatorship were designed to put the private sector in charge of education, granting them the freedom to configure their own educational projects. This is a model that makes sense on the

[23] JM Sanhueza and V Orellana, 'Análisis crítico de la reforma educacional de Bachelet (2014–2018)' in V Orellana (ed), *Entre el mercado gratuito y la educación pública* (Santiago, LOM Publishing, 2018) 280.

[24] Ibid, 287.

[25] Bellei (n 2) 127.

[26] Sanhueza and Orellana (n 23) 288.

[27] Bellei (n 2) 127.

assumption, as Salgado points out, that when faced with the need to distribute scarce goods, social rights can only be seen as rights to minimum benefits, as the correct way to allocate them would be to do so in accordance with each person's ability to pay for them.[28]

The first Coalition Governments tried to tackle some of the inconsistencies and issues of this system without questioning its fundamentals, notwithstanding the fact that the projects approved during the two administrations of President Michelle Bachelet, which were triggered by pressure from students and other social actors, managed to introduce substantial changes. In this regard, the prohibition against student selection, the elimination of the shared financing system and the enactment of the NEP should be inerpreted as an effort to guarantee that access to education is not conditioned by families' economic resources or purchasing power.

Despite the above, lingering issues remain. The most important, undoubtedly, is related to the fact that in the current system the state does not play a prominent or specific role. The aforementioned changes mainly aimed to establish a set of restrictions to the exercise of freedom of education as well as creating a new institutional framework that allowed the strengthening of public education without modifying the system's financing.[29] This becomes problematical because financing via vouchers makes it impossible to distinguish between the different types of educational institutions – as long as the private centres have the right to receive the same subsidy per student as public schools do – thus fostering a logic of competition between public and private schools.

To avoid this problem, the new Constitution must guarantee a social state model in which the administration is the primary agent in education. For social constitutionalism, there are certain goods and services that every person has access to on equal terms, regardless of their resources or social class. This carries a significant consequence, for the state to be seen, as in the 1980 Constitution, as a threat to freedom, but also, as a source of empowerment for citizens who have been excluded from the political process or the exercise of certain benefits.[30] Thus, the social dimension of rights justifies the obligation to change from a minimum or subsidiary benefits system in which the state is simply limited to competing with the private sector and where education is distributed by the market, to a model of universal and general benefits that will allow all students to develop their learning processes on an equal footing.[31] These considerations are relevant because they justify, among other things, the idea that the Constitution recognises the need to create a public education system that has a special category status as well as a financing method to fulfil the transformative role that education should play within society.

[28] C Salgado, 'El derecho a la educación en una nueva Constitución' in J Bassa et al (eds), *La Constitución que queremos* (LOM Publishing, 2019) 219.

[29] Sanhueza and Orellana (n 23) 288.

[30] D Lovera, 'Derechos sociales en una Nueva Constitución: el constitucionalismo transformador' in Bassa et al (n 28) 123.

[31] Ibid, 117.

This thesis is projected in two areas. While one is directly related to the provision of education, the other is linked to regulation of the educational service. In terms of the former, and as some authors accurately argue, the deepest intervention in state education, such as the creation of educational centres, cannot depend on the absence of initiative from the private sector.[32] The reason for this is that it is the first and foremost duty that the state takes on to guarantee the right to education. Therefore, it is a task that the state plays a leading role in and, consequently, cannot be delegated to the private sector. This point of view is thoroughly shared by the ICESCR:

> In this respect, two features of article 13 require emphasis. First, it is clear that article 13 regards states as having primary responsibility for the direct provision of education in most circumstances; State parties recognize, for example, that the 'development of a system of schools at all levels shall be actively pursued' (Art 13(2)(e)).[33]

Alternatively, and regarding the second aspect, the state assumes the duty to regulate the provision of education. In practice, even when human rights standards have an open-ended nature – that is to say, they do not force the public entity to take sides with a specific economic or development model – they do impose important normative and axiological limits on how they can conduct their activities. In this way, and according to their international obligations, the provision of education must be subjected to an intense state control, whether the service provider is a public or private entity. Amongst other things, this means that the administration must secure the regulation, continuity, gratuity, quality, equality, and feasibility of the cost of education.[34] This normative task is justified by the fact that education is a necessary condition for individuals to materialise their life plans, so nobody can be legally authorised to deny another individual their access to it, or to undermine the human rights of a student during their learning and formative process.

Certainly, this does not mean that the state must offer everyone the same formation. Evidently, students do not constitute a homogenous group and therefore public powers should introduce certain differences that allow the students to transform their abilities into effective operations, simply supporting the idea that: 'the criterion of distribution of the respective benefits [is] a criterion that rests on the recognition of the equality among all'.[35]

[32] E Irujo, *Las libertades en la enseñanza* (Madrid, Tecnos Publishing, 1982) 187. In the same sense: L Cotino, *El derecho a la educación como derecho fundamental. Especial atención a su dimensión social prestacional* (Madrid, Centre for Political and Constitutional Studies, 2012) 172.

[33] CESCR General Comment No 13: *The Right to Education* (Art 13), E/C.12/1999/10, 48.

[34] Cotino (n 32) 58.

[35] Atria (n 7) 61. A Henriquez, 'Some Conceptions about Distributive Justice and its Problems about the Enjoyment of the Right to Education' (2018) 17 *Revista de Derecho*, Faculty of Law of the Catholic University of Uruguay 49, 61.

Along the same line, the new Constitution should also move towards a more complex conceptualisation of the right to education. In fact, this guarantee does not simply consist in the right of access to education but in: (1) a dimension of availability, linked to the responsibility to secure a sufficient number of educational centres and the duty to guarantee that educational services are provided by competent and well-paid teachers; (2) a dimension of quality, associated with the duty to ensure that education is delivered without undermining the dignity of students and with the obligation to guarantee that the contents of said education follow certain purposes, related, among others, to the encouragement of the values that human rights embody; (3) a dimension of adaptability, related to the duty to adapt teaching to the needs of students and their respective communities; (4) and a final dimension of access, which will compel the state to remove all obstacles, economic or not, that constitute an impediment for individuals to access primary, secondary and tertiary education on an equal footing.[36] These different aspects are not included in the current constitutional text. Hence, their recognition is fundamental to effectively match the administration's actions with the objectives that sustain the concept of a social state.

However, I believe that the new Charter should also clearly establish that freedom of education not only protects the holder's subjective or individual interest, but constitutes one of the means the state has to guarantee the right to education, the justification being that the different rights and freedoms recognised in this field are functionally linked to the achievement of the objectives of education, which necessarily means that they must act as a channel to effectively ensure students' interests. The importance of this is that it opens means for the legislation to link the significant role that private patrons play in this matter with the social purposes that underlie the very idea of education, thus making it possible to limit the exercise of said role to ensure a general compliance with the objectives and standards established by the legal system regarding the protection of the right under consideration.[37] In other words, this implies that the Constitution must recognise the social function of freedom of education.

By comparison, we believe that it is important that the Constitution establish some of the principles that serve as a base or as a foundation for the Chilean education system. Following some of the proposals we have developed in other documents, we believe these principles could be:

(a) continuity of service: this can be devised as the duty the state has to ensure the continuous and efficient provision of educational services, to avoid any interruptions and, in case there are any, to take the necessary measures to fix them as soon as possible;

[36] Henríquez (n 14) 18.
[37] Ibid, 239.

(b) freedom of thought, of conscience and of religion: this consists of the obligation the administration must guarantee that students can choose their life options in compliance with their own decisions, belief, convictions, values, and hopes. Therefore, education plays a central role in the development of autonomy and critical thought;
(c) inalienability of students' fundamental rights: this can be seen in the prohibition against adopting measurements that could be considered discriminatory or arbitrary, both at the time of access, and throughout the development of the formative process. This obligation presents itself throughout the education system, whether in public or private schools'
(d) inclusion: this is given by the requirement to guarantee that both the learning environment and educational practices consider students' social, personal or health realities. Students do not constitute a homogeneous group. On the contrary, they are characterised by their personal and social diversity and, therefore, recognising this fact can have a great impact on the development of future educational policies that emerge under the new Fundamental Charter;
(e) gratuity: this covers the duty of the state to assume the direct costs (and in some cases, indirect ones) that education entails. It constitutes a central principle, as it aims to prevent the stratification of supply and the concentration of students with limited resources in low-quality institutions. Gratuity covers primary and secondary education, of course, but it must also be projected to higher or tertiary education;
(f) quality: in a broader sense, this principle involves the duty to guarantee students access to appropriate education so they can effectively develop their abilities, properly understand their surroundings, and exercise the rest of their fundamental rights.[38]

Lastly, I believe that the new Constitution must establish legal protection mechanisms that include the right to education. Even though the regulation of rights is by nature open-ended and imprecise in the current Constitution, the duties of the legislation cannot be fulfilled entirely and completely at their discretion, as they have an insurmountable limit in the so-called essential content of rights. This essential content corresponds to the content limited by the norms of both domestic and international law, which means that the right to education, with respect to fundamental laws, also has content that the authority cannot disregard. This content generates a series of obligations that are relatively specific, both in relation to the compelled individual, constituted by the state, as well as regarding all the actions it must undertake to accomplish its respective duties. Therefore, I believe there is no reason for the courts not to safeguard the positions of the fundamental rights that can be subsumed in the essential content

[38] Ibid, 337.

of the right under study, whether this comes from the semantic meaning of the corresponding norm or from a systematic and purpose-based interpretation, especially considering the international corpus in this matter. Otherwise, the system of legal sources would be subverted, the place of the Constitution as the supreme norm of the legal system would be undermined and the possibilities of maximising the exercise of students' rights would be reduced.[39]

V. CONCLUSION

Teaching and education constitute a form of community welfare. Hence, the distribution criterion the administration chooses can be none other than equality. However, during the dictatorship a series of transformations were implemented that sought to make the market responsible for distributing the provision of education. This model, which is based on families' payment capacity and the recognition of an extensive freedom of education, generated a series of consequences linked to the exclusion and segmentation of the supply of education, a fact that especially affected the most vulnerable sectors of the population. The first governments under the Coalition kept many of these elements in place but significant changes were made as of 2006 that sought to put an end to student selection, co-payment, and for-profit education. Nevertheless, the constitutional debate creates an opening that allows us to go one step further, insofar as the new Constitution moves towards a model of a social state that helps to strengthen the role that public education should play in the system as a whole, while incorporating the different dimensions of education, recognising the social function of freedom of education, including a series of principles that serve as a guide for the legislation to materialise these aspirations, and establishing mechanisms that allow their legal protection.

[39] Ibid, 205.

11

Integrating the Abidjan Principles on the Right to Education into the Constitution: Keys for the Chilean Process

VALENTINA CONTRERAS, VICENTE SILVA AND DELPHINE DORSI

I. INTRODUCTION

THE RIGHT TO education is not only a right in itself, but also an empowerment, multiplier and transformative right, 'an indispensable means of realizing other human rights'.[1] Thus, the right constitutes essential experiences and learning processes that enable people, individually or collectively, to develop their personalities and the maximum of their capacities, to be part of society and to interact with others and with their environment while fully respecting human rights.[2] From this perspective, it has been recognised in various international and regional human rights treaties[3] and in political commitments made in international forums.[4]

Despite the importance of the right to education, normative gaps in its understanding and interpretation of the right hindered its implementation, especially

[1] UN Committee on Economic, Social and Cultural Rights, General Comment No 13: Right to Education, UN doc E/C.12/1999/10 (1999), para 1.

[2] UN Committee on the Rights of the Child, General Comment No 1: Purposes of Education, UN doc CRC/GC/2001/1 (2001), paras 1–2.

[3] Art 26 of the Universal Declaration of Human Rights; Arts 13 and 14 of the International Covenant on Economic, Social and Cultural Rights; UNESCO Convention against Discrimination in Education; Art 24 of the Convention on the Rights of Persons with Disabilities; Art 10 of the Convention on the Elimination of All Forms of Discrimination against Women; Arts 28 and 29 of the Convention on the Rights of the Child; Art 13 of the San Salvador Protocol; Art 2 of Protocol 1 of the European Convention on Human Rights; Art 17 of the European Social Charter; Art 11 of the African Charter on the Rights and Welfare of the Child and Art 12 of the protocol of the African Charter on Human Rights.

[4] Goal No 4, Sustainable development goals (SDG), 2030 Agenda.

in a context of growing privatisation and commercialisation of education. It is to respond to these challenges that the Abidjan Principles on the human rights obligations of States to provide public education and to regulate private involvement in education (hereafter Abidjan Principles or the Principles) were adopted in February 2019. The Abidjan Principles compile existing standards, jurisprudence and practice on the right to education, presenting guidelines for states to guarantee public, free, quality education, and to regulate private actors' involvement in the provision of education.

This chapter argues that the Abidjan Principles could provide practical and legitimate guidance to address constitutional gaps in the right to education in Chile, particularly on critical themes in the Chilean context such as the content of education, the organisation, governance, and financing of education systems, the role and limitation of private schools and the regulation of private education. The Chilean constitutional process offers a unique institutional opportunity to integrate for the first time the most up-to date and comprehensive understanding of the right to education into the process of developing a new constitution, through the Abidjan Principles.

II. THE CONSTITUTIONAL PROTECTION OF THE RIGHT TO EDUCATION

According to Nino, a constitution 'is a political-normative instrument that establishes a set of fundamental rules for distributing power, organising life in common and guaranteeing the rights of all. Therefore, as the supreme legal norm, all laws and regulations must be aligned with the values, principles and norms enshrined by constitution'.[5] The constitution is like an essential roadmap 'to guide the destinies of the country'.[6]

Constitutional and legal incorporation is one of the essential and appropriate means of realising the right to education at the domestic level. As the Committee on Economic, Social and Cultural Rights points out, in many cases the legal incorporation of economic and social rights is not only appropriate but indispensable.[7] The constitution enables the existence of other appropriate measures for the fulfilment of the right to education, such as the availability of judicial remedies and other measures 'of an administrative, financial, educational and social'[8] nature. In other words, in order to implement public policies

[5] C Nino, *Fundamentos de derecho constitucional: análisis filosófico, jurídico y politológico de la práctica constitucional* (Buenos Aires, Editorial Astrea 2013) 1.

[6] Ibid, 1.

[7] UN Committee on Economic, Social and Cultural Rights, General Comment 3: The nature of States parties obligations (Art 2, Para 1, of the Covenant), UN doc E/1991/23 (1990), para 3.

[8] Ibid, para 7.

to develop a system of public schools, to design inclusive education strategies and even to put in place courts of law to protect people from violations of the right to education, the constitution can play a crucial role.

As a roadmap, the constitution is a constant reminder of the goals to be achieved by the state, which is particularly important in the case of social rights whose realisation is to be achieved progressively. The constitutionalisation of the human right to education, therefore, requires the design and implementation of plans, programmes and educational policies aimed at making it effective in practice.

III. THE ABIDJAN PRINCIPLES AND THE RIGHT TO EDUCATION

In 2019, 57 of the most qualified experts on the right to education adopted the Guiding Principles on States' human rights obligations to provide public education and to regulate private actors' involvement in education, known as the Abidjan Principles.[9]

In a global context of increasing privatisation and commercialisation of education, in which private interests and profitability take more prominence than respect, protection and realisation of the right to education[10] the Abidjan Principles provide states with a guide to address the potential tensions between states' obligations to guarantee provision of public, free, quality education for all without discrimination, and to respect the liberty to choose and establish private schools, applying a human rights framework to private actors' involvement in education.[11]

The Principles provide key reference points to address these tensions, reaffirming states' obligations to respect, protect and fulfil the right to education, both nationally and extra-territorially.[12] This instrument provides specific guidance to states to meet their obligations when private actors are involved in the provision of education, which includes the adoption of regulation, monitoring and accountability measures. Thus, the Abidjan Principles offer useful guidelines to re-design the organisation of education systems in accordance with international human rights standards.

Since their adoption, the usefulness of these Principles has been explicitly recognised by international and regional human rights bodies,[13] including the UN Human Rights Council in 2019 and 2021, and the African Commission

[9] Abidjan Principles, 2019, available at www.abidjanprinciples.org.

[10] Ibid, Introduction.

[11] S Aubry and D Dorsi, 'Towards a Human Rights Framework to Advance the Debate on the Role of Private Actors in Education' (2016) 42(5) *Oxford Review of Education* 1.

[12] Abidjan Principles, 2019, Introduction.

[13] A full list of the bodies recognising the principles is available at www.abidjanprinciples.org/en/support/official-recognition.

of Peoples' and Human Rights in 2019 and 2020. The Special Rapporteur on Economic, Social, Cultural and Environmental Rights of the Inter-American Commission on Human Rights also said of the Abidjan Principles that they are 'a valuable specialised source for the interpretation of this issue in the framework of the Inter-American system'.[14]

IV. TENSIONS IN THE CHILEAN CONTEXT

The tensions the Abidjan Principles seek to address have been at the heart of the public debate in Chile for decades and their main roots lie in the constitutional framework.[15]

The Pinochet regime put in place market policies in education which were enshrined in the constitution and maintained after the dictatorship, establishing an understanding of education as a consumer good. This understanding constitutes a structural barrier to changing the governance of the education system, and thus to truly guarantee education as a human right, as the international human rights law mandates.[16] It led to a re-conceptualisation of the freedom of education as merely a form of private entrepreneurial freedom. This reductionist approach was criticised by the UN Special Rapporteur on the Right to Education in his report on Chile,[17] the UN Committee on Economic, Social and Cultural Rights,[18] and the UN Committee on the Rights of Child.[19]

Chile's 1980 Constitution, as revised in 2015, set up a framework for education that is unbalanced towards private education. In particular, it addresses the right to education in Art 19.10 and it specifically protects 'freedom of education' in a separate paragraph, in Art 19.11. Article 19.10 carefully sets a limited obligation for the state to 'finance a free system' of education, but not to provide it. Article 19.11 guarantees 'the right to open, organize and maintain educational establishments', as well as 'the right to choose the educational establishment for their children'.

The framing of these liberties provides a higher level of protection for private education than the obligation to 'respect for the liberty of parents' to choose a

[14] OAS Special Rapporteur on Economic, Social, Cultural and Environmental Rights, Business and Human Rights: Inter-American Standards, 2019.

[15] M Ramos, 'Hemos llegado a un punto en que el éxito de los colegios privados está produciendo un daño al sistema público de educación', *CIPER* (5 April 2020), www.ciperchile.cl/2020/04/05/hemos-llegado-a-un-punto-en-que-el-exito-de-los-colegios-privados-esta-produciendo-un-dano-al-sistema-publico-de-educacion/.

[16] Ibid.

[17] UN Special Rapporteur on the Right to Education, Report on Chile, UN doc A/HRC/35/24/Add.1 (2017).

[18] UN Committee on Economic, Social and Cultural Rights, Concluding Observations: Chile, UN doc E/C.12/CHL/CO/4 (2015), para 30.

[19] UN Committee on the Rights of the Child, Concluding Observations: Chile, UN doc CRC/C/CHL/CO/4-5 (2015), paras 67–68 and 69–70.

school other than a state school, and the 'liberty of individuals and bodies to establish and direct educational institutions', which can be found in international law, in particular in Art 13(3) and 13(4) of the International Covenant on Economic, Social and Cultural Rights (ICESCR). Equally, while international human rights law puts a limitation on the liberty to choose or establish a private school, which must 'conform to such minimum educational standards as may be laid down or approved by the State' (ICESCR, Art 13(3)), no such similar limitation can be found in the Chilean Constitution. In addition to these elements specific to the provisions on education, the 1980 Chilean Constitution does not protect non-discrimination and equality in the enjoyment of the right to education or any other right, further limiting any attempt to protect equal quality of education for all without distinction of wealth or income.

The tensions between the obligation of the state to provide public education and the liberty of parents to choose private schools are rooted in the neoliberal norms enshrined in the Constitution of 1980. Although the fundamental charter consecrates diverse components of the right to education in Art 19 paragraphs 10 and 11, the text does not possess a human rights approach,[20] insofar as it only guarantees access to education, without including additional elements that constitute this right.[21] From a human rights-based approach, the current Constitution has a series of shortcomings:[22] (a) it puts freedom of education before the right to education; (b) it does not guarantee access to justice in case of rights violations; (c) it does not provide participation and governance mechanisms; (d) it does not protect individuals against discriminatory acts; (e) it does not guarantee the quality of educational provision; (f) it does not ensure the necessary adaptability of education to territories, identities or student needs; and (g) it does not ensure a lifelong learning process. These are critical issues that need to be considered in the reform of the education system in Chile, which the Abidjan Principles can help to resolve.

V. LEGAL INCORPORATION OF THE RIGHT TO EDUCATION IN LIGHT OF THE ABIDJAN PRINCIPLES

In accordance with international human rights law,[23] states are required to enforce human rights domestically through all appropriate measures, be they legislative, administrative, economic, judicial or otherwise (Art 2(1) ICESCR).

[20] UN Special Rapporteur Extreme Poverty and Human Rights, Report on Chile, UN doc A/HRC/32/31/Add.1 (2016), para 25.

[21] UN Committee on Economic, Social and Cultural Rights (n 1), para 6.

[22] J González et al, *Constituyamos Otra Educación, Una Mejor Sociedad Es Posible: 10 nudos constitucionales en educación y experiencias internacionales destacadas para inspirar el debate nacional* (2020), www.summaedu.org/wp-content/uploads/2020/10/CONSTITUYENTE-DOC_FINAL_PAG.pdf.

[23] For example, Art 2(1) of the International Covenant on Economic, Social and Cultural Rights.

Among these measures, the constitutional framework offers the greatest level of protection of rights in the legal order.

Both the UN Committee of Economic, Social and Cultural Rights and the UN Special Rapporteur on Extreme Poverty and Human Rights[24] have highlighted Chile's obligation to fully recognise and grant necessary legal protections to economic, social and cultural rights in the text of the new constitution.[25] The recognition of the right to education as a human right is a fundamental aspect of the obligations that the state of Chile has assumed since the ratification of treaties protecting the right to education, including the ICESCR in 1972 and the Convention of the Rights of the Child (CRC) in 1990, in a global environment in which education is one of the most constitutionally protected social rights.[26]

The Abidjan Principles offer a reference point for the development of a new constitutional framework for the right to education in Chile. As a compilation of states' binding obligations,[27] drawing in particular from the ICESCR and the CRC, the Abidjan Principles offer a useful tool to ensure that the new Chilean Constitution is in line with the most recent authoritative interpretations of the right to education.[28]

The Principles have a normative basis, grounded in the provisions of international human rights law which the Chilean state has an obligation to respect, protect and fulfil.[29] A series of factors exist which justify the legitimacy of this instrument before the state, including the independence and expertise of the drafters and signatories, the diversity of voices it includes, its rigour and persuasion, its practicality, and the validation process through which it was constructed.[30] Attending to the general provisions of international law, the specific construction of the Abidjan Principles may be useful in the practice of creating awareness regarding the violations of the right to education, identifying normative gaps, informing the design and implementation of public policies relating to education, and offering guidelines to enable those directly affected by violations of the right to education to seek reparations, while simultaneously offering states an essential tool for accountability.[31]

Regarding the political and social character of Chile, the Abidjan Principles acquire an additional importance. They could be an extremely useful tool to

[24] UN SR Extreme Poverty and HR (n 20), para 71.

[25] UN Committee on Economic, Social and Cultural Rights (n 18), para 7.

[26] C Jung et al, 'Economic and Social Rights in National Constitutions' (2014) 62(4) *American Journal of Comparative Law* 1043.

[27] Abidjan Principles, p 13.

[28] M Sepúlveda, 'Human Rights Guiding Principles: A Forward-Looking Retrospective' in F Adamson et al (eds), *Realizing the Abidjan Principles on the Right to Education. Human Rights, Public Education and the Role of Private Actors in Education* (Cheltenham, Edward Elgar, 2021) 27.

[29] Ibid.

[30] Ibid, 33–40.

[31] Ibid, 29–30.

guide discussions in the context of the constitutional process, and achieve profound transformations in the Chilean education system through their incorporation into law.

VI. ALIGNING THE CONSTITUTION WITH THE RIGHT TO EDUCATION

The Abidjan Principles were developed to offer a coherent understanding of the right to education to enable states and other stakeholders to analyse and respond to the contemporary trends and challenges in education, including the privatisation and commercialisation of education.[32] Thus, they are particularly relevant in the context of the constitutional process in Chile, where privatisation and commercialisation are central issues. The Abidjan Principles can enable innovative policy and ideas for the future reforms of the education system.

A. Define the Content and Aims of Education in a Comprehensive Manner

The existing constitutional text considers that 'the objective of education is the full development of the individual in different stages of their life'.[33] This formulation is a step forward with regard to provisions of past Chilean constitutions, which placed the state – and not the individual – at the centre of educational activity.[34] However, its wording could be improved by the incorporation of the education objectives as stated in international treaties and reflected in the Abidjan Principles. International law gives a dual role to education: the full development of human personality and human dignity; and the contribution to the achievement of public good and the construction and maintenance of healthy, open, transparent, tolerant and fair societies, which are non-discriminatory in character and provide a favourable environment for the realisation of human rights.[35] For instance, Art 13(1) of the ICESCR states that 'education shall be directed to the full development of the human personality and the sense of its dignity, and shall strengthen the respect for human rights and fundamental freedoms', and 'enable all persons to participate effectively in a free society, promote understanding, tolerance and friendship among all nations and all racial, ethnic or religious groups, and further the activities of the United Nations for the maintenance of peace'.

[32] J Mowbray, 'Is There a Right to Public Education?' in Adamson et al (n 28) 52.
[33] Constitución Política de la República de Chile, 1980, Art 19 no 10.
[34] Regarding this, see: Constitution of Chile, 1925, Art 10; Constitution of Chile, 1833, Arts 119, 144 and 145; Constitution of Chile, 1828, Arts 114–122; Constitution of Chile, 1823, Arts 38(4), 58(5), 220(3), 254, 255, 256, 257 and 261; Constitution of Chile, 1822, Arts 47(19) and 230–234.
[35] Abidjan Principles, Preamble, para 1.

The adoption of a comprehensive framework such as this one has the capacity and the potential to inspire all subsequent regulations around a common objective: the development of the person and the community.

In comparative law, this kind of formulation is common and can be found in countries with diverse traditions such Cuba,[36] Ecuador,[37] Spain,[38] Greece,[39] Iceland,[40] Mexico,[41] Norway,[42] and Portugal.[43] For example, Art 24 of the 2011 Draft Constitution of Iceland reads: 'Education shall aim at achieving comprehensive development for each individual, critical thinking and consciousness of human rights, democratic rights and obligations'.

B. Guarantee the Availability of Free, Inclusive, Quality Public Education for All

The Abidjan Principles help clarify the nature and scope of the right to public education.[44] Although the ICESCR and the CRC recognise the guarantee of universal access and the progressive free education at all levels – responsibility for which lies with the states, these treaties only indirectly address the role of public education. However, since their adoption a range of sources in international law have unpacked the obligation to provide this public education,[45] and how private education may act only as an addition or supplement to public education.[46]

The Abidjan Principles express this obligation in the Overarching Principle 2, which reads: 'States must provide free, public education of the highest attainable quality to everyone within their jurisdiction as effectively and expeditiously as possible, to the maximum of their available resources'.

The Abidjan Principles subject the provision of education to the guarantees relating to the provision of public services, obligations that extend to private educational institutions.[47] In conceptualising education as a public service, 'the State ceases to limit its action to the preservation of liberty and the guarantees

[36] Art 32.
[37] Art 27.
[38] Art 27.
[39] Art 16(2).
[40] Art 24, 2011 Draft Constitution.
[41] Art 3.
[42] Art 109.
[43] Art 73.
[44] General Principle 2 and Overarching Principle 29.
[45] Mowbray (n 32) 57.
[46] Ibid, 46.
[47] Abidjan Principles, numeral 19. Other elements can also be found in numerals 11, 12, 13, 31, 37 and 39.

of individual rights – private property and free trade – and becomes the direct protagonist of economic growth and social progress'.[48]

Although the text of the 1980 Constitution considers the obligation of the state to promote and guarantee pre-primary, primary and secondary education, this mandate is limited solely to the duty to finance a free system.[49] It obviates any other consideration linked to the organisation of state activity around a true public education service, within a human rights-respecting framework, namely, an accessible and non-discriminatory service that responds to the needs of its users and is culturally appropriate, participatory, of sufficient quality, adequately financed, transparent and responsible.[50]

Some countries have constitutionalised the idea of public education as an organising principle of society. Among the nations taking this approach are Côte d'Ivoire,[51] Costa Rica,[52] Denmark,[53] Ecuador,[54] France,[55] The Netherlands,[56] Mexico,[57] Portugal,[58] and Switzerland.[59] For example, Art 10 of the Constitution of Côte d'Ivoire states:

> The State ensures the promotion and development of general public education, technical education and professional training as well as the expansion of all sectors, according to international standards of quality and in relation to the needs of the labour market (…).

C. The Limitation of Freedom of Education and the Regulation of Private Actors in Education

Freedom of education, including the liberty of parents to choose for their children a school other than a public school, and the liberty to establish and direct private schools, as established in human rights treaties, is not absolute.

The original spirit that inspired this freedom was to allow parents to impede the conditioning of their children by a state, and permit parents with strong beliefs or linguistic necessities to educate their children in line with these

[48] A Troncoso, 'Dogmática Administrativa y Derecho Constitucional: el caso del servicio público' (1999) 57 *Revista Española de Derecho Constitucional* 87, 98.

[49] Constitution of Chile, 1980, Art 19 N° 10.

[50] The Global Initiative for Economic, Social and Cultural Rights, *States' Human Rights Obligations Regarding Public Services The United Nations Normative Framework* (GI-ESCR 2020) 3–4.

[51] Art 10.

[52] Art 77.

[53] Art 76.

[54] Arts 28–347(1)(2).

[55] Constitution of Chile, preamble, October 27, 1946.

[56] Art 23(3)(4).

[57] Art 3.

[58] Arts 74(2)–75(1).

[59] Art 62(1)(2).

requirements.[60] However, this provision has been increasingly reinterpreted and co-opted through the installation of a neoliberal project which has led to an increase of commercialisation and the retreat of the state.[61] Under this paradigm, the Chilean Constitution established a priority right 'to open, organise and maintain educational institutions' without any other 'limitations than those imposed by ethics, decency, public order and national security', ensuring the parents' right to 'choose the educational establishment for their children'. Following this logic, any regulatory attempt has been seen as state intervention seeking to expropriate potential profits.

A 'strong emphasis on choice helps to turn citizens into consumers shopping for the best "deal" for their child, rather than community members supporting a school that belongs to the whole community'.[62] At the same time, the conceptualisation of the freedom of education as absolute produces a perverse effect whose exercise often materially diminishes the rights and outcomes of less fortunate children.[63]

In this sense, Guiding Principle 48 of the Abidjan Principles recalls that these freedom are not absolute, and that international human rights law imposes a series of specific and concrete limits on their exercise. Among these limits are: not supplanting or replacing public education and not creating adverse systemic impacts on the right to education, including the generation or maintenance of disparities of opportunity or outcomes for some groups in society, and not adversely affecting the capacity of the state to realise the right to free, quality public education.

On this matter, the constitutional process offers Chile the opportunity to adapt the constitutional guarantees on freedom of education to human rights standards, including the assurance that the existence of private actors does not lead to the commercialisation of education,[64] and that, in the event that private education is financed with public funds, the guarantee of the right to education without discrimination is safeguarded.[65]

D. Guarantee Good Governance of the Public Education System

The contribution of the Abidjan Principles in governance matters is substantial.[66] The Abidjan Principles recall states' 'immediate obligation to take all measures

[60] J Härmä, 'Evidence on School Choice and the Human Right to Education' in Adamson et al (n 28) 152–53.

[61] Ibid, 153.

[62] Ibid, 152.

[63] Ibid, 152.

[64] Guiding Principle 48.c.3.

[65] Art 66.d.

[66] Governance is a critical topic in the Abidjan Principles, with various Guiding Principles dedicated to this issue, in particular: 20, 21, 32, 42, 45, 48, 55, 66, 81 and 83.

to address ineffective governance, the lack of transparency, the lack of accountability, or corruption, which may adversely affect the realisation of the right to free, quality, public education'.[67] They also lay out the obligation to establish a participative education governance system where all stakeholders are represented, including children, students, the parents or the legal guardians, teaching staff, and other members of the education system, trade unions and civil society.[68]

There is a considerable gap in the Chilean constitution on this matter, since it limits itself to timidly mention that 'the community should contribute to the development and improvement of education',[69] without establishing any way to fulfil this duty. Other constitutions follow a different approach, including those of Cuba,[70] Ecuador,[71] Spain,[72] Greece,[73] Indonesia,[74] Mexico[75] and Portugal,[76] which offer a wide variety of participatory mechanisms for educational communities and systems. For example, Art 77 of the Portuguese Constitution states:

> Democratic participation in education. 1. Teachers and students shall possess the right to take part in the democratic management of schools, as laid down by law. 2. The law shall regulate the forms in which teachers', students' and parents' associations, communities and scientific institutions participate in drawing up the education policy.

E. Establish the Rights to Equality and Non-Discrimination

The Abidjan Principles recall the obligation of states to take all the necessary measures to protect and guarantee the rights to equality and non-discrimination in education. For instance, they reiterate the obligation of states to adopt all the necessary measures to eliminate all forms of discrimination in the enjoyment of the right to education, on prohibited grounds including direct and indirect discrimination, harassment and lack of reasonable adjustments, and multiple, intersectional, associative, and perceptive discrimination.[77] They also recall states' obligation to design and adopt a national gender-sensitive

[67] Abidjan Principles, Overarching Principle 42.
[68] Ibid, 32.
[69] Constitution of Chile, 1980, Art 19 N° 10.
[70] Art 32(d).
[71] Art 347(11).
[72] Art 27(5)(7).
[73] Art 16(5).
[74] Art 22D(3).
[75] Art 3.
[76] Art 77(1)(2).
[77] Abidjan Principles, Guiding Principle 24. See also Guiding Principles 55 and 73 for other provisions against discrimination.

education strategy, responsive to the needs of girls and women and transformative for all.[78]

Equality, non-discrimination and the related segregation in the education system are critical elements that the new constitution could improve, and are entirely absent from the 1980 Constitution. This includes the need to incorporate a gender lens and to emphasise the instrumentality of a non-sexist education to bring about social progress.

On a comparative level, many constitutions have adopted a variety of provisions to safeguard equality, inclusion and the prohibition of discrimination in education. Among them are the founding charters of South Korea,[79] Côte d'Ivoire,[80] Cuba,[81] Ecuador,[82] Slovakia,[83] Slovenia,[84] Spain,[85] Finland,[86] Hungary,[87] Italy,[88] Japan,[89] Mexico,[90] Norway,[91] Portugal,[92] Singapore[93] and Turkey.[94] Furthermore, some of them include specific provisions that address gender equality, such as those of Cote d'Ivoire,[95] Ecuador[96] and Poland.[97] In fact, Art 33(2) of the Polish Constitution states that 'men and women shall have equal rights, in particular, regarding education …'.

F. Guarantee Adequate Funding for Public Education

The Abidjan Principles develop the crucial importance of funding education[98] and emphasise the need to prioritise the funding of public education and to only fund private education institutions when they strictly adhere to a series of substantive, procedural and operational requirements.[99] The Abidjan Principles recall the obligation of states to provide free, public education of the

[78] Ibid, numeral 21.
[79] Art 31(1).
[80] Arts 32–33.
[81] Art 44.
[82] Arts 29, 46, 47, 57(14)(21), 340, 343–347(10).
[83] Art 34(1)(2e).
[84] Arts 52–64.
[85] Art 27.
[86] Art 16.
[87] Art 68(2).
[88] Arts 33–38.
[89] Art 26.
[90] Art 2(B I, V, VIII)–3.
[91] Art 109.
[92] Arts 73–74(1)(2).
[93] Art 16(2).
[94] Art 42.
[95] Art 10.
[96] Art 43(1)
[97] Art 32-2.
[98] See section IV. Financing; Overarching Principle 5 and Guiding Principle 64.
[99] Guiding Principles 63–74.

highest possible quality to all persons under their jurisdiction as effectively and expeditiously as possible, using the maximum of their available resources.[100] They specify that the threshold of maximum available resources cannot be lower than the levels set by national and international commitments to education financing, such as the percentage of GDP established in development goals.[101]

International declarations such as the 2011 Incheon Declaration, indicate that states should dedicate at least 6 per cent of their GDP and/or at least 20 per cent of their national expenditure to achieve quality education for all.[102] Constitutions such as those of Costa Rica[103] and Indonesia[104] already guarantee a national education budget within their fundamental texts. Article 78(2) of the Costa Rican constitution reads: 'In State education, superior [education] included, public expenditure will not be inferior to the annual eight percent (8 per cent) of the gross domestic product, in accordance with the law …'. Therefore, in the process of drafting the new constitution, Chile could ensure an adequate level of funding for public education by including some related provisions to that effect.

G. State Accountability

As in other human rights instruments, the Abidjan Principles place a general obligation on states to take all effective measures to ensure the realisation of the right to education.[105] According to them, some of the ways in which this obligation must be fulfilled are through the establishment of adequate accountability mechanisms[106] and monitoring.[107] These instruments can take the form of judicial mechanisms, but they can also be implemented as quasi and non-judicial means, including 'parliamentary oversight, monitoring by National Human Rights Institutions operating in accordance with the Paris Principles, civil society organisations, or other domestic, human rights-compliant quasi-judicial mechanisms',[108] and the incorporation of compliance monitoring tools. Monitoring instruments should meet all human rights principles such as participation, transparency, access to information, inclusivity and

[100] Overarching Principle 2.
[101] Guiding Principle 15.
[102] Also, the 2015 Incheon Declaration recommends that states allocate at least between 4% and 6% of their GDP, and/or at least between 15% and 20% of their total expenditure in education (Educación 2030, 2016, p 9).
[103] Art 78.
[104] Art 31(4).
[105] Overarching Principle 4.
[106] Overarching Principle 7.
[107] Overarching Principle 7.
[108] Guiding Principle 80.

non-discrimination;[109] also, their results should be public and lead to the necessary improvements of legislation, policies and practices.[110]

The incorporation of state liability, accountability and monitoring methods in the new constitution of Chile is a paramount element to ensure the effectiveness of the right to education – and more generally of all social rights. This could prevent the problems that excessive judicialisation can produce at an institutional and budgetary level. At the same time, they could fill two critical requirements of a democratic society of the twenty-first century: flexibility of state action to meet people's needs; and incorporation of communities' perspectives through the use of human-centred design in public services.

Constitutions such as the ones from Ecuador,[111] Spain,[112] Estonia,[113] The Netherlands,[114] Mexico,[115] Switzerland,[116] and Turkey,[117] have taken steps specifically towards the establishment of mechanisms of monitoring, but further improvement could be made by Chile in its new process of constitutional architecture. Article 23(8) of the Constitution of The Netherlands says: 'The Government shall submit annual reports on the state of education to the States General'. Thus, Chile's opportunity to lead is to be seized.

H. Make the Right to Education Justiciable

The Abidjan Principles require states to ensure the availability of prompt, accessible, effective, procedurally fair and independent grievance and redress mechanisms – including, where necessary, judicial remedies – to enable any rights holder or other interested party, such as public interest groups, to have the ability to claim rights and seek redress for any human rights abuse by an actor involved in education.[118] This contribution may fill a profound gap within the 1980 Constitution, which only guarantees the enforcement of freedom of education through the 'recurso de protección' under the reductionist terms set out previously.[119]

Although the nature of enforceability mechanisms varies on a comparative level, constitutions such as those of Argentina,[120] Colombia[121] and Estonia[122]

[109] Guiding Principle 82.
[110] Guiding Principle 82.
[111] Art 346.
[112] Art 27.8.
[113] Art 37.
[114] Art 23.8.
[115] Art 3, IX.
[116] Art 62.
[117] Art 131.
[118] Abidjan Principles, Guiding Principle 89. See also Guiding Principle 80.
[119] Constitution of Chile, 1980, Art 20.
[120] Art 43.
[121] Art 86.
[122] Art 15.

consider the right to education as a justiciable right. Article 86 of the Constitution of Colombia reads:

> Every individual may claim legal protection before the judge, at any time or place, through a preferential and summary proceeding, for himself/herself or by whoever acts in his/her name, the immediate protection of his/her fundamental constitutional rights when the individual fears the latter may be jeopardized or threatened by the action or omission of any public authority.

VII. CONCLUSION

In February 2019, the Abidjan Principles were adopted by a diverse group of human rights experts through a legitimate process to tackle the global challenges of privatisation and commodification of education.

The example of Chile becomes relevant: the 1980 Constitution, alongside the education reforms that followed an exclusively market-oriented logic, played an essential role in the commodification of education.

Given this panorama, and in accordance with international human rights law, Chile has the obligation to align the international right to education with its domestic regulatory framework.

The Abidjan Principles are a helpful legal instrument that can guide the discussions on the constitutionalisation of the right to education, to emphasise key elements in the constitution that are necessary for the establishment of an educational system founded on the respect of social justice.

This chapter has shown how the Abidjan Principles can be used to resolve critical points of pre-existing tensions related to the right to education. The Principles can help to ensure that: (1) public education prevails over merely entrepreneurial freedom; (2) equality and non-discrimination are treated as mainstreaming principles of the system; (3) governance mechanisms allow for the participation of civil society when it comes to education; (4) education is adequately funded; and (5) legal mechanisms are in place to provide effective remedies for violations of the human right to education.

The use of the Abidjan Principles in the Chilean constitutional process would ensure that the provision of education covers all the dimensions of the right to education, including its societal role. This opportunity to incorporate the Principles in the Constitution would also guarantee the fulfilment of international obligations adopted by Chile decades ago, while transforming the legal basis of an educational system historically rooted in discrimination and inequality.

12

Taking the Right to Adequate Housing Seriously in Chile's Next Constitution: Building from Scratch

KOLDO CASLA AND VERÓNICA VALENZUELA

I. INTRODUCTION

THIS CHAPTER INTRODUCES the right to adequate housing as part of the right to an adequate standard of living. The first section presents the content and significance of this right in light of international and comparative law and practice. Second, the chapter explores some of the legal and policy implications of enhancing the status of the right to adequate housing in Chile's Constitution, specifically in relation to the responsibilities of housing developers, the legal recognition of the social function of housing and home-ownership, and the need to protect tenants with strong habitability standards and security of tenure in the private rental sector. Taking seriously the right to housing as part of the right to an adequate standard of living can contribute to addressing the root causes of poverty and inequality in Chile.

II. A LOOK AT INTERNATIONAL HUMAN RIGHTS LAW AND COMPARATIVE PRACTICE

Article 25 of the Universal Declaration of Human Rights proclaims in its first paragraph that:

> everyone has the right to a standard of living adequate for the health and well-being of himself and of his family, including food, clothing, housing and medical care and necessary social services, and the right to security in the event of unemployment, sickness, disability, widowhood, old age or other lack of livelihood in circumstances beyond his control.

The right to adequate housing is part of the right to an adequate standard of living. It is recognised in Art 11(1) of the International Covenant on Economic,

Social and Cultural Rights, Art 27(4) of the Convention on the Rights of the Child, Art 5(e) of the International Convention on the Elimination of All Forms of Racial Discrimination, and Art 14 of the Convention on the Elimination of All Forms of Discrimination Against Women. All of these treaties have been signed and ratified by Chile, and the country needs to abide by them in good faith as a matter of international law; internal law is no justification for any country's failure to abide by international human rights obligations (Arts 26 and 27 of the Vienna Convention on the Law of Treaties).

In accordance with Art 34 of the Charter of the Organization of American States, countries agree to dedicate every effort to achieve 'adequate housing for all sectors of the population'. In order to achieve such goal progressively, 'by legislation or other appropriate means', states must 'adopt measures, both internally and through international cooperation, especially those of an economic and technical nature' (Art 26 of the American Convention on Human Rights).

In Europe, Art 31 of the Revised European Social Charter of 1996 proclaims the right to adequate housing. The European Committee of Social Rights monitors states' compliance with the European Social Charter in its different versions and with its additional protocols. Among other things, this committee has established that the legal, social and economic protection of families includes the adequate provision of housing, which extends to security from unlawful evictions where legally established rules are not being respected or where the rights of the persons concerned are not being sufficiently protected.[1]

Although not explicitly mentioned in the African Charter on Human and Peoples' Rights (Banjul Charter), the African Commission on Human and Peoples' Rights has interpreted that the right to adequate housing is implicit in the Banjul Charter, as the substance of the right can be inferred from other rights recognised therein, including the right to health, the protection of family, and the right to property.[2]

The right to housing is indeed closely linked to the right to private and family life, and the corresponding right to home. Proclaimed also in the current Chilean Constitution of 1980 (Arts 19(4) and 19(5)), the right to home should be interpreted in light of international human rights law, including Art 17 of the International Covenant on Civil and Political Rights, ratified by Chile. In interpreting this provision, the UN Human Rights Committee has established that the prohibition on 'arbitrary interference' with the enjoyment of one's home 'is intended to guarantee that even interference provided for by law should

[1] European Committee of Social Rights, *European Roma Rights Centre v Greece*, Collective Complaint No 15/2003, Decision on the Merits of 8 December 2004, paras 24 and 51.

[2] African Commission of Human and Peoples' Rights, *Social and Economic Rights Action Center (SERAC) and Center for Economic and Social Rights (CESR) v Nigeria*, Communication No 155/96, Ruling of 27 May 2002, para 60.

be in accordance with the provisions, aims and objectives of the Covenant and should be, in any event, reasonable in the particular circumstances'.[3]

Housing is much more than a roof over one's head, and much more than a mere commodity. Housing, as observed by the UN Committee on Economic, Social and Cultural Rights (CESCR), 'should be seen as the right to live somewhere in security, peace and dignity'.[4] The CESCR has identified seven criteria to determine the adequacy of housing: (1) legal security of tenure, including protection from forced evictions, irrespective of the type of property and tenure (homeownership, rental, informal settlement, etc); (2) availability of services, materials, facilities and infrastructure, including access to natural and common resources, all of which is essential for health, security, comfort and nutrition; (3) affordability, including protection from unreasonable rent levels and increases, so as not to compromise or threaten the attainment and satisfaction of other essential needs and rights; (4) habitability, in terms of protection from cold, damp, heat, rain, wind and other threats to health and safety; (5) accessibility, paying particular attention to the requirements of groups and individuals at greater risk of harm, disadvantage and discrimination; (6) location, allowing access to employment, healthcare services, schools, transport and other facilities, bearing environmental concerns in mind as well; and (7) cultural adequacy, using materials and tools that recognise and express appropriately the cultural identity and diversity of the population.[5]

The persistent non-payment of rent and other serious breaches of contractual obligations can justify the need for an eviction. However, in the words of the UN CESCR, such eviction 'should be carried out in strict compliance with the relevant provisions of international human rights law and in accordance with general principles of reasonableness and proportionality'.[6] The committee has added that the eviction of people living in rental accommodation may be compatible with international human rights law, but only when 'the eviction is provided for by law and is carried out as a last resort, and (when) the persons concerned have had prior access to an effective judicial remedy, in order to ascertain that the measure in question is duly justified'.[7] An eviction related to a rental contract between individuals can, therefore, affect and potentially infringe socio-economic rights the state is bound to respect, protect and fulfil.[8]

[3] UN Human Rights Committee, *General Comment No 16: Article 17 (Right to Privacy), The Right to Respect of Privacy, Family, Home and Correspondence, and Protection of Honour and Reputation*, UN doc HRI/GEN/1/Rev.1 at 21 (1988), para 4.

[4] UN CESCR, *General Comment No 4: Right to Adequate Housing*, UN doc E/1992/23 (1991), para 7.

[5] Ibid, para 8.

[6] UN CESCR, *General Comment No 7: Forced evictions*, UN doc E/1998/22 (1997), paras 11 and 14.

[7] UN CESCR, *Ben Djazia and Naouel Bellili v Spain*, Communication No 5/2015, UN doc E/C.12/61/D/5/2015 (2017), para 15.1.

[8] Ibid, para 14.2.

The proportionality test

> entails examining not only the consequences of the measures for the evicted persons but also the owner's need to recover possession of the property. This inevitably involves making a distinction between properties belonging to individuals who need them as a home or to provide vital income and properties belonging to financial institutions'.

These factors should be borne in mind when ruling on the possible postponement or suspension of an eviction.[9] Furthermore, before an eviction is executed, public authorities must ensure that nobody will be rendered homeless or vulnerable to human rights violations as a result of the eviction.[10]

In *Ben Djazia and Bellili v Spain* (2017), the UN CESCR recommended that Spanish authorities should adopt measures 'to ensure that in judicial proceedings in relation to the eviction of tenants, defendants are able to object or lodge an appeal so that the judge might consider the consequences of eviction and its compatibility with the Covenant'.[11] Eviction orders can only be carried out 'once the State has taken all essential steps, to the maximum of available resources, to ensure that evicted persons have alternative housing'.[12] States must also ensure an adequate level of 'coordination between court decisions and the actions of social services which can result in an evicted person being left without adequate accommodation'.[13] The proportionality test may require that an eviction order is made conditional on the 'requirement that administrative authorities intervene and assist the occupants in order to mitigate the impact of the eviction'.[14] It may also require postponing 'an eviction while the competent authorities negotiate with the persons concerned regarding the available alternatives'.[15]

International comparative practice shows that the enhancement of the right to adequate housing can result in specific policies that, in turn, can improve the living conditions of particularly vulnerable people. Starting with the proportionality assessment in the case of evictions, for example, in Scotland the law distinguishes between mandatory and discretionary grounds for eviction, and in the latter case the homeowner is required to prove that certain circumstances make the eviction justifiable, and a judge will determine the necessity of the eviction under those circumstances, before authorising it.[16] Similarly, both Germany

[9] UN CESCR, *López Albán v Spain*, Communication No 24/2018, UN doc E/C.12/66/D/37/2018, para 11.5.

[10] UN CESCR, *General Comment No 7: Forced evictions* (n 6), para 16.

[11] UN CESCR, *Ben Djazia and Naouel Bellili v Spain* (n 7), para 21.

[12] Ibid.

[13] Ibid.

[14] UN CESCR, *Gómez-Limón Pardo v Spain*, Communication No 52/2018, UN doc E/C.12/67/D/52/2018, para 9.6.

[15] Ibid.

[16] Private Housing (Tenancies) (Scotland) Act 2016.

and the Netherlands give their judges the power and the responsibility to pay attention to the personal circumstances of tenants taking into account the legitimate interests of landlords and tenants.[17]

In the case of England, the Homelessness Reduction Act 2017 gives local authorities additional responsibilities to those that have existed since the 1970s. Similar legislation exists in Scotland and Wales. UK law requires social services of local authorities to evaluate the causes and context in which the loss of a home may potentially arise in a given case, including the circumstances and needs of household members, particularly when children are involved. Local authorities must intervene at least 56 days in advance of the date when the loss of the home is likely to occur, often as a result of an eviction in the private rental sector.[18] Social services can offer financial assistance to pay the rent, or they may look for alternative housing options in the public or private rental sector in the area.

Between 2013 and 2017, several regions in Spain reformed their housing laws to include fiscal incentives and/or punitive measures targeted at dwellings kept deliberately empty by the owners for a long period of time. Legislation in these regions established that homeownership must serve a social function, namely, the satisfaction of a housing or habitation need. Houses kept out of the market do not meet the legally recognised essential content of homeownership.[19] Spain's constitutional court concluded that these regional laws were a constitutionally permissible and a fair instrument to develop the right to adequate housing while respecting the right to private property at the same time, both of which are recognised in Spain's 1978 Constitution.[20]

In relation to equality and non-discrimination, which are core principles of international human rights law, two examples are worth noting. In the application of international and comparative law and practice, in June 2020, the Supreme Court of Mexico urged the national institute of statistics to generate and compile disaggregated information about the population living in informal settlements. The Mexican Supreme Court observed that such data would provide more sophisticated information about the extent of poverty in those settlements, and about the impact that the allocation of public resources and other poverty alleviation measures might be having on the population.[21] In the same vein, the UK's Equality Act 2010, in force in England, Wales and Scotland, requires public authorities to have due regard to the need to eliminate discrimination,

[17] M Vols et al, 'Human Rights and Protection against Eviction in Anti-social Behaviour Cases in the Netherlands and Germany' (2015) 2 *European Journal of Comparative Law and Governance* 156.

[18] Housing Act 1996, Pt VII: Homelessness, modified by Homelessness Reduction Act 2017.

[19] Spain's Constitutional Court, Judgments 93/2015, 14 May (Legal Justification No 13), 16/2018, 22 February (Legal Justification No 5), and 32/2018, 12 April (Legal Justification No 7).

[20] Spain's Constitutional Court, Judgment 16/2018 (Legal Justification No 17).

[21] Mexico's Supreme Court, *Techo Mexico v INEGI*, Amparo en Revisión 635/2019, Judgment of 17 June 2020.

harassment and victimisation, advance equality of opportunity, and foster good relations. Judicial and quasi-judicial bodies monitoring compliance with this legal duty regularly require the gathering of disaggregated data as a means to end direct and indirect discrimination.[22]

III. CONSTITUTIONALISING THE RIGHT TO ADEQUATE HOUSING IN CHILE: WHAT IT MEANS IN PRACTICE

As observed by the former UN Special Rapporteur on Adequate Housing, Leilani Farha, specific policies implemented in the last four decades around the world favoured the retreat of public housing, its privatisation, the deregulation of construction and market, and the expanding role and unprecedented dominance of financial markets and corporations, all of which resulted in the disconnect of housing from its social function and its treatment primarily as a financial asset instead.[23] The commodification of housing, ie treating housing as a mere commodity and not as a human right, had significant consequences in Chile. We cover some of them in this section.

A. The State and Private Housing Developers: Building Blocks of Inequality

Housing is not only a human right; it is also the physical space where individuals develop their personality, where families grow and share their lives. The right to housing is closely interrelated with other human rights. A home's location affects access to several other rights and services, including education, work and health.

Chile faces extreme levels of economic and social inequality.[24] The average income of the richest 10 per cent of the population is 27 times that of the poorest 10 per cent, exceeding the average of OECD countries.[25] The income Gini coefficient for Chile in 2017 (latest available data) was 0.47, which places it as the second most unequal country in the OECD.[26]

Household wealth is even more unequally distributed than income. Research published in 2019 shows that Chile was the sixth most unequal OECD country

[22] Equality Act 2010, s 149.

[23] UN Special Rapporteur on Adequate Housing as a component of the right to an adequate standard of living, and on the right to non-discrimination in this context, Report on the financialization of housing (2017), UN doc A/HRC/34/51, para 1.

[24] UN Special Rapporteur on Extreme Poverty and Human rights, Report on his mission to Chile, UN doc A/HRC/32/31/Add. (2016), para 13.

[25] A Chapman, *Global Health, Human Rights and the Challenge of Neoliberal Politics* (Cambridge, Cambridge University Press, 2016).

[26] 'Income inequality', OECD Data: data.oecd.org/inequality/income-inequality.htm.

in terms of concentration of wealth: the richest 10 per cent of people owned nearly 60 per cent of the wealth (data from 2015–16).[27]

Regional inequalities are at least as acute as income and wealth inequalities. After his official mission to the country, the former UN Special Rapporteur on Extreme Poverty and Human Rights, Philip Alston, observed that Chile experiences a 'large geographical inequalities between regions and within cities';[28] people living within the same area experience significant differences in their income and wealth levels.

The relationship between public policies concerning housing and structural inequality is undeniable. As noted by the former Special Rapporteur on Adequate Housing, Leilani Farha, three historical conditions have influenced the housing situation in Chile: (1) the fact that laws and regulations from the time of the military regime are still in force; (2) the blind reliance on private market solutions; and (3) 'the resultant geographic segregation of the population based on socioeconomic status, with the poorest living on the outskirts of cities or in precarious conditions'.[29]

In this regard, most social rights from international human rights instruments are not adequately incorporated in the 1980 Constitution. The right to health, the right and freedom to education and the right to social security are weakly entrenched,[30] both in relation to the content of the rights and to the mechanisms available to hold authorities to account. The right to adequate housing is not included in the constitutional bill of rights.

Moreover, the 1980 Constitution was adopted in a context of the radical privatisation of social benefits promoted by Pinochet.[31] Four decades later, in line with that spirit of privatisation, private developers play a central role in the provision of housing, while the state has a subsidiary role.

Despite the lack of constitutional entrenchment of the right to adequate housing, in the opinion of the former UN Special Rapporteur on Adequate Housing, 'Chile has successfully managed to address a significant portion of its quantitative housing deficit, and to some extent also its qualitative deficit, and has put in place programmes to diversify tenure systems'.[32] However, public policies concerning housing provision have been developed with an exclusive

[27] OECD, *Society at a Glance 2019: OECD Social Indicators* (OECD Publishing, 2019) 98–99.

[28] UN Special Rapporteur on Extreme Poverty and Human Rights, Report on his mission to Chile (n 24), para 14.

[29] UN Special Rapporteur on Adequate Housing, Report on her mission to Chile, UN doc A/HRC/37/53/Add.1 (2018), para 21.

[30] R Bustos, 'Nueva constitución y derechos sociales: Hacia un nuevo paradigma' in E Chía and F Quezada (eds), *Propuestas para una nueva constitución (originada en democracia)* (Santiago, Fundación Igualdad, 2015) 229.

[31] D Lovera, 'Derechos Sociales en la Constitución del 80 (… y del 89, y del 2005)' in C Fuentes (ed), *En nombre del pueblo debate sobre el cambio constitucional en Chile* (Santiago, U. DP and Fundación Böll, 2010) 226.

[32] UN Special Rapporteur on adequate housing, Report on her mission to Chile (n 29), para 18.

focus on private property and overreliance on the private market.[33] Such structure has proved to be unsuccessful so far in fulfilling the right to adequate housing in light of international human rights standards.

Under the private market, housing becomes an asset that responds to supply and demand logic, thus low-income groups tend to be segregated from such system. In Chile, the private market approach to housing, as well as other factors, impacted on housing prices, which increased 37.2 per cent between 2011 and 2019, while in the same period wages rose by only 24.7 per cent. Hence, the property prices index average is 7.6, which means, on average, a family must allocate their full salary for 7.6 years to buy the home where they live.[34]

The increased prices of housing and real estate assets have also contributed to enhance wealth inequality and exclusion. Concerning Chile, the appropriation of land by large-scale investors and speculators 'has meant that inner-city redevelopment has displaced many traditional residents, exemplifying "the intertwined roles of the state and assorted holders of economic capital in the production, distribution and representation of urban exclusion and segregation"'.[35]

Chile's housing public policy has historically been focused on providing solutions for particularly vulnerable groups. However, under this paradigm, the state has also acted as a financer of the private real estate market through public subsidies. Private real-estate builders, developers and financial institutions are the main actors in the housing sector.[36]

Public subsidies are economic contributions from the state to low and middle-income families who need support to finance the purchase of their first home. The applicant families are required to pay a proportion of the cost out of personal savings, and the state 'covers the difference', while middle incomes groups 'require larger savings and a mortgage to help finance the cost of the unit and the State pays a smaller subsidy … Private builders are contracted to build the units'.[37] The model 'constitutes an incentive for segregation, because it continues to promote density of subsidized housing built on cheap land, usually located at the periphery of cities and without services or employment opportunities'; the model contributes to further discrimination, segregation, and exclusion of vulnerable groups, such as the poor, migrants, indigenous people, and women.[38]

[33] I Silva et al, *Habitar en dignidad: hacia el derecho a la vivienda en la nueva Constitución* (Santiago, Techo-CHILE, Fundación Vivienda y GI-ESCR, 2020) 30.

[34] F Hurtado, 'Índice de acceso a la vivienda (Price Income Ratio)', Cámara Chilena de la Construcción, August 2019, www.cchc.cl/uploads/archivos/archivos/INDICE_DE_ACCESO_A_LA_VIVIENDA_-_28_agosto_2019.pdf.

[35] UN Special Rapporteur on Adequate Housing, Report on the financialization of housing (n 23), para 36.

[36] UN Special Rapporteur on Adequate Housing, Report on her mission to Chile (n 29), para 24.

[37] Ibid, para 26.

[38] Ibid, paras 29–30.

In the 2010s, the state introduced public policies that enabled low and middle sectors to access housing through public housing programmes, such as the lease programme (*programa de arriendo*), or the housing choice solidarity fund (*fondo solidario de elección de vivienda*), which contributed, to some extent, to reduce the quantitative deficit in houses. According to official data, the housing deficit decreased by a quarter between 2002 and 2017, from 521,957 to 393,613 houses.[39]

Research shows that 'the lowest income quintile did not necessarily receive more housing subsidies than the other quintiles'.[40] Also, the state has imposed other requirements on the granting of subsidies for homeownership, such as a permanent residence permit, which have an impact on the access of the immigrant population to this type of benefit.[41] Only 2.2 per cent of housing subsidies for homeownership were awarded to immigrants between 2015 and 2019.[42] The UN CESCR recommends that public policies and legislation should 'not be designed to benefit already advantaged social groups at the expense of others'.[43]

Although public policies promoted by the state may have helped to reduce the housing deficit,[44] the number of informal settlements has increased dramatically since 2011, which has led to 81,643 families living in 969 informal settlements in 2021, the highest number since 1996.[45] Despite the growth in the homebuilding sector, housing remains unaffordable for many people, raising questions about the extent to which the private market, on its own, can provide the necessary resources and mechanisms to satisfy access to adequate housing.

Chile 'lacks national urban planning policy guidelines based on human rights'.[46] This further impairs the full enforcement of the right to adequate housing, since this deficiency 'appears to have caused fragmentation and inconsistency in the decision-making processes about land, creating strong incentives for some local governments to prefer a concentration of high-income residents'.[47] The current paradigm on housing and homeownership urgently requires a review, since it positions housing as a commodity, stripping it of its human right status.

[39] Chile's Minister for Housing and Urbanism, Public Account 2019, www.minvu.cl/wp-content/uploads/2019/06/CUENTA-PUBLICA-resumen-ejecutivo-2019-2.pdf.

[40] A Casgrain, 'La apuesta del endeudamiento en la política habitacional chilena' (2010) 25 *Revista Invi* 155, 164.

[41] P Roessler et al, *Informe 3: Acceso a la vivienda y condiciones de habitabilidad de la población migrante en Chile* (Santiago, Servicio Jesuita a Migrantes, 2020) 3.

[42] Ibid, 2.

[43] UN CESCR, *General Comment No 4: Right to Adequate Housing* (n 4) para 11.

[44] Casgrain (n 40) 157.

[45] F Vergara et al., *Catastro Nacional de Campamentos 2020–2021 Report* (Santiago, Techo-Chile, 2021), www.ceschile.org/wp-content/uploads/2020/11/Informe%20Ejecutivo_Catastro%20Campamentos%202020-2021.pdf,

[46] UN Special Rapporteur on Adequate Housing, Report on her mission to Chile (n 29) para 34.

[47] Ibid, para 34.

The constitutionalisation of the right to adequate housing can help reduce material inequalities in Chile. But the constitutional recognition of rights is not enough. The state should also adopt other practical measures to ensure the fulfilment of this right. An active role and commitment of the state is required to address the root causes of housing segregation, including via the public provision of housing for people who cannot afford it in the private sector on their own, as well as the recognition of the social function of homeownership.

B. The Social Function of the Right to Property and Homeownership

Article 19(24) of the Constitution of 1980 recognises the right to private property. Also, it states that only the law can set 'limitations and obligations that derive from its social function', which includes the general interests of the nation, national security, the public utilities and health, and the preservation of the environment. Thus, while the Constitution sets the social function as a possible limitation to the right to private property, it does not define what it is meant by *social function*. Instead, it only provides a list of elements that *could* be considered as constitutive of such social function.

Despite how broad the elements may seem, the Chile's Constitutional Court has interpreted them restrictively.[48] For instance, it has held that the general interests of the nation include those:

> legal interest[s] that are directly related to the whole nation, and never, however important it may be, to a sector of it, and that relates, basically, to the superior benefit of the political society as a whole, without any reference to social, economic or other categories or groups.[49]

Moreover, the 1980 Constitution includes provisions that allow fundamental rights guaranteed therein to be amended by law, as long as the law does not affect or restrict the essence of the right of property. Article 19(24)(3) provides that:

> no one can, in any case, be deprived of his or her property, the assets affected or any of the essential faculties or powers of the domain, but by virtue of a general or special law that authorises expropriation for public utility or national interest, *qualified by the legislator*. (emphasis added)

This means that an absolute majority of deputies and senators in office must vote in favour of such law. Article 19(26) establishes that 'the assurance that the legal precepts which, by mandate of the Constitution, regulate or complement the guarantees that it establishes or that limit them in the cases that it authorises it, shall not affect the rights in their essence'. The Chilean Constitutional

[48] Chile's Constitutional Court, Judgment 334/2001, 21 August 2001 (Legal Justification No 21).
[49] Ibid (Legal Justification No 22).

Court, taking into consideration both provisions, has held that the rights to use, enjoy and dispose of goods are inherent or essential prerogatives derived from private property, and cannot be restricted by law.

The right to property, in the Chilean constitutional doctrine, stands as a practically absolute right subject only to a few limitations provided by law under restrictive circumstances. Thus, 'the initiatives that emerge from the State to democratise the use of land are incessantly slowed down by the legal dogma of private property'.[50]

In the words of the former Special Rapporteur on Adequate Housing, Raquel Rolnik, 'property has a vital social function including adequate housing of the urban poor'.[51] A new constitution for Chile should contribute to redefining the meaning of homeownership and housing. Housing has a social function that can be part of the content of the right to private property when it affects homeownership. Legislators and policymakers should consider exploring different alternatives deriving from the social function of property, such as tax incentives and penalties to large and/or corporate homeowners who keep properties deliberately empty and out of the residential rental market.

C. Secure Tenancy and Habitability Standards in the Housing Rental Sector

Chilean authorities have not paid sufficient attention to housing affordability. Over the years, the price of rents has significantly increased, affecting smaller homes. It has been said that 'the real cause of rising rents would be the increasing concentration of homeownership acquired for rental purposes … with rental charges that ensure the profitability of these investments'.[52]

The current legislation does not include any provision concerning protection from unreasonable rent levels and increases. In contrast, the state introduced public policies that enabled low and middle classes to access rental housing through temporary housing benefits. Beneficiary families receive an amount which is paid monthly with a maximum limit and may be used consecutively or fragmented over a period, according to the geographic location of the district where the leased housing is located.[53] As in the case of subsidies for the purchase

[50] F Alarcón et al, 'Derecho a una vivienda adecuada en Chile: Una mirada desde los campamentos' in T Vial (ed), *Informe Anual sobre Derechos Humanos en Chile* (Santiago, Universidad Diego Portales, 2016) 111.

[51] UN Special Rapporteur on adequate housing as a component of the right to an adequate standard of living, and on the right to non-discrimination in this context, Raquel Rolnik, UN doc A/HRC/25/54 (2013), para 5(4).

[52] E López and N Herrera, 'Arriendos por las nubes: efecto de la creciente concentración de la propiedad', *Ciper* (July 2018), www.ciperchile.cl/2018/07/25/arriendos-por-las-nubes-efecto-de-la-creciente-concentracion-de-la-propiedad/.

[53] Decree 52, which approves regulations for the housing rental subsidy program of the Chile's Minister for Housing and Urbanism, 10 June 2013.

of housing, in the rental subsidy the applicant families are required to pay a proportion of the rental cost out of personal savings, and the state covers the difference.

Housing benefits can play an important role in facilitating access to housing for people who may otherwise have no access in the private sector. However, without adequate regulation, housing benefits can also result in rising inequalities, as they effectively constitute a transfer of resources from public accounts to private landlords. This can be particularly problematic when dealing with corporate landlords or with large landlords, namely, landlords owning a large number of residential properties, who tend to be in the upper end of society in terms of income and wealth distribution. The transfer of public resources from the State to wealthy or relatively wealthy private landlords is also problematic when the private rental sector law does not guarantee an adequate degree of security of tenure for tenants, and when housing law does not include habitability standards. That is, in fact, part of the problem in Chile.

The right to private property is protected through an emergency constitutional remedy. According to Art 20 of the Constitution, anyone who suffers deprivation, disruption or threat in the legitimate exercise of the right to private property by arbitrary or illegal acts or omissions may file a claim before the court of appeals, which shall immediately take measures to restore the rule of law and ensure the due protection of the affected party. This constitutional device has been successfully used by tenants suffering harassment from landlords: courts have accepted claims and have stopped landlords from expelling tenants and from taking their notion of justice into their own hands.[54]

The rights of tenants are also preserved by a series of regulations and other legal instruments. In light of statute no 18.010, of 1982, amended in 2003, in contracts in which the rental term has been agreed month by month, and in those of indefinite term, homeowners can put an end to the residential lease anytime through eviction. Evictions can only be carried out judicially or by personal notification made by a notary. The eviction notice is two months, and the period will be increased by one month for each full year that the tenant has been in the property; the said term plus the increase may not exceed six months in total.

Eviction orders are carried out with no analysis of reasonableness and proportionality, which is contrary to the international human rights standards voluntarily accepted by Chile. As indicated earlier, as a matter of international human rights law, everyone at risk of eviction should be entitled to have the proportionality and reasonableness of such eviction examined by an independent actor, a judge, on a case-by-case basis.[55]

[54] Supreme Court of Chile, Apelación de recurso de protección 21072-2019, Judgment of 8 August 2019; Court of Appels of Santiago Chile, Recurso de Protección 637462-2019, Judgment of 25 September 2019.

[55] UN CESCR, *General Comment No 7: Forced evictions* (n 6); UN CESCR, *Ben Djazia v Spain* (n 7).

The UN Special Rapporteur on Adequate Housing lamented that, when an eviction is about to be carried out, Chilean authorities do not ensure that 'alternative accommodation is available or comply with other international human rights obligations'.[56] This is contrary to international human rights law: the state must ensure that no one is rendered homeless as a result of an eviction.[57] Alternative temporary accommodation must not put personal safety at risk, cannot become a long-term solution, must not separate family members, and must provide space to respect individuals' privacy.[58]

The current legal framework in Chile does not require landlords to ensure habitability standards that are adequate for residential purposes. Unless both parties agree otherwise, Art 1924 of Chile's Civil Code only includes the general rule that the landlord must keep the property in the state of being used for the purpose for which it has been rented.[59]

The lack of legal framework to ensure habitability in the private rental sector has resulted in the abuse of particularly vulnerable communities and low-income households. Migrants are particularly affected by lack of protection of their rights in the private rental sector.[60] Some migrants have denounced being 'exploited in the private housing market by landlords who overcharged or who offered costly but precarious living conditions'.[61] The UN Special Rapporteur on Extreme Poverty and Human Rights observed during his mission to Chile in 2015 that 'migrants often live in overcrowded, unsanitary and unhygienic conditions'.[62]

The UN Special Rapporteur on Adequate Housing recommended Chile in 2018 to 'modernize legislation regarding rental accommodation to better protect the rights of tenants and set in place adequate regulation for private landlords',[63] as well as to 'ensure the accountability of private actors with regard to their human rights obligations'.[64]

[56] UN Special Rapporteur on adequate housing, Report on her mission to Chile (n 29) para 52.

[57] UN CESCR, *General Comment No 7: Forced evictions* (n 6) para 16.

[58] UN CESCR, *El Goumari and Tidli v Spain*, Communication No 85/2018, UN doc E/C.12/69/D/85/2018 (2021), para 9.

[59] Law 21,325, of April 2021, not yet in force at the time of writing, amended Law 18,101, of 1982, on renting of urban properties with regard to abusive overcrowding. The amendment provides that the renting of dwellings or rooms that do not comply with the minimum conditions of habitability of the General Ordinance on Urban Planning and Construction ('Ordenanza General de Urbanismo y Construcciones') will be illegal, and sets financial penalties for those who do not comply with these regulations: www.bcn.cl/leychile/navegar?idNorma=1158549&idParte=10221475.

[60] Roessler et al (n 41) 1.

[61] UN Special Rapporteur on Adequate Housing, Report on her mission to Chile (n 29) para 63.

[62] UN Special Rapporteur on Extreme Poverty and Human Rights, Report on his mission to Chile (n 24) para 63.

[63] UN Special Rapporteur on Adequate Housing, Report on her mission to Chile (n 29) para 86(j).

[64] Ibid, para 86(n).

IV. CONCLUDING REMARKS

The UN Committee on Economic, Social and Cultural Rights in 2015, and the Special Rapporteur on Extreme Poverty and Human Rights in 2016, expressed their concern that economic, social and cultural rights, including the right to adequate housing, are not properly recognised in the 1980 Constitution and, as a consequence, there are not adequate institutional and judicial mechanisms in place to provide remedies and reparations to people for whom the right to adequate housing remains an unfulfilled promise.[65]

The CESCR issued a number of recommendations to make the right to housing real in Chile, with a view to adopting a comprehensive housing strategy that would give priority to most vulnerable people, including those living in informal settlements, rural areas, or inadequate conditions; such strategy should protect against forced evictions, prohibit segregation, and allocate adequate funding, with effective monitoring and accountability.[66]

The adoption of a comprehensive strategy is essential. A new paradigm should switch from blind reliance on the private market towards an active role and commitment of the state in the provision of housing. The model must be based on the principle that homeownership is a special form of private property over a good that exists to serve a public function that is at least as important as its private function: apart from satisfying an investor's legitimate private interest, a house exists to give people a place to live.

Courts exercising constitutional jurisdiction should consider ways to promote spaces for litigants to be involved and participate. For a number of years, the South African constitutional court has issued 'meaningful engagement' orders urging the parties to resolve social rights disputes through dialogue.[67] The South African court has 'created a deliberative space in which [plaintiffs], a group with minimal political or social influence, were given a real voice in the decision-making process'.[68] It should be noted that, in late 2019, the Chilean Supreme Court exceptionally accepted a remedy of protection filed by a local district (neighbourhood) council against a community formed by members of an informal settlement, ordering all parties involved (which included also police, city council and administrative bodies) to take coordinated action in order to find a

[65] UN CESCR, Concluding Observations: Chile, UN doc E/C.12/CHL/CO/4 (2015), para 7; UN Special Rapporteur on Extreme Poverty and Human Rights, Report on his mission to Chile (n 24) paras 25–26.

[66] UN CESCR, Concluding Observations: Chile (n 64) para 26; UN Special Rapporteur on Adequate Housing, Report on mission to Chile (n 29) para 84.

[67] A Pillay, 'Toward Effective Social and Economic Rights Adjudication: The Role of Meaningful Engagement' (2012) 10(3) *International Journal of Constitutional Law* 732; S Liebenberg, 'The Participatory Democratic Turn in South Africa's Social Rights Jurisprudence' in K Young (ed), *The Future of Economic and Social Rights* (Cambridge, Cambridge University Press, 2019).

[68] S Fredman, *Human Rights Transformed: Positive Rights and Positive Duties* (Oxford, Oxford University Press 2008) 121.

global and effective solution to the situation of the members of the community and protect their rights on the basis of equality.[69]

Chile has the chance to finally take seriously the right to housing. The deafening silence about adequate housing in the 1980 Constitution has contributed to a weakening of this right in the domestic order, to the detriment of the Chilean people, particularly of most vulnerable households. 'It would be naïve to think that adopting a bill of constitutional social rights would ensure their protection'[70] on its own, but the constitutional entrenchment of social rights 'plays a subsidiary, but important supporting role in the multi-institutional scheme of protecting social rights'.[71] Chile's unique and profoundly democratic constitutional moment provides an excellent opportunity to build the right to adequate housing from scratch.

[69] Supreme Court of Chile, Apelación de recurso de protección 22.086-2019, Judgment of 30 October 2019.

[70] J King, *Judging Social Rights* (Cambridge, Cambridge University Press, 2012) 2.

[71] Ibid, 18.

13

Health Rights in the New Chilean Constitution

ALEJANDRA ZÚÑIGA-FAJURI

I. INTRODUCTION

A KEY RIGHTS issue to be addressed by the constituent convention drafting a new charter for Chile is the content and scope of health rights. The notion that a just society needs equitable universal health coverage is a powerful one. It assumes that everyone, regardless of class, ethnicity, disability or gender, should be guaranteed equal access to a basic set of health goods, a decent healthcare. Long achieved by most developed and some developing nations, in Chile this goal remains unmet despite implementation of the 2005 AUGE health reform. The moral basis advanced in this chapter for constitutional social rights content vacates libertarianism and embraces liberal egalitarian political theory. To agree on a fair constitutional wording of health rights, it suggests that the rationing criteria of health economics – which seek to maximise limited resources – be applied only at the macro- and not at the micro-distributive level. It further argues that efficiency principles cannot be applied to all allocation decisions lest they lead to unfair outcomes and examines the libertarian normative model in the current Chilean Constitution and its evolution over time. Finally, for the rationing of health resources, it proposes a liberal egalitarian model that enables the changes required to achieve equity and efficiency objectives.

II. A MORAL FOUNDATION FOR HEALTH RIGHTS

On issues of healthcare, Norman Daniels notes three fundamental questions of justice: does health – and therefore healthcare and other factors that affect health – hold special moral importance? When are health inequalities unjust? How can health needs be fairly met in the face of resource constraints?[1] If we

[1] N Daniels, *Just Health: Meeting Health Needs Fairly* (Cambridge, Cambridge University Press, 2008) 11.

can explain why societies do and should give special moral importance to health needs, then we may be able to characterise the basis of our obligation to protect health. If we can explain when health inequalities are unjust, then we will have a better idea of what factors affecting health and its distribution we are obliged to modify through social policy. Finally, if we know how to make fair and legitimate priority- and limit-setting decisions about meeting health needs under resource constraints, then we can guide our actions toward more just outcomes under non-ideal conditions.[2] From early childhood vaccinations to the care needed to treat illness or recover from an accident, this is a resource without which it would be impossible to protect the opportunity or capability to function as free, equal citizens. The impact of healthcare on people's lives requires us to provide a strong moral foundation for the recognition and guarantee of a right to health protection whose distribution, as a fundamental right, should not be left to the market.

The libertarian theory of justice[3] morally underpinning the 1980 Chilean Constitution supports a form of mercantilism that leaves distribution to the market and forgoes tax policies ensuring the poorest receive a decent minimum of care. We hold that the theory of justice that should underpin the new Chilean Constitution is liberal egalitarianism, which argues a duty to provide a public system that guarantees a minimum of healthcare for all, based on John Rawls' notion of fair equality of opportunity.[4] Robert Nozick, a leading libertarian, dismisses the notion of social rights because libertarianism opposes coercive taxation. He argues that state activity should be limited to protecting against force, theft, fraud, and so on. 'Any more extensive state will violate a persons' right not to be forced to do certain things and is unjustified'.[5] There should be no public education, healthcare, transportation, roads, or parks, as all involve coercive taxation of some people against their will, violating the principle of 'from each as they choose, to each as they are chosen'.[6] Egalitarians, however, are troubled by the great differences in the distribution of initial resources according to social positions allocated at birth. Wealth comes not from individual talent and effort, as Nozick would have us believe, but from brute luck and inheritance. As Rawls notes, given that the distribution of natural endowments is morally undeserved and social institutions allow the better-off to exploit these endowments and retain the even greater benefits they provide, it is fair to support resource distribution mechanisms that ensure equal opportunity.[7]

Rawls' *Theory of Justice*, then, provides the basis for health rights and for a public obligation to guarantee universal minimum protection. His principles

[2] Ibid, 16.

[3] W Kymlicka, *Contemporary Political Philosophy. An Introduction* (Oxford, Oxford University Press, 2002) 102.

[4] J Rawls, *A Theory of Justice* (Oxford, Oxford University Press, 1971).

[5] R Nozick, *Anarchy, State and Utopia* (Oxford, Basic Books, 1974) ix.

[6] Kymlicka (n 3) 104.

[7] Rawls (n 4).

of justice hold that no one should have less than they would receive in a fair division of primary goods and that social cooperation should allow not only general improvement, but especially improvement of the worst off. This political theory underpins a basic needs principle. This, Rawls notes, is 'a lexically prior principle requiring that citizens' basic needs be met'.[8] In other words, this principle must be satisfied for the other principles of justice to be satisfied. The basic needs principle that Rawls conceptualises as a 'constitutional essential' in democratic society includes a basic right to healthcare. Based on Rawls, Daniels explains the ethical importance of equal opportunity in healthcare. He writes that those macro-distributive decisions – such as what kind of services should be available, who should have or enjoy them, and on what basis and how the financing burden should be distributed – must be based on a certain notion of justice, so that healthcare claims must be grounded on a general theory of distributive justice or 'theory of health justice'. In *Just Health Care*, Daniels claims that health is morally special not just because of its effect on one's ability to be an active member of society, but also because of its effects on the different projects that constitute a life plan.[9]

Daniels defines health as the absence of disease and disease as departure from species-typical functioning. He notes the notion of 'society's normal opportunity range', defined as 'the array of life plans reasonable persons are likely to develop for themselves' in a given society.[10] The extent of this array is partly determined by the typical functioning of a member of the human species. Daniels goes on to characterise an 'individual share' of society's opportunity range as the part of the normal opportunity range open to individuals, given their talents. Since the contents of the normal opportunity range are indexed to species-typical functioning, an individual's departure from them can be expected to reduce her share – ie poor health diminishes opportunity. Using the principle of equality of opportunity, Daniels argues that these curtailments are unjust and that society is under an obligation to prevent them by meeting health needs when possible.[11] As a 'normal range' is also determined by individual skills and abilities, he notes that equal opportunity does not require all to be equal; it requires equal opportunity for those with similar skills and talents.[12] It is enough that the less advantaged receive compensation for their natural bad luck. The public duty to provide all with a minimum standard of care rests on how inequalities in 'normal functioning' due to illness or disability restrict available opportunity.

Liberal egalitarian theory, then, argues that: (1) healthcare is a particularly important social good insofar as it contributes to equality of opportunity and

[8] J Rawls, *Political Liberalism* (Columbia University Press, 1993) 7.

[9] N Daniels, *Just Health Care* (Cambridge University Press, 1985) 60.

[10] N Daniels, *Just Health: Meeting Health Needs Fairly* (Cambridge University Press, 2008) 43.

[11] B Sachs, 'Lingering Problems of Currency and Scope in Daniels's Argument for a Societal Obligation to Meet Health Needs' (2010) 35(4) *Journal of Medical Philosophy* 402.

[12] N Daniels et al, *Benchmarks of Fairness for Health Care Reform* (Oxford, Oxford University Press, 1996).

ensures a certain minimum capacity to participate in society; (2) despite the importance of this asset, the state sets rationing mechanisms due to limited social resources and to the constant expansion of need. However, based on the ideal of 'equality of opportunity', the state should provide appropriate medical services regardless of ability to pay. This reinforces the ethical justification for universal access to health services.[13]

III. MODERN HEALTHCARE SYSTEMS

Scientific and technological advances without parallel in the history of medicine, coupled with, inter alia, an ageing population, emerging diseases, and the prevalence of chronic diseases, have raised health costs to an extent national budgets find difficult to bear. The unprecedented ability to save lives has led to striking demographic changes. The longer people live, the more prone they are to suffer from chronic disease and disabilities, and the greater the demand for care. Forced to define the share of total resources to be spent and how they are to be allocated, what kind of system provides the fairest distribution of healthcare? If public care aims to enable the basic capabilities of the entire population, states should provide full coverage of certain needs in order to narrow the health equity gap. The inequality created by regressive health systems is evident in countries, such as Chile, that were the target of 'libertarian' experiments in the 1980s. They encouraged across-the-board privatisation, minimal investment in public health, and segregation of rich and poor by allowing the former to buy superior coverage from private insurers. The massive inequalities caused by these policies were noted by the World Health Organization (WHO) in its 2000 report, which ranked Chile among countries with the lowest rates of health equity.[14] In 2004, this led Chile to introduce the ambitious healthcare reform called AUGE (Explicitly Guaranteed Universal Access).

What is the 'right to health'? The WHO defines health as 'a state of complete physical, mental and social well-being and not merely the absence of disease or infirmity' (Art 12, International Covenant on Economic, Social and Cultural Rights). But as Daniels correctly notes, the WHO definition risks turning all social philosophy and policy into healthcare.[15] For severely disabled or sick people such a broad definition would set an unattainable standard, as there are times when no amount of medical care or resources will make a sick person better, let alone make them healthy again. Moreover, such an expectation would force the state to spend all its resources on healthcare, precluding the pursuit

[13] P De Lora and A Zúñiga-Fajuri, *El derecho a cuidado sanitario. Un análisis desde las teorías distributivas de la justicia* (Madrid, IUSTEL, 2009).

[14] World Health Organization, *The World Health Report 2000. Health Systems: Improving Performance* (WHO, 2000).

[15] Daniels (n 10).

of other important social goods. Therefore, although a proper understanding of health must give relevance to its social construction – that is, noting that it is part of a historical process of understanding and redefining illness – health rights cannot exceed the duty to provide the services needed to maintain, restore or provide normal functioning (or its equivalent, if possible). As conceptual narrowness is required, in line with Boorse we say that 'health is the absence of pathology', where 'pathology' refers to deviation from the natural functional organisation of a typical member of a species.[16] As such, preventive health institutions are the gateway to the system and the first mandatory requirement for the state. However, as not all deviations from normal can be prevented, a second tier of protection by deviation-correction institutions that rehabilitate and restore normal functioning is needed. As not all treatments can cure illness, the elderly and the chronically ill need a third tier. A fourth tier concerns delivery of health services to those who cannot possibly meet Rawls' idealisation, ie the terminally or seriously physically or mentally ill. These tiers, Daniels writes, seek to maintain normal functioning because prevention is better than cure and cure is better than having to compensate for loss of function. All these institutions are required if equality of opportunity is to be preserved.[17]

Given a shortage of resources and the wide range of procedures available, investment in healthcare must account for the likelihood of success, ie the efficiency of delivery. Investment should be limited to what is proven to work and therefore forms part of the basic health basket – the decent minimum. Entrenching a fair, efficient health protection system in the new Constitution requires understanding that the issue of allocating limited health resources has two distinct levels of analysis, known as the tragic first- and second-tier dilemmas. At the first, macro-distributive tier, it is important to establish how much of something there should be, ie what to produce and at what cost. Applied to health systems, this requires agreeing on the priorities that will, in principle, be guaranteed as a minimum[18] based on cost-efficient calculations. Disability-adjusted life years (DALY), for example, combine a measure of morbidity and premature deaths, while quality-adjusted life years (QALY) provide a weighting function for states to quantify the health benefits obtained by intervention. Both measures of health sacrificed and gained quantify a normal functioning concept of health.[19] In the micro-distribution tier, the quandary is how to allocate available resources. Second-tier tragic dilemmas are tied to the standards used to choose patients. Although in theory all have a right to healthcare, helping everyone at once is not possible and priorities must be set. The main principle is 'need',

[16] C Boorse 'Rebuttal on Health' in JM Humber and RF Almeder (eds), *What Is Disease? Biomedical Ethics Reviews* (Totowa, NJ, Humana Press, 1997).

[17] Daniels (n 10) 47.

[18] TL Beauchamp and JF Childress, *Principles of Biomedical Ethics*, 5th edn (Oxford, Oxford University Press, 2001).

[19] Daniels (n 10) 38.

without detriment to personal responsibility, quality of life, or life expectancy.[20] Should the most seriously ill be always prioritised? Is it ethical to give an organ to a terminally-ill elderly patient rather than to a younger person with no associated illnesses?[21]

IV. HEALTH RESOURCE ALLOCATION MODELS

Agreeing on the first level of distribution requires a basic consensus on the nature of health services and their place in the overall organisation of society and the state. This includes an overriding consensus that healthcare is a fundamental social good that benefits individuals and society through better living standards and increased cohesion.[22] Although financing and provision vary widely among countries, the WHO favours general tax- and social insurance-based systems founded on solidarity, which implies cross-subsidies from the healthy to the sick, from men to women, from the wealthy to the less well-off, from the young to the old, and from individuals to families.[23] As to a constitutionally useful proposal for regulation of health rights, several options exist, depending on the nature of the system. A health financing model is 'progressive' if the share of income paid out for healthcare rises with earnings, 'proportional' if the share of income paid out is the same for all earnings levels, and 'regressive' if the share of income paid out falls as earnings rise. Most countries finance the bulk of health expenditures from one or more of four sources: taxation; social insurance contributions; out-of-pocket payments; and private insurance premiums.[24]

Research into health system equity metrics suggests that the overall progressivity of a financing system depends on the mix of sources and the rules linking contributions to income. On the delivery side, the degree of inequality depends on the extent to which someone's income (or ability to pay) influences the probability of seeking care when ill and on the amount of care received once initial contact is made. The influence of income is likely to be greater the larger the various pecuniary and non-pecuniary costs individuals incur in utilising medical care.[25] Another way to categorise health systems is: (1) fully private

[20] A Zúñiga-Fajuri, 'Autonomía, salud y responsabilidad: ¿Se puede responsabilizar al enfermo "culpable" de su enfermedad?' in M Gascon et al (eds), *Derecho sanitario y bioética (Cuestiones actuales y retos futuros)* (Valencia, Tirant Lo Blanch, 2011).

[21] Á Puyol, 'Ética y priorización en las listas de espera de la sanidad' in *Listas de espera: ¿lo podemos hacer mejor?* (2009) 29 *Cuadernos de la Fundació Víctor Grífols i Lucas*, n 18.

[22] R Saltman, 'The Western European Experience with Health Care Reform' (The European Observatory on Health Care Systems, 2002) 2, www.researchgate.net/publication/239925245_The_Western_European_Experience_with_Health_Care_Reform.

[23] Ibid.

[24] A Wagstaff et al, 'Equity in the Finance and Delivery of Health Care: Some Tentative Cross-country Comparisons' (1989) 5(1) *Oxford Review of Economic Policy* 107.

[25] Ibid.

financing through private insurance purchases and direct patient payments to providers; (2) public subsidies supporting the market purchase of private insurance; (3) single-source, universal, publicly financed insurance, with a parallel private sector offering coverage for the same services (ie the UK); and (4) single-source, universal, publicly financed insurance with no parallel private sector (ie formerly Canada). The Canadian model was amended following *Chaoulli v Quebec (Attorney General)*, a 2005 Supreme Court decision which declared that outlawing private health insurance was unconstitutional. The Court held that waiting lists delaying certain surgical procedures in the public system increased the risk of patient mortality or harm. To Hurley, the evidence shows that single-funded systems deliver better service when parallel systems are not allowed, as these take up resources the public system needs to deliver timely, quality services to all.[26] The UK health model (the NHS was founded in 1948) is the classic example of single-source, universal, first-dollar (ie not deductible) publicly-financed insurance, with a parallel private sector offering coverage for the same services.[27] These models aim to increase both utility and fairness and are founded on three ethical principles: universality; comprehensiveness; and free access. This means providing free comprehensive healthcare to all regardless of age, class, gender, location, or other factors.[28] This is understood as an expression of the more fundamental principle of treating everyone according to their healthcare needs.

V. THE CHILEAN HEALTHCARE ALLOCATION MODEL

Chile's 1980 Constitution, drafted under a dictatorship, reflects the convictions of libertarian ideologues and libertarian theories that decry redistribution of social resources.[29] National jurisprudence and doctrine, for their part, have insisted that social rights are mere statements of intent and therefore that the state and the courts are not required to enforce them.[30] The 1980 Constitution also laid out the basis of the current healthcare system by regulating, inter alia, a public and private sector for healthcare provision and the freedom to choose between them. It also established that the state is responsible for regulating

[26] J Hurley, 'Ethics, Economics, and Public Financing of Health Care' (2001) 27 *Journal of Medical Ethics* 234–39.

[27] C Hughes, *Accidental Logics: The Dynamics of Change in the Health Care Arena in the United States, Britain, and Canada* (Oxford, Oxford University Press, 1999).

[28] R Crisp, 'Treatment According to Need: Justice and the British National Health Service' in R Rhodes et al (eds), *Medicine and Social Justice. Essays on the Distribution of Health Care* (Oxford, Oxford University Press, 2002) 134.

[29] JP Unger et al, 'Chile's Neoliberal Health Reform: An Assessment and a Critique' (2008) 5(4) *PLoS Med* e79.

[30] A Zúñiga Fajuri, 'Justicia y racionamiento sanitario en el Plan AUGE. Dilemas bioéticos asociados a la distribución de recursos escasos' (2011) 17(1) *Acta Bioethica* 73.

social security, which covers healthcare. The Chilean Constitution acknowledges the right to health protection as follows:

> **Article 19(9)**
>
> The State protects free and equal access to measures for the promotion, protection and recovery of health and for the rehabilitation of individuals. It is also responsible for the coordination and control of health-related measures. It is a special duty of the State to ensure the implementation of health-related measures, whether provided by public or private institutions, in the form and conditions prescribed by law, which may include requiring mandatory premiums. Every person shall have the right to choose the healthcare system, public or private, he or she wishes to join.

The reforms of the early 1980s changed the system structure and operation, establishing a National Health Fund (FONASA), private health insurers (ISAPRE), and decentralisation of the National Health Service (SNS), which became a network of independent administrations spread throughout the country.[31] Unlike other countries, the Chilean healthcare system is not funded from general taxes, as recommended by the WHO. Rather, it is financed by a mandatory 7 per cent payroll deduction that allows contributors to 'choose' between the private system and the public system, which covers almost 80 per cent of the population. In both cases co-payment is required, except for those living in poverty, and amounts depend on type of treatment chosen. FONASA is a public agency that collects and manages funds provided by the national health budget and by mandatory contributions from workers unable to afford an adequate private plan. ISAPREs, designed to manage the contributions of customers who can afford better care, offered over 8,000 different plans designed according to sex, age, health risk, supplementary premiums, and co-payment. They focus on higher-income clients with lower health risks (in 2003, the mean income of ISAPRE members was over four times that of FONASA members). In some years, the profit margins of ISAPREs have exceeded 20 per cent.[32]

Chile's mixed healthcare system, with public subsidies supporting the purchase of private insurance, has strongly regressive financial consequences and exhibits massive differences in treatment for rich and poor patients. While overall health indicators remain satisfactory, major differences exist in certain areas and populations, including nearly 10-year differences in life expectancy, depending on district. While infant mortality averages 10 per 1,000 live births, alarming variations exist between regions and may be double or triple that in

[31] 'Study and Proposal of a New Legal Framework for the Private Health System', Presidential Advisory Commission for the Study and Proposal of a New Legal Framework for the Private Health System, www.researchgate.net/publication/296672012_Estudio_y_Propuesta_de_un_Nuevo_Marco_Juridico_para_el_Sistema_Privado_de_Salud.

[32] N Homedes and A Ugalde, 'Privatización de los servicios de salud: las experiencias de Chile y Costa Rica' (2002) 16 *Gaceta Sanitaria* 54.

some areas.[33] The private system, based as it is on segregating by risk, charges different premiums to men, women, the elderly and the young. Adult women pay up to four times more than men for a health plan. Moreover, the share of ISAPRE members over 60 drops dramatically as they face premiums up to eight times higher than those of young adults,[34] which often forces them to move to FONASA. This regressive system has stayed in place because modifying it has been politically impossible, even after the 2005 AUGE reforms. And since AUGE stands for 'explicitly guaranteed universal access', this has led to a large number of challenges being filed before the Constitutional Court.[35] What were the consequences of the AUGE reform from a legal standpoint and in relation to the constitutional content of health rights? How important was it for a constitutional understanding of health rights? Prior to 2004, the public system would guarantee no service beyond emergency care.[36] Access was discretionary and local health administrations could cite lack of resources, with no need for further explanations.[37] Moreover, the constitutional rule regulating private insurers was construed only in terms of freedom, ie the right to purchase coverage in the open market. As such, during the first 20 years of the Constitution, access to healthcare was based not on need (it was not a precondition) but on ability to pay.

Law 19966 of 25 August 2004 set up a regime of explicit health guarantees (GES) benefiting all residents regardless of age, sex, education, ethnicity, sexual orientation or income, arguably marking the beginning of an era of universality in Chilean healthcare. But as noted, even if a certain standard is recognised and guaranteed, not all health services are equally important, as some may improve quality of life, but others save lives. It therefore becomes necessary to choose which health needs should be met when unlimited coverage is unattainable. The GES reform required public and private providers to supply health plans containing the basic priorities and explicit guarantees enshrined in the law, including access, timeliness (opportunity), quality, and financial protection.[38] Access is the

[33] H Sánchez and C Albala, 'Desigualdades en salud: adulto en comunas del Gran Santiago' (2004) 132 *Revista Médica de Chile* 4; J Vega et al, 'Chile: Socioeconomic Differentials and Mortality in a Middle-Income Nation' in T Evans (ed), *Challenging Inequalities in Health: From Ethics to Action* (Oxford, Oxford University Press, 2001).

[34] M Pollack, 'Equidad de Género en el Sistema de Salud Chileno' (2002) *Financiamiento del Desarrollo series No 123, CEPAL*, Santiago.

[35] The Chilean judiciary's website notes that about 70% of motions for protection of fundamental rights heard annually are filed against ISAPREs: A Zúñiga-Fajuri, 'When Constitutional Justice has the Last Word on Healthcare. The Case of Chile' (2014) 44(2) *International Journal of Health Services*.

[36] The constitutional right to health protection is regulated in Law 18469, as amended by Law 19650 (1999). The law bars medical centres from requiring cash or other surety for emergency medical care.

[37] Art 11, Law 18469: 'Health centers will provide covered benefits using the physical and human resources available'.

[38] A Zúñiga-Fajuri, 'Justice and Health Rationing in the AUGE Plan. Bioethical Dilemmas Associated with the Distribution of Scarce Resources' (2001) XVII *Acta Bioethica* 1.

notion that everyone should be guaranteed a priority set of services, with both private insurers and public health services providing a mandatory benefits package; opportunity alludes to a maximum timeframe for receiving care at each stage; quality involves the procedures and technologies necessary to treat a medical condition, and financial protection relates to the maximum families should spend on healthcare per year. Destitute and low-income persons are exempt, but for the rest, co-payment cannot exceed 20 per cent of a reference price posted by health authorities.[39] Without needing to amend the Constitution, these guarantees gave healthcare a new meaning that was recognised by some courts as a fundamental right with specific content involving explicit access, quality, opportunity and cost guarantees. The reform redefined and broadened the core of constitutional health rights, helping construe them as a human right with an enforceable service content. In Alexy's words, 'when a right exists, it is also justiciable'.[40] That said, full enforcement of health rights is a pending assignment, as some of the flaws of the AUGE reform still remain. Discrimination on age grounds has not gone away, key medical conditions are still off the GES list, and some of the jurisprudence still fails to see why the courts should protect health rights.

VI. PROPOSAL TO ENSHRINE HEALTH RIGHTS IN THE NEW CHILEAN CONSTITUTION

Health reform in Western Europe shows that it is possible to uphold certain health policy values and principles that include cost-containment strategies and an optimal mix of public and private providers. Small differences aside, the general social consensus that recognises health rights contains certain basic elements. First, that healthcare is both an individual right and a social good, as most curative and preventive services are construed first and foremost as goods that benefit both individuals and society. Second, that to guarantee equity, it is essential to aim for solidarity-based funding mechanisms (ie general taxes, universal social insurance systems). Based on WHO guidelines, Chile's national health system covers the health priorities that account for the highest mortality and morbidity rates and stand at the core of constitutional health rights. Yet, contrary to the fairness values that inspired the reforms, discriminatory rationing criteria can still slip in at the implementation stage. In fact, while the 2004 reforms initially sought to specify selected diseases based on epidemiological indicators (DALY) in order to guarantee treatment for all, age restrictions unrelated to epidemiological criteria were imposed on over 70 per cent of treatments on purely financial grounds.

[39] G Bastías et al, 'Health Care Reform in Chile' (2008) 179(12) *Canadian Medical Association Journal* 1289.

[40] R Alexy, *A Theory of Constitutional Rights* (Oxford, Oxford University Press, 2002).

Contrary to the principles that ought to regulate health rights in the new Constitution, the current system continues to restrict access to basic services on grounds of patient age or place of residence.

Absent incentives to properly address the needs of high-risk members, ISAPREs attract mostly low-risk individuals, creating a fragmented market in which low-risk consumers are charged low premiums and vice versa. No private health insurance plan is well designed for low-income buyers, creating serious equity problems. The issue has become so widespread that thousands of claims filed against ISAPREs – which overall account for nearly 70 per cent of the court system caseload – are often settled by accepting the abuse of basic rights. The new Constitution should uphold healthcare equity principles at both the macro-distributive and micro-distributive levels and universally guarantee the benefits predefined in a basic package. Age-based restrictions should be banned and only egalitarian health rationing mechanisms based on fair, objective criteria – such as patient condition or order of precedence in waiting lists – should be allowed. At the micro-distributive field, as Harris notes, 'when there are no resources to save everyone, we must choose those who will not be saved in a way that does not appear to be an unfair preference'.[41] Patient age or income level should not be a factor.

VII. CONCLUSION

Because it involves goods and services needed to achieve or maintain species-typical normal functioning, health resource distribution is a key concern for modern society. Impairment of normal species functioning reduces the range of individual opportunity to construct a life plan or concept of the good. As such, providing universal access to healthcare requires delivering basic and preventive care through public or mixed health systems. The WHO has stated that service delivery should be grounded on a standard of need and not be distributed by ability to pay.[42] The Chilean health system, with help from private insurers, ought to be capable of providing universal access to comprehensive coverage based on universality (the basic plan should cover 100 per cent of the population under standard terms and conditions), coverage (inclusion of all medically necessary health services), and free access (at least for the needy). Policies covering the basic care package defined by law should be offered without discrimination by sex or age. In short, the new Constitution can lay the foundations for a model of resource allocation that deems healthcare a fundamental human right that the state should universally provide through a national health system. Chile can supersede its regressive model by changing its sources

[41] J Harris, 'Micro-allocation: Deciding between Patients' in H Kuhse and P Singer (eds), *A Companion to Bioethics* (Blackwell Publishing, 2001).

[42] World Health Organization, *Commission on Social Determinants of Health* (WHO, 2009).

of funding and ensuring wealth redistribution through progressive taxation. The state must monitor the use of cost-efficiency health rationing criteria, restricting application at the macro-distributive level and scaling them down as much as possible at the micro-distributive level in order to avoid arbitrary discrimination in access to care.

14

The Right to Social Security in Chile's Constitution: Considerations and Opportunities

ALEXANDRA BARRANTES

I. CHILEAN CONTEXT: THE SOCIAL CONTRACT AND THE ROLE OF SOCIAL SECURITY

OVER THE PAST few years, Chilean society has experienced generalised social unrest and discontent, creating a significant amount of turmoil rooted in the questioning of the legitimacy of the existing social contract, and of the relationship of Chileans with the state and its institutions.

This questioning of the legitimacy of the country's social security system was already apparent well before the October 2019 social mobilisation as Chileans expressed their dissatisfaction with what they believed to be a not fully inclusive social security system that prioritised private individualised pensions. There was resentment against the private sector-administered pension scheme requiring each citizen to save for retirement by paying into an individual account during their working years.[1] At the core of these tensions are the constitutional principles upon which the Chilean contributory social security is based: individual, private ownership.[2] As such, one of the key issues with Chile's current social security system can be described as follows:

> The design of the contributory pillar of the pension system in Chile was based on individual savings, drawing on the premise of ensuring that each worker is the owner of his/her savings. This premise contrasts with the key social security principle which involves ensuring income in old age by distributing risk socially. The contributory component of the Chilean pension system, based on individual capitalization with only workers themselves paying contributions to protect themselves from the risks of

[1] International Labour Organization, *Nota Informativa. Consideraciones sobre seguridad social, seguridad de ingresos, pensiones y el 10% de ahorros de los trabajadores en las AFP en el contexto de la COVID-19 en Chile* (ILO, 2020).

[2] Ibid.

> old age, lacks solidarity and inter- and intra-generational arrangements that distribute this social risk.[3]

In 2020, a series of consultations undertaken in Chile highlighted a worrying context of increasing discontent with the existing social contract with the state and the frustration with the lack of change. The consultations pointed to an unmet societal demand for better social protection, for a state able to address the risks individuals face throughout the course of their lives and for a transformation of the relationship between the state and its citizens.[4]

Added to the negative socio-economic impacts of the Covid-19 pandemic, this festering social discontent and resentment speaks eloquently of the inequalities and lack of social cohesion in Chile. A study undertaken by the Ministry of Social Development and Family[5] points directly at this questioning of the state's institutional capacity to address citizens' needs. The study finds a surge in perceptions around social injustice: citizens perceive there to be a lack of dignity in the delivery of public services and they see differential access to social rights based on social class. Trust in institutions is clearly diminishing and the belief that work is insufficiently compensated in terms both of earnings and retirement benefits is growing. Upwards social mobility expectations have clearly been dealt a blow.[6]

The results of a survey showed worrying levels of perceptions among Chilean citizens of their social rights:[7] 22 per cent were aware of their rights in terms of health and 19.3 per cent of their educational rights, but only 5.9 per cent knew they had a right to a decent retirement pension. Asked which rights they perceived to be most vulnerable, 20.7 per cent named health first, followed by the right to a decent retirement pension (16.8 per cent). In response to a question about the protection of their right to a decent pension, 12.8 per cent perceived this right to be fully protected, 52.6 per cent considered it to be somewhat protected, and 34.7 per cent considered it to be not protected at all.

This deep social discontent underlines the apparent inability of the current political and institutional system in Chile to adequately address its citizens' demands, leading to a weakened sense of belonging in society.[8] The constitutional framework of Chile, encompassing individual, privatised social security,

[3] Ibid, 3. Translated by author from original source.

[4] Pontificia Universidad Católica de Chile, Universidad de Chile, and Tenemos que Hablar de Chile, *Resultados Preliminares: Seis Hallazgos de Los Primeros 1.000 Diálogos* (2020).

[5] Ministerio de Desarrollo Social y Familia, *Informe Final Consejo Asesor para la Cohesión Social. Diagnóstico para una aproximación a la cohesión social en Chile y recomendaciones para fortalecer el aporte de la política social* (2020).

[6] Ibid.

[7] Instituto Nacional de Derechos Humanos y ClioDinamcia Consulting, *Resultados de la IV Encuesta Nacional de Derechos Humanos* (2018).

[8] Macarena Lobos Palacios, 'Panel Derechos Sociales y Una Nueva Constitución' Presentación Seminario *CEPAL* (2020) www.cepal.org/sites/default/files/presentations/presentacion_mlobos_25112020.pdf.

is partly responsible for this lack of ability of the state to provide answers: the state plays a subsidiary role in the provision of services provided by the private sector. Furthermore, there is an obvious lack of defining social security principles such as universality, sufficiency, solidarity and equality, among others.[9] It should be pointed out that the Chilean Constitution is not neutral in this regard, since in its very first article it outlines a subsidiary role for the state that 'affects the manner in which the beneficiary of the rights complies with the obligation to satisfy the social security, health and educations services'.[10]

II. SOCIAL SECURITY AND ITS ROLE IN SOCIETY

The constitution of the International Labour Organization (ILO), established in 1919, declares the obligation to provide adequate protection for the life and health of workers in all occupations, extending social security measures to provide a basic income to all those in need of such protection and comprehensive medical care, including provisions for child welfare and maternity protection. This desire to provide social security and social justice was a crucial instrument in the socio-economic development of many countries, forging social cohesion, strengthening democracy, and becoming an essential function of the so-called welfare states in European countries.[11] Thus, many countries have incorporated these concepts into their constitution in the form of human rights, as the incorporation of social rights in a country's constitution has been seen as contributing towards social distributive justice efforts.[12] Based on the concept of social justice, social security promotes solidarity among the active and inactive members of society (intergenerational solidarity), among high and low income groups, and in this way it can contribute to human dignity, equality, social inclusion, empowerment, and stable democracies.[13]

The right to social security is enshrined in the framework of human rights at both the regional and global level, including in Arts 22 and 25 of the Universal Declaration of Human Rights,[14] the International Covenant on Economic, Social and Cultural Rights (Arts 9 and 11), the Convention on the Rights of the Child (Art 26), the Additional Protocol to the American Convention on Human Rights in the area of Economic, Social, and Cultural Rights (more commonly

[9] Ibid.

[10] M Henríquez, 'La actual Constitución no es compatible con las demandas sociales' (2020) 4 *Ciper Académico*, www.ciperchile.cl/2020/02/04/la-actual-constitucion-no-es-compatible-con-las-demandas-sociales/, translated by author from original source.

[11] A Egorov (ed), 'The Right to Social Security in the Constitutions of the World. Broadening the Moral and Legal Space for Social Justice', vol 1 ILO Global Study (ILO, 2016).

[12] C Jung et al, 'Economic and Social Rights in National Constitutions' (2014) 62(4) *American Journal of Comparative Law* 1043.

[13] Egorov (n 11).

[14] UNGA Resolution, Universal Declaration of Human Rights, A/RES/3/217 A (United Nations, 1948).

known as the 'Protocol of San Salvador' Art 9) and the ILO Social Protection Floors Recommendation No 202. This latter document provides a set of principles and guidance to countries, emphasising 'the universality of protection based on social solidarity' and 'the overall and primary responsibility of the State' in enacting basic social security.[15]

The investment in state-run public services such as education, health and social security in the so-called welfare states of Europe was part of a drive to achieve greater social justice, lasting peace and stronger democracies.[16] This in turn served to increase citizens' confidence in their government, reinforcing the social solidarity on which social security systems depend and thus strengthening the virtual circle: greater investment in social services leads to increased welfare, and more confidence in the government's ability to manage the risks, vulnerabilities and contingencies to which all individuals are exposed at some stage during their lifecycle.

A solid normative framework based on the constitutional recognition of the right to social security is the foundation on which the state, as duty bearer, can establish an inclusive social security system. Moreover, such a framework is crucial to the gradual expansion of social security coverage, enabling the State to work progressively towards universal coverage.

III. RIGHT TO SOCIAL SECURITY: PRINCIPLES AND THE IMPORTANCE OF A RIGHTS-BASED APPROACH

A rights-based approach to social security implies framing the debate and political decisions on fundamental human rights and principles, including those of equality and solidarity, among others.[17] This focus lends the conceptual and normative framework for implementing integral and universal social protection systems, in stark contrast to social protection measures envisaged from the point of view of the responsibility of the individual, of largely private pension schemes and the fragmentation of services, all of which exclude many citizens from coverage. These are two contrasting social protection paradigms: one based on fundamental rights, entitlements and the protection of individuals during the course of their lives, and the other a fragmented system relying on charity and the provision of social assistance for 'the others', 'the poor', or the 'deserving poor'.[18]

[15] ILO, Social Protection Floors Recommendation, No 202 (2012).

[16] Egorov (n 11).

[17] A Barrantes, 'Why Are Human Rights Considerations Fundamental to Inclusive and Lifecycle Social Protection Systems?' (Pathways Perspectives, 30, 2020). www.developmentpathways.co.uk/publications/why-are-human-rights-considerations-fundamental-to-inclusive-and-lifecycle-social-protection-systems/.

[18] S Kidd, 'Citizenship or Charity: The Two Paradigms of Social Protection' (Pathways Perspectives, 25, 2017) www.developmentpathways.co.uk/publications/designing-social-protection-schemes-charity-citizenship-paradigm/.

Encompassing the fundamental principles of human rights within the area of social security requires an adequate legal and institutional framework; long-term strategies; the adoption of coherent, integral and coordinated policies; and respect for the principles of equity and non-discrimination, among others.[19] Applying human rights principles to social security is not just a matter of rhetoric: implementing programmes and services within a social protection framework means that the State must respect human rights standard and principles in carrying out the obligations it has assumed.

Beyond the fact that social security rights are legally binding, human rights consideration are fundamental to the building of inclusive, lifecycle-based social protection systems.[20] The following are some of the main reasons.[21]

Human rights provide the framework of standards and guiding principles along the lines of which social protection programmes and services are to be implemented. Furthermore, by establishing a social contract between the state and individuals, a rights-based approach can strengthen social cohesion and place human dignity at the centre of the relationship. As right holders, individuals should be seen as active agents of change rather than merely passive beneficiaries of social security programmes and services.

A human rights-based approach also involves the incorporation of lifecycle considerations into social security realms. Individuals of all ages are exposed to risks and vulnerabilities and may be confronted at some point in their lives with any number of possible contingencies; being rights holders is therefore of fundamental importance when such occasions arise. Unlike social security systems focused on targeting 'the poorest of the poor' for reasons of fiscal austerity, a rights-based approach requires the state to maximise the use of available resources and progressively work towards achieving the right to social protection for everyone within the context of a more inclusive system.

The inclusive nature of lifecycle social protection systems, together with the fact that they cover large portions of a population, helps address shocks and risks more efficiently, allowing responses to reach a higher number of affected households. Such systems also provide access to updated information, facilitating rapid implementation of transfers/services and coverage expansion, if necessary.[22] Besides, the issue of who is 'deserving' of transfers and/or other forms of government support becomes highly questionable, especially in the context of pandemics such as the current one.[23]

[19] M Sepúlveda and C Nyst, *The Human Rights Approach to Social Protection* (Helsinki, Ministry for Foreign Affairs of Finland, 2012).

[20] Barrantes (n 17).

[21] Ibid.

[22] S Kidd and D Sibun, 'What Has the Covid-19 Crisis Taught Us about Social Protection?' (Pathways Perspectives, 29, 2020) www.developmentpathways.co.uk/publications/what-has-the-covid-19-crisis-taught-us-about-social-protection/.

[23] M Ravallion, 'On the Virus and Poor People in the World' (2020) Blog in The Economics of Poverty, https://economicsandpoverty.com/2020/04/02/on-the-virus-and-poor-people-in-the-world/.

Finally, a rights-based approach means that adequate attention is paid to the whole policy process, instead of merely focusing on social security policy outcomes. The obligations of the state are not restricted to the content of the policies but also apply to the implementation process of these policies,[24] from the design and regulation of the programmes and services to implementation in the field. It is of essence that the entire process incorporates the principles of human dignity and non-discrimination instead of being centred solely on efficiency in achieving outcomes.

IV. BRIEF COMPARATIVE SUMMARY OF SOCIAL SECURITY RIGHTS AS ENVISAGED IN CONSTITUTIONS ACROSS THE GLOBE

Following the conceptual thread of the discussion outlined above, the importance of a constitutional framework guaranteeing the right to social security cannot be over-emphasised. The inclusion of rights at the constitutional level reflects the fundamental values and beliefs of a society[25] and in the case of the right to social security, provides the cornerstone for these social policies to be fully embraced and implemented.[26] The inclusion of the right to social security in a constitution also adds a strong moral dimension by safeguarding against the unjust negation of human dignity and providing income security.[27]

Constitutional recognition of rights imposes obligations on the state to coordinate the articulation of the responsible state institutions, develop the necessary legislative norms, and put in place the necessary judicial processes.[28] Constitutional guarantees serve to safeguard human rights through institutional mechanisms that ensure compliance with these rights and protecting citizens against regressive fiscal austerity measures that impact negatively on social rights.[29] In addition, a country's legal framework can ensure superiority of legally binding international human rights instruments over domestic law.

A constitution that recognises the right to social security, guaranteed by the state, is of immense importance to a cohesive social contract, because it can capture the support of the majority of citizens and not just the existing beneficiaries of social security services and programmes.

However, there are different ways in which the right to social security is embedded in constitutions across the globe, varying from loosely worded commitments to very specific provisions. The general pattern that emerges is: to

[24] Sepúlveda and Nyst (n 19).

[25] A Ben-Bassat and D Momi, 'Social Rights in the Constitution and in Practice' (2008) 36(1) *Journal of Comparative Economics* 103.

[26] G Montt and A Coddou, 'El Derecho a La Seguridad Social En Chile y El Mundo: Análisis Comparado Para Una Nueva Constitución', *Informes Técnicos*, 14 (OIT Cono Sur, 2020).

[27] Egorov (n 11).

[28] Ibid.

[29] Ibid.

affirm social security as an individual human right; or to define the state's responsibilities in the provision of social security; or to follow an approach that classes social security among the guiding principles of state policy.[30]

Most constitutions refer to the provision of social security services and social assistance in general terms, responding to specific risks or vulnerabilities to which individuals might be exposed to during their lifecycles.[31] Another set of constitutions – fewer – make reference to concepts of income security, minimum wage levels and/or social pensions.[32]

A global study[33] on the incorporation of economic, social and cultural rights in constitutions identified various levels of inclusion. In 42.8 per cent of cases the rights are justiciable, liable to be brought before a court of law, whereas in 26.3 per cent of cases the rights are merely aspirational. In this latter group of countries, the right to social security is not legally binding but rather is 'articulated through general guidelines that steer public policies'.[34]

The constitutions of some Latin American countries are among the most advanced and detailed in matters of social security (even more notable in the case of recently adopted/amended constitutions) and the majority of countries in the region have incorporated wide-reaching social security provisions.[35] In addition to incorporating social security provisions that cover a range of risks over an individual's lifecycle, Latin American constitutions also show a trend towards greater state responsibility and wider inclusion of such social security measures, extending for instance to domestic and/or rural workers.[36]

In the case of Argentina, for example, the constitutional reforms of 1957 and 1994 (Art 14 bis) enshrine the right to social security and in line with Keynesian interventionism, social policies became more universal in nature, based also on collective rights.[37] Moreover, the Argentine constitution gives priority to international human rights norms over domestic law. Article 14 bis reads:

> The State shall grant the benefits of social security, which shall be of an integral nature and may not be waived. In particular, the laws shall establish: compulsory social insurance, which shall be in charge of national or provincial entities with financial and economic autonomy, administered by the interested parties with State participation, with no overlapping of contributions; adjustable retirements and

[30] International Labour Conference, 'Social Security and the Rule of Law: General Survey Concerning Social Security Instruments in Light of the 2008 Declaration on Social Justice for a Fair Globalization' (ILO, 2011).

[31] Egorov (n 11).

[32] Ibid.

[33] E Rosevear et al, 'Justiciable and Aspirational Economic and Social Rights in National Constitutions' in KK Young (ed), *The Future of Economic and Social Rights* (Cambridge, Cambridge University Press, 2019).

[34] Montt and Coddou (n 26).

[35] International Labour Conference (n 30).

[36] Ibid.

[37] L Halperín et al, 'Políticas Sociales en la Argentina : Entre la Ciudadanía Plena y el Asistencialismo Focalizado in La Contención del Pauperismo' (Universidad de Buenos Aires, CEPED, 2008).

> pensions; full family protection; protection of homestead; family allowances and access to a worthy housing.[38]

Another example is that of Ecuador and its most recent constitutional reform process of 2008. In Art 34 the reformed constitution establishes the right to social security through adherence to the principles of solidarity, obligation, universality, equity, among others. For its part, the state commits to guaranteeing this right, making particular reference to those engaged in unpaid work at home and autonomous workers.[39] The new constitution also establishes that:

> The right to social security is a right of all persons and it cannot be waived, and it shall be the State that must bear the prime duty and responsibility for this right. Social security shall be governed by the principles of solidarity, obligation, universality, equity, efficiency, subsidiarity, adequacy, transparency and participation, to meet individual and collective needs. The State shall guarantee and ensure the full and effective exercise of the right to social security, which includes persons who carry out unpaid work in households, livelihood activities in the rural sector, all forms of self-employed and who are unemployed.[40]

As such, Ecuador is an example of the trend towards greater inclusiveness in coverage of social security systems and establishes some of the fundamental principles of inclusive social security systems.

In the context of a region where constitutions have the highest average number of entrenched social rights and incorporate more justiciable social rights than any other region,[41] Chile stands out with an outdated legal framework that does not allow for the right to social security to be adequately protected. In the case of Chile, the constitution currently in force does not guarantee its citizens equal and universal access to social security rights. In general terms the constitution 'embeds a neoliberal economic model, making it very difficult for citizens to exercise their social rights'.[42] Implicit in this model is the fact that the state does not guarantee social security rights but rather 'the State must satisfy the need for a system of social security superintendence whereby citizens can claim against administrative infringements of regulatory/legal norms but not against constitutional norms'.[43]

Article 19 of the current Chilean Constitution therefore regards social security not from the perspective of the universality of rights and the right to social security in itself, but in terms of an individual's right to choose between public or private social security provisions, an approach that necessarily leads to a

[38] National Argentine Constitution, English version.

[39] Constitution of the Republic of Ecuador, 2008.

[40] Constitution of the Republic of Ecuador, English version.

[41] Jung et al (n 12).

[42] R Uprimmi, Derechos sociales en Chile: obstáculos y oportunidades constitucionales, Video, 2020, https://www.youtube.com/watch?v=_mOM8bAx5dA, translated by author from original source.

[43] Montt and Coddou (n 26), translated by author from original source.

large degree of precariousness in the exercise of these rights.[44] Furthermore, instead of promoting greater social integration and/or cohesion through access to social services and programmes, this perspective is actually conducive to the opposite trend, creating segregation and fragmentation within the provision of social security services by the state.[45] Thus, this limited interpretation of social security rights in Art 19 does nothing to contribute towards the solidarity pillar required to finance universal social security systems.

Beyond the recognition of social rights within the framework of a national constitution, the welfare of a population depends ultimately on the material access to these rights. Given all of the arguments mentioned above, with the Constitution in its current form, access to the right to social security by most Chileans cannot be guaranteed.

V. CONCLUSION

Based on the principles discussed above, the incorporation of the right to social security in the new constitution to be drawn up in Chile can, if based on the principles discussed throughout this chapter, undoubtedly contribute to greater social cohesion throughout the country.

Enshrining respect for human dignity and the right to social security based on principles and standards of solidarity, universality, equity and sustainability is a crucial step in building a new social contract that establishes rights and obligations in line with the expectations of Chilean society. The current inequities, social grievances and lack of public trust in state institutions and their policies can be channelled towards achieving a greater sense of social belonging and social justice and improving the level of interaction with the State.

Given the segmented and fragmented nature of social security service provision in Chile today, achieving social cohesion will depend in large measure on the social security system becoming more inclusive.[46] The widespread social discontent and negative impacts of the Covid-19 pandemic provide a window of opportunity for the country to pay heed to the clamour for a more just society, more accessible social services and greater respect for human rights and human dignity by rebuilding the social contract.[47]

The current crisis can, therefore, be used to reformulate the social security system to reflect basic principles and standards such as solidarity, equity, universality, human dignity, adequacy of benefits, non-discrimination, and social

[44] J Bassa, 'Seguridad social y proceso constituyente: hacia un pacto social inclusive', Video, Serie de conversatorios 'Derechos sociales y proceso constituyente: re(imaginando) el Chile del siglo XXI', 2020 www.youtube.com/watch?t=2563s&v=FgrbydBDIM4.

[45] Ibid.

[46] Ministerio de Desarrollo Social y Familia (n 5).

[47] ILO (n 1).

inclusion, as well as ensuring transparency and participation.[48] The incorporation of the right to social security in Chile's new constitution could also constitute a key step towards a progressive expansion of social security coverage.

This inclusive, lifecycle approach to social security furthermore facilitates a heightened level of preparedness for natural disasters and sanitary, health and socio-economic emergencies such as the current pandemic. Events like these make it clear that it is not just the lower socio-economic segments of society that require a social security system to fall back on. The whole of society is susceptible to facing vulnerabilities and shocks, to job instability, loss of income etc. at some stage of their lives. The best answer to deal with these risks and vulnerabilities is through an inclusive, rights-based system of social security enshrined in the national constitution.

[48] ILO (n 15).

15

Environmental Issues in a New Constitution

VERÓNICA DELGADO AND DOMINIQUE HERVÉ

I. INTRODUCTION

CONSTITUTIONS SET DOWN a fundamental consensus on a nation's future. Although Chile holds places of significance in matters of biodiversity, the country's relationship with the elements of nature that enable life and growth has broken down and Chileans are losing them fast.[1] Circumstances are changing rapidly, and significant uncertainty exists as to what can happen, and when, should humanity continue to mismanage the planet and ignore the impact of climate change.

Although institutional progress has been made, this chapter argues that it falls short of what is needed. The difficulties and challenges Chile is facing are not mere issues of good management or governance – of the environmental impact assessment system, for example. The issues will not go away with discrete legislation on water resources, glaciers, biodiversity, land management, forestry, or fisheries. The current constitutional framework and interpretations have undermined the necessary reforms. To bring about a truly transformative shift in society, Chile requires a fairer, greener constitution.

II. THE CONSTITUTION OF 1980: OBLIVIOUS TO THE COLLECTIVE NATURE OF ENVIRONMENTAL ISSUES

In matters of the environment, the Constitution of 1980 distinguishes between rights, obligations, and principles.[2] We propose to include in this category not only those provisions concerning environmental protection, but also the natural

[1] OECD-ECLAC, *OECD Environmental Performance Reviews: Chile 2016* (OECD Publishing, 2016) 41.

[2] E Costa et al, '¿Receptividad deliberativa? El derecho al medio ambiente en la discusión constituyente de Chile 2016–2017' (2020) 248 *Revista de Derecho Universidad de Concepción* 169.

resource ownership regime.[3] Additionally, we include other equally relevant provisions (ie those that regulate decentralisation, land and basin management, indigenous rights, and taxation).

Current constitutional provisions are out of step with the times, limited (especially in terms of the rights and duties involved), and more concerned with safeguarding free enterprise and ownership of natural resource concessions than protecting the environment. While few in number, these rules have been successfully leveraged to block restrictions meant to protect nature or secure a collective benefit, and more generally, to tip the balance toward unrelenting economic growth – water resources being a prime example. As such, a new constitution should also enshrine other matters relevant to fully support an environmentally oriented development.

A. Rights, Obligations, and the Motion for Environmental Protection

Article 19(8)(1) of the Chilean constitution sets out a fundamental right: 'The Constitution shall guarantee all people the right to live in a pollution-free environment. The State shall ensure that this right is not infringed and shall safeguard the preservation of nature'.

To uphold this right, the Constitution (Art 20) provides recourse to a type of legal action called a motion for environmental protection. However, whilst these actions can be brought against illegal acts or omissions they cannot be brought against purely arbitrary acts or omissions; this makes them much more restrictive than guarantees on private property or free enterprise. In a sector noted for few provisions and ample discretion, this can be a serious hurdle.

In actual practice, motions for environmental protection will safeguard related rights only within a highly distinct scenario: living in a pollution-free environment. Based on the letter of the provision, the courts have long interpreted these safeguards to apply only to humans and to deny them when asserted to protect dolphins, seals, trees, or other fauna and flora. The courts have further restricted their rulings to specific scenarios where life and limb are at stake, turning down requests for environmental protection when no specific rule on pollution was infringed. Some courts have recently ruled based on quality of life standards, such as claims involving offensive odours, although Chile has no such standards. In exceptional yet highly relevant cases, recent case law has extended protection to scenarios involving manifest impairment of wetland integrity, although most such rulings remain rather anthropocentric (ie to prevent flooding of populated areas, guarantee the water supply).[4]

[3] D Hervé and G López, 'El medio ambiente y el desafío de una nueva Constitución' in R Lorca et al (eds), *La Hoja en Blanco* (Editorial La Pollera, 2020) 199.

[4] Court of Appeals of Concepción, case 6412 (2018), as confirmed in Supreme Court, case 22196 (2018) and Supreme Court case 118 (2018).

Significantly, in 2005 the Constitution was amended to add the possibility to appeal omissions. The original language contemplated only acts, clearly to deter claims against a state that at the time knew little about environmental issues. This was a positive development, especially when governments fail to act or to properly coordinate with other competent authorities, as in the salmon spills off Chiloé Island,[5] and the mass poisonings in the towns of Quintero and Puchuncaví.[6] Still, the Chilean Constitution made environmental obligations incumbent only on government, effectively giving private individuals and corporations a free pass on sustainable development. Moreover, it required the state to preserve nature but said nothing about its associated social and cultural elements. The Constitution also failed to clearly state the purpose or rationale for preserving nature. Had these considerations been contemplated, they would have given more breadth to nature as a collective challenge and more strength to environmental rights and responsibilities challenged by individual rights.

Failure to acknowledge the collective nature of the interests at stake has practical consequences that can and should be averted. For example, allowing only the personally affected to bring suit detracts from the public interest and hinders environmental protection.[7] While efforts have been made to expand legal standing based on Bermúdez's adjacent surroundings argument,[8] the Chilean Supreme Court often rejects environmental cases based on a finding of no standing.[9] The Court has even taken the time to write that motions for environmental protection cannot be brought by members of the public, finding that this is the case when, for example, legislators, mayors or grassroots leaders go to court in the name of the people.[10] Expanded legal standing could help improve access to environmental justice and secure more effective jurisdictional protection.[11]

B. Restrictions on Other Rights and Limits on Property Rights on Environmental Grounds

Article 19(8)(2) of the Constitution contains wording to help address clashes of rights: 'To protect the environment, the law may restrict certain rights or

[5] P Moraga et al, 'Sentencia Corte Suprema 22 May 2018' (2018) *Actualidad Jurídica Ambiental*, www.actualidadjuridicaambiental.com/jurisprudencia-al-dia-iberoamerica-chile-principio-de-prevencion-y-precaucion-vertidos-medio-marino/.

[6] Supreme Court case 5888 (2019).

[7] Hervé and López (n 3) 206.

[8] J Bermúdez, *Fundamentos de derecho ambiental*, 2nd edn (Ediciones Universitarias de Valparaíso, 2014) 64–65 and 134–36.

[9] Supreme Court ruling in cases 8213 (2011), 3141 (2012), 4755 (2012), 3146 (2013), 3294 (2013), 7677 (2013), 14937 (2013), 6590 (2014), 10759 (2014), 14263 (2014), 21973 (2014), 26829 (2014), 24932 (2017), and 12729 (2018).

[10] Supreme Court ruling in cases 4777 (2011); 8213 (2011); 2463 (2012); 4755 (2012), 5888 (2019) and 45.059 (2017).

[11] V Delgado, 'La protección del Medio Ambiente a través de las acciones populares del artículo 948 del Código Civil de Andrés Bello: un estudio histórico-comparativo' in M Martinic and

freedoms', notably the right to acquire all manner of assets, to free enterprise, and to own property. Clashes are also addressed by the express inclusion of the notion of the 'conservation of environmental assets' among the social functions of ownership. Art 19(24)(2) states:

> The law shall set out the manner in which property shall be acquired, used, enjoyed and disposed of, as well as the limits and obligations arising from its social functions. These include the requirements of the general interest of the nation, national security, the public good, public health, and the conservation of environmental assets.

But the lawgiver faces a major stumbling block in Art 19(26): no such restrictions will 'detract from the essence of these rights'.

The case law of the Constitutional Court and other Chilean courts of law shows that cases involving the social function of the environment are few and far between, and the criteria upheld are not at all clear.[12] This provision's potential to restrict rights on environmental grounds '[h]as not been a determining factor in achieving a greener form of development, arguably due to the unusual force of the natural resource ownership regime'.[13] Sharing this critique, Galdámez refers to these undeveloped, seldom-used provisions as 'sleeper clauses'. The critique points to a regulatory flaw, as motions for constitutional protection, although meant to safeguard basic environmental rights, are actually unable to enforce state obligations or restrict other rights on environmental grounds. These issues would be best enshrined elsewhere in the constitution – ie in the definition of the institutional framework – so as to enable their application across the board.[14]

C. The Natural Resource Ownership Regime

Chief among this class of provisions is Art 19(23)(1):

> [The Constitution shall guarantee all people] The freedom to acquire and own all manner of assets save for those made common to all by nature or which belong to the nation as a whole, as provided for by the law. The foregoing is without prejudice to provisions elsewhere in the Constitution.

This clause, a fundamental pillar of the present economic system, enshrines the freedom to own anything and everything, natural resources included, save only

M Tapia (eds), *Sesquicentenario del Código Civil de Andrés Bello. Pasado, presente y futuro de la codificación Tomo II* (Chile, Lexis Nexis, 2005) 907.

[12] R Guzmán, *Derecho Ambiental Chileno* (Chile, Planeta sostenible, 2012) 72–76.

[13] Hervé and López (n 3) 209.

[14] L Galdámez, 'Constitución y medio ambiente: algunas ideas para el futuro' (2018) 9 *Revista de Derecho Ambiental* 72, 72–75, 89 and 90. See also L Galdámez, 'Los deberes de protección estatal, cláusula presente (aunque dormida) en la Constitución de 1980: una fórmula constitucional frente al cambio climático' in P Moraga (ed), *La protección del medio ambiente: reflexiones para una reforma constitucional* (Editorial Jurídica de Chile, 2019) 77–85.

for public property as defined in the law. The Constitution effectively asserts a wide-ranging right to privately own elements of nature, leaving it to the law to exclude some by declaring them public property.

Only mining resources are constitutionally held to be absolute, exclusive, inalienable and imprescriptible public property (Art 19(24)(6)).[15] Coastal and water resources are declared public property in the Civil Code and the Water Code. And geothermal resources have been so declared by special legislation.[16]

However, after introducing the rule and the exception – the freedom to own anything except assets that belong to the nation or are common to all – Art 19(24)(9)(11) of the Constitution adds a highly contentious clause on the ownership of rights held by private parties over mineral and water resources: 'Title to mining concessions is protected by the constitutional guarantees herein'; […] 'The water rights held by private parties, as recognised or established under the law, will confer title to them on their owners'.

The Chilean Constitution expressly provides for ownership of water rights and other concessions and rights granted to use elements of nature. Incongruously, the law states that no title of ownership will accrue to marine or aquaculture concessions.[17]

In a phenomenon known as the commodification of rights,[18] Art 19(24) entrenches and assures ownership of intangible rights.[19] '[The Constitution shall guarantee all people] The right to own all kinds and manner of tangible and intangible assets'.

What are the implications of the Constitution recognising a right to own rights? And why does it reiterate this notion in respect of elements of nature? The Constitution states, in Art 19(24):

> No one, under any circumstances, shall be deprived of her property, of the assets owned or of any of the essential attributes and prerogatives of title except by virtue of general or special legislation allowing expropriation thereof by reason of public or national interest, as duly qualified by the lawgiver.

In other words, anyone who holds recognised, legally constituted mining concessions or water rights owns the right to use and exploit them and cannot be deprived of this property, or of the essential prerogatives thereof, except through legislation. For good measure, expropriated rights holders are entitled to preferential compensation and treatment: they must be indemnified in full, at market value, before the state can take possession.[20] While not owners of the resources

[15] Hervé and López (n 3) 209.

[16] D Hervé, *Justicia ambiental y recursos naturales* (Chile, Ediciones Universitarias de Valparaíso, 2015).

[17] Ibid, 238.

[18] R Domínguez, 'Aspectos de la Constitucionalización del Derecho Civil Chileno' (1996) 93 *Revista de Derecho y Jurisprudencia* 127.

[19] Hervé (n 16) 238.

[20] M Guiloff and C Salgado, 'El derecho de propiedad privada y la tutela de los bienes públicos' in R Lorca et al (eds), *La Hoja en Blanco* (Editorial La Pollera, 2020) 269–71.

per se, which remain public property, they do own the right to use and exploit them. The legal shield is perfected by giving rights owners an unrestricted ability to file for protection. So, while the Constitution may allow the law to impose limits and obligations on property rights based on the social function of ownership, such limits have practically never been imposed in respect of water rights or natural resource concessions. This arrangement, which determines and delimits the powers of the state over publicly owned natural resources, is the key to understanding the legal regime applicable to natural resource management. By guaranteeing private parties the right to own rights over publicly owned natural resources, the Constitution effectively privatises those resources. The end result is that the rights of the state as administrator are significantly weaker than the property rights of private parties.[21]

D. Other Provisions Related to the Environment

With regard to environmental matters, the new Chilean Constitution should also contain other equally relevant provisions, that either warrant revision from their existing version or need to be added.

i. Indigenous Rights

The Chilean Constitution of 1980 says nothing in relation to indigenous rights, even though they were being embraced throughout the region at the time.[22] Yet, native rights, natural resource rights, and protection of the environment are inextricably intertwined. And since the indigenous rights debate intersects environmental issues, reference is made to the relevant instruments in international human rights law, notably the ILO Convention Concerning Indigenous and Tribal Peoples (Convention 169, 1989) and the United Nations Declaration on Indigenous Rights (2007).

Significantly, the case law of the Inter-American Court of Human Rights recognises the following indigenous rights under Convention 169: (1) over the total lands and territories they occupy or otherwise use (Arts 13 and 14); (2) over the natural resources pertaining to their lands and territories, which include participating in their use, management, and conservation (Art 15(1)); (3) where the state retains ownership, the right to be consulted before exploration or exploitation is permitted, to participate in the benefits of such activities,

[21] Hervé (n 16) 298–99.

[22] J Aylwin, 'Los derechos de pueblos indígenas en la nueva Constitución' in V Contreras et al (eds), *Derechos sociales y el momento constituyente de Chile: Perspectivas globales y locales para el debate constitucional, Tomo I: Chile, desigualdad y derechos sociales* (Global Initiative for Economic, Social and Cultural Rights, Human Rights Centre University of Essex, Universidad de Concepción, 2021).

and to receive fair compensation for damages sustained as a result thereof (Art 15(2)); and (4) the right to be informed of the environmental impact of any activities conducted on their lands (Art 7(3)).

Entrenching the collective rights of indigenous peoples over their territories and natural resources, especially the rights to be consulted and to participate in the benefits, is fully consistent with adoption of a new, fairer, greener constitution. Although indigenous consultation is well entrenched in domestic law, constitutional recognition will help consolidate mechanisms, especially on the protection of nature and the environment in indigenous lands, that are yet to be effectively applied.[23] Enshrining a right to participate in the benefits would be just as relevant, since establishing the appropriate domestic mechanisms remains a pending assignment.[24] Constitutional recognition would also help guarantee environmental equity and justice, principles that are key to achieving a socially transformative constitutional arrangement.

ii. Decentralisation

As Chile is one of the most centralised countries in the OECD and reforms remain inadequate, territorial development will require the new constitution to move forward on decentralisation.[25]

Recent reforms include the creation of regional governments and direct election of both regional councillors (2014) and regional governors (2021).

A scheduled transfer of powers gave regional governments new roles in land use, production, and social and cultural planning and urban centres with populations of 250,000 and greater will be able to set up metropolitan areas for ease of municipal coordination.

However, key challenges remain: (1) the regional economic agenda is still mostly set by the central government; (2) public spending has a sector-based logic that blocks funding of integrated regional initiatives;[26] and (3) critical environmental decisions are made at the central level, a method that fails to adequately address regional differences and imbalances concerning pollution, water shortages and other environmental burdens.

A 2016 OECD report pointed out that local leaders lacked the autonomy and resources to play a more substantive role in managing the environment and

[23] D Hervé and D Bascur, 'La protección de los derechos de las comunidades indígenas en el SEIA por parte de los tribunales ambientales: ¿avances o retrocesos?' (2019) 11 *Revista Justicia Ambiental* 197.

[24] D Hervé and S Pérez, 'Adecuación de la legislación interna a los estándares impuestos para la administración de los recursos naturales' in J Contesse (ed), *El Convenio 169 de la OIT y el derecho chileno. Mecanismos y obstáculos para su implementación* (Heinrich Boll Foundation, Ediciones UDP, 2012) 15.

[25] OECD, *Making Decentralisation Work in Chile: Towards Stronger Municipalities* (OECD Publishing, 2017).

[26] Ibid.

adapting national policy to local needs. For example, regional governments currently have no say on the air and water quality measurements needed to identify stressed or contaminated areas and implement prevention or clean-up plans. In fact, although the OECD report warned about a large number of polluted ecosystems, not one water resource clean-up plan was implemented.[27] Moreover, projects submitted to the environmental impact assessment system are reviewed by committees consisting entirely of central government appointees, and while Chile had its first democratically-elected governors in 2021, they will not sit on these committees. Also required is a stronger municipal role concerning drought, forest fires, flooding, and other effects of climate change.

iii. Land and Basin Management

One of Chile's key water management shortcomings is poor river basin management, which causes most water resources to be managed in isolation from changes in land use. Absent any planning, key decisions tend to be made by water rights owners. Other users are not consulted, and vulnerable communities and ecosystems are not ensured a supply. The 1980 Constitution says nothing about critical water uses, and leaves resource allocation up to the market.[28] The mentioned OECD report advised Chile to 'resume institutional and regulatory reforms with the purpose of adopting an integrated river basin management system to unify planning and regulation of water quantity and quality'.[29]

Equally concerning is weak land use management, especially in rural areas. Such urban planning as exists is based on centrally-formulated city plans. There has been some progress, such as giving regional governments an increased say in land management plans and requiring land use instruments to undergo strategic environmental assessment. But as the OECD report rightly adds, 'both the integration of environmental considerations into land use plans and public participation in their development need improvement'.[30] In actual practice, however, few protected areas exist, especially in unregulated land. Changes in land use depend on sector authorities who lack an ecosystemic perspective and, for good measure, conduct little or no monitoring. As a result, vast expanses of native forest have been turned into farmland or residential property outside any form of planning.

The impact is highly significant, especially in terms of biodiversity loss, depletion of ground and surface water, and aquifer contamination from

[27] OECD-ECLAC (n 1) 28.

[28] V Delgado, 'La regulación de las aguas subterráneas en el derecho de aguas de Chile: liberal, incompleta y poco ambiental' in V Delgado and J Luis Arumí (eds), *El modelo chileno de regulación de las aguas subterráneas: Críticas desde el derecho ambiental y las ciencias ambientales* (Tirant Lo Blanch, 2021) 83.

[29] OECD-ECLAC (n 1) 46.

[30] Ibid.

agrochemicals and septic tanks. In addition, especially in areas such as agriculture and forestry, the time-honoured central policy has been to encourage resource exploitation and subsidise automated irrigation and agrochemical use without impact assessment. Regional land management plans – a recent innovation not yet in effect – are a step forward, but their design leaves something to be desired. In effect, these plans are only binding on discrete projects submitted to the environmental impact assessment system, and since decisions impacting rural lands are the sole preserve of the central government, they cannot create new protected areas. Urban land is a happy exception, since local authorities can request recognition of, for example, urban wetlands, which once approved are protected under land planning instruments.

iv. Taxation

Green taxes are a levy on allowable environmental disruptions.[31] Intended to protect the environment while boosting fiscal revenues,[32] green taxes hold economic players accountable for the impact of their activities, encourage cleaner technologies, and deter egregiously contaminating activities.[33] In Chile, as instruments of government policy, green taxes must conform to the principles and purposes laid out in the environmental, taxation and general provisions of the Constitution, such as Art 1(4), which asserts that the function of the state is to foster the common good.

However, recent recourse to green taxes has sparked some debate on their constitutionality, particularly with a 2014 tax reform that introduced a charge on fixed-source emissions. Some question the state's authority to levy taxes for non-fiscal purposes, others that green taxes overlook ability to pay and try to regulate environmental behaviour 'by financially impacting property rights or assets.'[34] As Art 19(20) of the Constitution prevents levying taxes for specific purposes, their use in environmental protection remains restricted.[35] It remains unclear whether green taxes agree with its taxation guarantees. The constitutional framework may therefore be in need of revision, as green taxes can contribute to much more than cleaner technologies. From a redistributive standpoint, they can help offset the environmental burden caused by the negative externalities they are intended to address, and by recognising specific environmental issues, they can help channel resources for reparations or redress.

[31] M Matus, 'Particularismos e imposibilidades de los impuestos a las emisiones en la Constitución Política de Chile. Estudio Preliminar' (2015) 42(3) *Revista Chilena de Derecho* 1035, 1038.

[32] R Tobia, 'Una mirada comparada sobre los tributos ambientales en Chile y España' (2019) 12 *Revista de Derecho Ambiental* 7.

[33] Ibid.

[34] Tobia (n 32) 16.

[35] Ibid, 18.

III. A GREENER CONSTITUTION

While not every difficulty and challenge can be addressed in a new constitution, laying a foundation for sustainability will clearly need new provisions that should be as realistic and flexible as a fast-evolving climate scenario requires.

As a twenty-first century constitution and the first to be written after adoption of the 2015 Paris Agreement and the 2030 Agenda for Sustainable Development, a truly environmentally-friendly constitution should embrace the growing outcry for environmental protection.[36] This shift in focus is all the more crucial relative to what needs to be replaced: a system so bent on guaranteeing individual freedoms and ownership rights, it fails to recognise the collective interest when imposing environmental obligations.

The 1980 Constitution '[e]nables an institutional model that keeps the State from addressing environmental issues with enough authority to place the common good ahead of the private interest'.[37] Such a transformation requires the three pillars of sustainability to be built up: approach resource use from an ecosystemic perspective; preserve the environment for future generations; and keep populations and the environment safe by ensuring that all decision-making is participatory and based on both scientific and ancestral knowledge. Explicit constitutional recognition of global climate change issues would be a very concrete step forward.

A new constitutional framework should begin by acknowledging Chile's environmental wealth. The 1980 Constitution makes no mention of the fact that Chile is endowed with a vast natural diversity spanning from vast oceans to towering mountain ranges. Treasuring and highlighting Chile's unique features is far from a purely testimonial issue. Focusing attention on the country's rich biodiversity and landscapes and identifying the threats they face from the 1980 Constitution implies setting priorities capable of impacting the subsequent interpretation of other constitutional principles, including those enshrining rights and responsibilities.

Were the current structure to be maintained, experience suggests that important changes ought to be introduced, especially as regards rights, responsibilities, and legal protections. For example, the collective nature of the interests at stake must be recognised, especially with regard to who is accorded legal standing to petition the courts when the public interest is involved – why not everyone, as in Portugal, Paraguay, and Colombia? At a minimum, legal standing should be expanded to other bearers of the collective interest, including expert organisations and groups and those acting on behalf of the ecosystem and future generations. Proposals already on the table include constitutional class actions and an environment ombudsman.[38]

[36] Costa et al (n 2).

[37] Hervé and López (n 3) 212.

[38] FIMA NGO, 'Bases para una Constitución Ecológica en Chile', www.fima.cl/wordpress/wp-content/uploads/2020/11/BASES-PARA-UNA-CONSTITUCIO%CC%81N-ECOLO%CC%81GICA-v.-25.11.20-1.pdf.

Environmental rights should contemplate wider scenarios than mere pollution prevention, step back from anthropocentric stances, and consider overall ecosystem integrity. Noteworthy comparative experiences include the constitutions of Brazil (Art 225), Argentina (Art 45), France (Art 1 of the Charter on the Environment), Paraguay (Art 7), Costa Rica (Art 50), and Ecuador (Art 14), which set out a right to a healthful and balanced environment. This means recognising the cycles of nature, as only a balanced ecosystem will deliver its provisioning, regulating, and cultural services. An integral approach to the ecosystem would also enable a broader focus than shielding people from contamination and preserving a few ecosystems in formally protected areas. As to responsibilities, doubtlessly one of the most crucial issues in the coming constitutional debate, we have noted that current Chilean standards do not make the grade.

Argentina (Art 41), Brazil (Art 225), Colombia (Arts 95(2)(8) and 8), and France (Arts 2, 3 and 4 of the Charter on the Environment, attached to the Constitution) make it incumbent on everyone to protect, prevent harm to, and even defend the environment. In Chile, in contrast, obligations accrue only to the state and go no further than protecting the right to live in a pollution-free environment and at preserving nature, a task construed as protecting certain valuable areas. The comparative experience, however, yields many notable approaches based on environmental and ecological education and research (Arts 8 and 9 of the French Charter on the Environment). Germany's Basic Law (Art 20(a)), for example, requires the state to take legislative, executive and judicial action to protect 'the natural foundations of life and animals', citing its responsibility toward future generations. More recent charters require the state to maintain and restore essential ecological processes (Brazil, Art 225), protect environmental diversity and integrity, and regulate exploitation of natural resources, including their conservation, restoration and replacement (Colombia, Arts 79 and 80), and conserve ecosystems' capacity for natural regeneration (Ecuador, Art 395). Pennsylvania (Arts I and 27) and Hawaii (Arts XI and 1 and 7) require governments to conserve and maintain public natural resources 'for the benefit of all', including future generations.[39] This is also explicit in the Bolivian Constitution, which requires the state to ensure that natural assets are conserved and used for the benefit of all (Art 346).

Also in need of revision are the approaches used to restrict free enterprise and ownership of resource rights or concessions. The notion of the commodification of rights, ie the ownership of intangible assets, has become accepted doctrine in Chile. Unless or until abolished, a crucial point to understand is that ownership of intangible assets, or of mere rights or concessions, cannot be equated to or guaranteed as other kinds of ownership, especially when it involves publicly owned assets that the state must protect and maintain. Constitutional protection

[39] M Blumm and Z Schwartz, 'The Public Trust Doctrine Fifty Years After Sax and Some Thoughts on Its Future' (2021) 1 *Public Land & Resources Law Review* 44, 52; C Bauer et al, *Protección de la naturaleza y una nueva Constitución para Chile: Lecciones de la doctrina del Public Trust* (Chile California Conservation Exchange, 2020).

of ownership of rights does not mean, as often construed in Chile, that owners have title to the originating regulation.[40] A greener constitution should therefore identify the strategic elements of nature and safeguard them for the benefit of all, including future generations. It should set effective limits and obligations on the state and private parties or, alternatively, enact compensation mechanisms designed to ensure that the public good prevails over the private interest. The social function of ownership is a notion that requires regulation on general rather than specific terms. Instead of being construed as exceptional grounds for the setting of limits, the social function of ownership should help explicate private property and its regime. This is an essential principle that actively configures the social function of ownership.[41] In this respect, a point of interest is the Colombian constitution (Arts 58 and 333), which restricts private property guarantees where the common good, the public interest, or the environmental and cultural heritage are concerned. It also requires private interests to yield to the public interest, asserting that ownership is a social function with inherent ecological obligations.

In Chile, a new constitutional framework would also require embedding certain basic principles designed to both ensure sustainability and rise to the challenges posed by the twenty-first century. These principles include: (1) participation in environmental decision-making, which includes the rights to justice and information; (2) intra- and intergenerational environmental justice (in its distributive phase), which implies a fairer allocation of burdens and benefits and sharing the economic, social and environmental wealth originating in nature;[42] and (3) non-retrogression, whereby protections of the quality and integrity of ecosystems and peoples' lives cannot be rolled back. Other potential candidates include the preventive, precautionary, and sustainable development principles. All of these basic principles would preclude the government of the day from scrapping long-term policies and goals and relaxing environmental standards for economic or political reasons.

Indigenous rights over territories and natural resources should also be entrenched, especially the right to be consulted and to partake in the benefits of the use and exploitation of natural resources. A determined effort must be made to achieve territorial equity, an undertaking that requires decentralised decision-making and land and basin management plans capable of addressing environmental disparities between urban and rural areas. Above all, Chile needs to become a decentralised country and grant new autonomy to regional and municipal governments. It needs polycentric governance from the ground up and local governments with broader prerogatives, especially on environmental and climate matters.[43]

[40] Guiloff and Salgado (n 20) 268.
[41] Ibid, 267.
[42] Hervé (n 16) 25–74.
[43] M Billi et al, *Gobernanza policéntrica para la resiliencia al cambio climático: análisis legislativo comparado y ley de marco climático en Chile* (Estudios Públicos, 2020) 160.

Several constitutions have adopted inspiring approaches to the complex issue of balancing land use and environmental protection. France (Art 6 of the Charter on the Environment), for example, requires government policy to further sustainable development. In Portugal (Art 66(e)(f)), the state must integrate environmental goals across sector policy. Article 395 of the Constitution of Ecuador states that, as a matter of principle, 'cross-cutting environmental management policies shall be enforced at all levels. These will be mandatory for the State and for all individuals and entities'. Again, in Portugal (Art 66(2)(b)), the state must '[e]ffect and encourage land management plans ensuring suitable emplacement of activities, balanced socio-economic development, and protection of the landscape'. Along with local governments, it is further required to enforce environmental quality standards across urban centres. In Bolivia, only designated forest areas can be turned into farmland and special safeguards apply for water resources (Art 389). Several other constitutions consider river basins as a basic unit for priority water use and management.

Finally, allocating green tax revenues to areas directly impacted by taxed activities can help more equitably share environmental burdens and achieve a greater degree of environmental justice. This could take the form of tax-funded environmental endowments designed to allocate protection resources or to distribute benefits across the communities directly impacted by the issues addressed by green taxes.

Bibliography

Abidjan Principles on the Right to Education (2019).

Abramovich, V, 'De las violaciones masivas a los patrones estructurales: nuevos enfoques y clásicas tensiones en el Sistema Interamericano de Derechos Humanos' (2009) 63 *Revista Derecho PUCP*.

—— 'Responsabilidad estatal por la violencia de género: Comentarios sobre el caso "Campo Algodonero" en la Corte Interamericana de Derechos Humanos' in *Anuario de Derechos Humanos* (Universidad de Chile, Facultad de Derecho, Centro de Derechos Humanos, 2010).

Abramovich, V and Courtis, C, *El Umbral de La Ciudadanía. El Significado de Los Derechos Sociales En El Estado Social Consitucional* (Buenos Aires, Corporación Gráfica, 2006).

Ackerman, B, *We The People: Transformations* (Cambridge, MA, Harvard University Press, 1998).

African Commission of Human and Peoples' Rights, 420 Resolution on States' Obligation to Regulate Private Actors Involved in the Provision of Health and Education Services – ACHPR/Res 420 (LXIV) 2019.

Aguirre Briones, A, *Los grupos económicos chilenos en perspectiva histórica: entre la industrialización sustitutiva de importaciones y el neoliberalismo 1938–1988*, Doctoral thesis (Barcelona, Universitat de Barcelona, 2017).

Alarcón, FP, Cisterna, Silva V and Schönsteiner, J, 'Derecho a una vivienda adecuada en Chile: Una mirada desde los campamentos' in T Vial (ed), *Informe Anual sobre Derechos Humanos en Chile* (Santiago, Universidad Diego Portales, 2016).

Aldao, M and Clérico, L, 'El derecho social autónomo a la salud y sus contenidos. El caso Poblete Vilches y el examen de (in)cumplimiento de las obligaciones impostergables y no ponderables' in M Morales Antoniazzi and L Clérico (eds), *Interamericanización del derecho a la salud. Perspectivas a la luz del caso Poblete de la Corte IDH* (Queretaro, Instituto de Estudios Comparados del Estado de Querétaro, 2019).

Alemparte, B, 'Towards a Theory of Neoliberal Constitutionalism: Addressing Chile's First Constitution-making Laboratory' (2021) 1 *Global Constitutionalism* 1.

Allen, T, *The Right to Property in Commonwealth Constitutions*' vol 11 (Cambridge, Cambridge University Press, 2000).

Alexy, R, *A Theory of Constitutional Rights* (Oxford, Oxford University Press, 2002).

ANC, *Constitutional Guidelines for a Democratic South Africa* (1989).

—— *A Bill of Rights for a Democratic South Africa: Working Draft for Consultation* (1990).

Arato, A, 'Beyond the Alternative Reform or Revolution: Postsovereign Constitution-Marking and Latin America' (2015) 50 *Wake Forest Law Review* 891.

Atria, F, *Veinte años después, Neoliberalismo con rostro humano* (Santiago, Catalonia, 2013).

—— *Derechos sociales y educación: un nuevo paradigma de lo público* (Santiago, LOM, 2014).

—— *La Constitución Tramposa* (Santiago, LOM, 2015).

Atria, F, Salgado, C and Wilenmann, J, *Democracia y Neutralización: Origen, Desarrollo y Solución de la Crisis Constitucional* (Santiago, LOM, 2017).

Aubry, S and Dorsi, D, 'Towards a Human Rights Framework to Advance the Debate on the Role of Private Actors in Education' (2016) 42(5) *Oxford Review of Education* 1.

Auslander, GK and Gold N, 'Disability Terminology in the Media: A Comparison of Newspaper Reports in Canada and Israel' (1999) 48 *Social Science & Medicine* 1395.

Aylwin, J, 'Los derechos de pueblos indígenas en la nueva Constitución' in Global Initiative for Economic, Social and Cultural Rights, Human Rights Centre of the University of Essex and University of Concepción (ed), *Derechos sociales y el momento constituyente de Chile: Perspectivas globales y locales para el debate constitucional* (Santiago, GI-ESCR, 2021).

Barrantes, A, 'Hacia Sistemas Integrales de Protección Social?' in AD Cimadamore, A Ivo, C Midaglia and A Barrantes (eds), *Estados de Bienestar, Derechos e Ingresos Básicos en América Latina* (Ciudad de México, La Cuestión Social, Siglo XXI Editores, 2019).

—— 'The Golden Rule, Applied to Social Protection' *Development Pathways Blogs* (2019).

—— 'Why Are Human Rights Considerations Fundamental to Inclusive and Lifecycle Social Protection Systems?' *Pathways Perspectives* (2020).

Bassa, J, *Seguridad social y proceso constituyente: hacia un pacto social inclusivo.* 2020. Serie de conversatorios 'Derechos sociales y proceso constituyente: re(imaginando) el Chile del siglo XXI'. Youtube video.

Bastías, G, et al, 'Health Care Reform in Chile' (2008) 179(12) *Canadian Medical Association Journal* 1289.

Bauer, C, Blumm, M, Delgado, V, Guiloff, M, Hervé, D, Jiménez, G, Marshall, P and McKay, T, *Protección de la naturaleza y una nueva Constitución para Chile: Lecciones de la doctrina del Public Trust* (California, Chile California Conservation Exchange, 2020).

Beauchamp, TL and Childress, JF, *Principles of Biomedical Ethics* (Oxford, Oxford University Press, 2001).

Bellei, C, 'Study of Socioeconomic and Academic Segregation in Chilean Education' (2013) XXXIX *Estudios Pedagógicos* 325.

—— 'Evolución y contexto de las políticas educacionales sobre la educación pública en Chile' in C Bellei (ed), *Nueva educación pública, Contextos, contenidos y perspectivas de la desmunicipalización* (Santiago, Center for Advanced Research in Education, 2018) 19.

Bellei, C et al, 'La fragilidad de la escuela pandémica', *CIPER* (19 December 2020).

Ben-Bassat, A and Dahan, M, 'Social Rights in the Constitution and in Practice' (2008) 36(1) *Journal of Comparative Economics* 103.

Benhabib, S, 'Reason-Giving and Rights-Bearing: Constructing the Subject of Rights' (2013) 20(1) *Constellations* 38.

Berger, H et al, 'Central Bank Independence: An Update of Theory and Evidence' (2001) 15(1) *Journal of Economic Surveys* 3.

Bermúdez, J, *Fundamentos de derecho ambiental*, 2nd edn (Chile, Ediciones Universitarias de Valparaíso, 2014).

Bertelsen, R, 'El Estado empresario en la Constitución de 1980' (1987) 18 *Revista Chilena de Derecho* 115.

Bertrand, M and Mullainathan, S, 'Are Emily and Greg More Employable than Lakisha and Jamal? A Field Experiment on Labor Market Discrimination' (2004) 94 *The American Economic Review* 991.

Billi, M, Delgado,V, Jiménez, G, Morales, B, Neira, CI, Silva, MI and Urquiza, A, *Gobernanza policéntrica para la resiliencia al cambio climático: análisis legislativo comparado y ley de marco climático en Chile* (Chile, Estudios Públicos, 2020).

Birtha M, 'Nothing about CRPD Monitoring without Us: A Case Study on the Involvement of the Disability Movement in Policy-making in Zambia' (2013) 1 *ADRY* 115.

Blumm, M and Schwartz, Z, 'The Public Trust Doctrine Fifty Years after Sax and Some Thoughts on Its Future' (2021) 1 *Public Land & Resources Law Review* 44.

Böckenförde, EW, *Estudios sobre el Estado de Derecho y la democracia* (Madrid, Editorial Trotta 2000).

Bohoslavsky, JP, Fernández, K and Smart, S (eds), *Pinochet's Economic Accomplices. An Unequal Country by Force* (London, Lexington Books, 2020).

Bohoslavsky, JP and Rulli, M, 'Unraveling the Financial Assistance to the Pinochet's Regime' in JP Bohoslavsky, K Fernández and S Smart (eds), *Pinochet's Economic Accomplices. An Unequal Country by Force* (London, Lexington Books, 2020).

Bond, P, *Elite Transition – From Apartheid to Neoliberalism in South Africa*, 2nd revised edn (University of KwaZulu-Natal Press, 2005).

Bonilla Maldonado, D (ed), *Constitutionalism of the Global South: The Activist Tribunals of India, South Africa, and Colombia* (Cambridge, Cambridge University Press, 2013).

Boorse, CA, 'Rebuttal on Health' in JM Humber and RF Almeder (eds), *What Is Disease? Biomedical Ethics Reviews* (Totowa NJ, Humana Press, 1997).
Boyd, D, *The Environmental Rights Revolution: A Global Study of Constitutions, Human Rights, and the Environment* (Vancouver, UBC Press, 2011).
Brickhill, J (ed), *Public Interest Litigation in South Africa* (Claremont, Juta, 2021).
Brown, J, *South African's Insurgent Citizens: On Dissent and the Possibility of Politics* (London, Zed Books, 2015).
Bryde, BO and Stein, MA, 'General Provisions Dealing with Equality' in M Tushnet, T Fleiner and C Saunders (eds), *Routledge Handbook of Constitutional Law* (Abingdon, Routledge, 2012).
Bueno de Mesquita, B, Smith, A, Siverson, RM and Morrow, JD, *The Logic of Political Survival* (Massachusetts, MIT Press Books, 2003).
Bustos, R, 'Nueva constitución y derechos sociales: Hacia un nuevo paradigma' in E Chía and F Quezada (eds), *Propuestas para una nueva constitución (originada en democracia)* (Santiago, Fundación Igualdad, 2015).
Carbonell, M, 'Introducción general al control de convencionalidad' in D Valadés and LR González Pérez (eds), *El constitucionalismo contemporáneo, Homenaje a Jorge Carpizo* (Mexico, Universidad Nacional Autónoma de México, 2018).
Carruthers, D, 'Environmental Politics in Chile: Legacies of Dictatorship and Democracy' (2001) 22(3) *Third World Quarterly* 343.
Casgrain, A, 'La apuesta del endeudamiento en la política habitacional chilena' (2010) 25(68) *Revista Invi* 155.
Casla, K, 'The Democratic Case for Social Rights in Chile's Constitutional Moment' Petrie-Flom Center Harvard Law School (August 2020).
Cassese, A, *Study of the Impact of Foreign Economic Aid and Assistance on Respect for Human Rights in Chile*, UN doc E/CN.4/Sub.2/412, Vols I to IV (1978).
Cea, JL, 'Derecho constitucional chileno' II (Santiago, Ediciones UC, 2008).
Centro de Estudios Políticos, 'Estudio Nacional de Opinión Pública No 84' (December 2019).
Céspedes, LF and Valdés, R, 'Autonomía de bancos centrales: La experiencia chilena' (2006) 358(1) *Documentos de Trabajo, Banco Central de Chile.*
Comisión Asesora Presidencial para el Estudio y Propuesta de un Nuevo Modelo y Marco Jurídico para el Sistema Privado de Salud, *Informe* (2014).
Correa, J, '¿Ha llegado la hora de una Nueva Constitución?' (2013) *Anuario de Derecho Público 2013 de la Universidad Diego Portales* 21.
—— *Diálogos constitucionales* (Santiago, CEP, 2015).
Costa, E, Susaeta, N, Klenner, M and Ledesma, J, '¿Receptividad deliberativa? El derecho al medio ambiente en la discusión constituyente de Chile 2016–2017' (2020) 248 *Revista de Derecho Universidad de Concepción* 169.
Cotino, L, *El derecho a la educación como derecho fundamental. Especial atención a su dimensión social prestacional* (Madrid, Centro de Estudios Políticos y Sociales, 2012).
Courtis, C, 'Luces y sombras. La exigibilidad de los derechos económicos, sociales y culturales en la sentencia de los "Cinco Pensionistas" de la Corte Interamericana de Derechos Humanos' (2004) 6 *Revista Mexicana de Derecho Público*.
—— 'La protección de los derechos económicos, sociales y culturales a través del artículo 26 de la Convención Americana sobre Derechos Humanos' in C Courtis, D Hauser and G Rodríguez Huerta (eds), *Protección internacional de los derechos humanos. Nuevos desafíos* (Mexico, Porrúa-ITAM, 2005).
—— *Ni un paso atrás. La prohibición de regresividad en materia de derechos sociales* (Buenos Aires, Editores del Puerto-CEDAL-CELS, 2006).
—— 'Capítulo III – Derechos Económicos, Sociales y Culturales: Artículo 26. Desarrollo Progresivo' in C Steiner and P Uribe (eds), *Convención Americana sobre Derechos Humanos, Comentario* (Bolivia, Fundación Konrad Adenuaer, 2014).
—— 'Prologue' in M Morales Antoniazzi, L Ronconi and L Clérico, *Interamericanización de los DESCA. El caso Cuscul Pivaral de la Corte IDH* (Mexico, Instituto Max Planck de Derecho

Público Comparado y Derecho Internacional Público Instituto de Estudios Constitucionales del Estado de Querétaro Instituto de Investigaciones Jurídicas Universidad Nacional Autónoma de México, 2020).

Couso, J, 'The "Economic Constitutions" of Latin America: between Free Markets and Socioeconomic Rights' in T Ginsburg and R Dixon (eds), *Comparative Constitutional Law in Latin America* (Cheltenham, Edward Elgar, 2017).

—— 'The Possibilities and Limits of a Constitution-Making Transnational Legal Order: The Case of Chile' in G Shaffer, T Ginsburg and TC Halliday (eds), *Constitution-Making and Transnational Legal Order* (Cambridge, Cambridge University Press 2019).

Crenshaw, K, 'Demarginalizing the Intersection of Race and Sex: A Black Feminist Critique of Antidiscrimination Doctrine, Feminist Theory and Antiracist Politics' (1989) *University of Chicago Legal Forum* 139.

Crisp, R, 'Treatment According to Need: Justice and the British National Health Service' in R Rhodes, M Battin and A Silvers (eds), *Medicine and Social Justice. Essays on the Distribution of Health Care* (Oxford, Oxford University Press, 2002).

Cristi, R and Ruiz Tagle, P, *El constitucionalismo del miedo. Propiedad, bien común y poder constituyente* (Santiago, LOM 2015).

Daniels, N, *Just Health Care* (Cambridge, Cambridge University Press, 1985).

—— *Just Health: Meeting Health Needs Fairly* (Cambridge, Cambridge University Press, 2008).

Daniels, N, Light, D and Caplan, R, *Benchmarks of Fairness for Health Care Reform* (Oxford, Oxford University Press, 1996).

Dann, P, Riegner, M and Bönnemann, M (eds), *The Global South and Comparative Constitutional Law* (Oxford, Oxford University Press, 2020).

De Lora, P and Zúñiga-Fajuri, A, *The Right to Health Care. An Analysis from the Theories of Distributive Justice* (Madrid, IUSTEL, 2009).

De Otto, I, *Derecho constitucional* (Madrid, Ariel, 1999).

De Rosa, M, Flores, I and Morgan, M, *Inequality in Latin America Revisited: Insights from Distributional National Accounts*, World Inequality Lab – Technical Note 2020/02 (November 2020).

Deal M, 'Disabled People's Attitudes toward Other Impairment Groups: A Hierarchy of Impairments' (2003) 18 *Disability & Society* 897.

Délano, M, Luengo, A and Salazar, M, 'La mayoría de los ejecutivos claves del Grupo Edwards perteneció a la dictadura de Pinochet' *La Interferencia* (29 November 2020).

Delgado, V, 'La protección del Medio Ambiente a través de las acciones populares del artículo 948 del Código Civil de Andrés Bello: un estudio histórico-comparativo' in M Martinic and M Tapia (eds), *Sesquicentenario del Código Civil de Andrés Bello. Pasado, presente y futuro de la codificación Tomo II* (Chile, Lexis Nexis, 2005).

—— 'La regulación de las aguas subterráneas en el derecho de aguas de Chile: liberal, incompleta y poco ambiental' in V Delgado and JL Arumí (eds), *El modelo chileno de regulación de las aguas subterráneas: Críticas desde el derecho ambiental y las ciencias ambientales* (Valencia, Tirant Lo Blanch, 2021).

Delgado, V, Moraga, P and Farías, L, 'Sentencia Corte Suprema 22 May 2018' (2018) *Actualidad Jurídica Ambiental*.

Domínguez, R, 'Aspectos de la Constitucionalización del Derecho Civil Chileno' (1996) 93 *Revista de Derecho y Jurisprudencia* 127.

Drew, N, Funk, M, Tang, S, Lamichhane, J, Chavez, E, Katontoka, S and Pathare, S et al, 'Human Rights Violations of People with Mental and Psychosocial Disabilities: An Unresolved Global Crisis' (2011) 378 *The Lancet* 1664.

Dukes, R, *The Labour Constitution the Enduring Idea of Labour Law* (Oxford, Oxford University Press, 2014).

Dugard, J, 'Unpacking Section 25: What, If Any, Are the Legal Barriers to Transformative Land Reform?' (2019) 9 *Constitutional Court Review* 135.

Dugard, J, Madlingozi, T and Tissington, K, 'Rights-Compromised or Rights-Savvy? The Use of Rights-Based Strategies to Advance Socio-Economic Struggles by Abahlali base Mjondolo, the South African Shack-Dwellers' Movement' in HA García, K Klare and LA Williams (eds), *Social and Economic Rights in Theory and Practice: Critical Inquiries* (London, Routledge, 2015).

Economic Commission for Latin America and the Caribbean (ECLAC), *Social Panorama of Latin America 2018* (2019).

—— *América Latina y el Caribe ante la pandemia del COVID-19: efectos económicos y sociales* (United Nations, 2020).

—— *Panorama Social de América Latina* (United Nations, 2021).

Egorov, A (ed), *The Right to Social Security in the Constitutions of the World. Broadening the Moral and Legal Space for Social Justice* vol 1 (Geneva, ILO, 2016).

Eisenstadt, TA, LeVan, AC and Maboudi, T, *Constituents before Assembly: Participation, Deliberation, and Representation in the Crafting of New Constitutions* (Cambridge, Cambridge University Press, 2017).

El Desconcierto, *'Piñera y viuda de Luksic entre ellos: Cinco multimillonarios en Chile aumentaron su fortuna durante la pandemia'* (29 December 2020).

Elacqua, G, Montt, P and Santos, H, 'Evidencias para eliminar – gradualmente – el Financiamiento Compartido' (2013) 14 *Claves de Políticas Públicas* 1.

Elkins, Z, Ginsburg, T and Melton, J, *The Endurance of National Constitutions* (Cambridge, Cambridge University Press, 2009).

Elster, J, *Ulysses Unbound: Studies in Rationality, Pre-commitment, and Constraints* (Cambridge, Cambridge University Press, 2000).

Embid Irujo, A, *Las libertades en la enseñanza* (Madrid, Tecnos, 1982).

Evans, E and Reher, S, 'Disability and Political Representation: Analysing the Obstacles to Elected Office in the UK' (2020) IPSR (online first).

Evans, E, Howlett, S, Kremser, T, Simpson, J, Kayess, R and Trollor, J, 'Service Development for Intellectual Disability Mental Health: A Human Rights Approach' (2012) 56 *Journal of Intellectual Disability Research* 1098.

Falabella, A, 'School Markets in Chile and the Emergence of the New Public Management: The Fabric of Policies between a Neoliberal Dictatorship Regime and Center-left Democratic Governments (1979–2009)' (2015) 36(132) *Educação e Sociedade* 699.

Falabella, A and Ilabaca, T, 'Cómo terminar con el lugar privilegiado de la educación privada en Chile' *CIPER* (21 December 2020).

Faranaaz, V, 'Realising the Right to Basic Education: The Role of the Courts and Civil Society' (Claremont, Juta, 2019).

Fermandois, A, *Derecho Constitucional Económico* (Santiago, Ediciones Pontificia Universidad Católica de Chile, 2010).

Fermandois, A and García, JF, 'Compatibilidad entre el derecho a la libre contratación y la fijación de salarios por ley (a propósito de la Ley 20.281 sobre sueldo base)' (2010) 37 *Revista Chilena de Derecho* 343.

Fernández Neira, K and Garcés Fuentes, M, 'Pesquera Arauco and Colonia Dignidad Cases' in JP Bohoslavsky, K Fernández and S Smart (eds), *Pinochet's Economic Accomplices. An Unequal Country by Force* (London, Lexington Books, 2020).

Ferrada, JC, 'La constitución económica de 1980. Algunas reflexiones críticas' (2000) 11 *Revista de Derecho* 47.

—— 'La autonomía del Banco Central de Chile: Reflexiones acerca de este modelo institucional de gestión de la política monetaria' (2003) 30(1) *Revista Chilena de Derecho* 151.

Ferrer Mac-Gregor, E, Morales Antoniazzi, M and Pantoja, R (eds), *Inclusión, Ius Commune y justiciabilidad de los DESCA en la jurisprudencia interamericana. El caso Lagos del Campo y los nuevos desafíos* (Instituto de Estudios Constitucionales del Estado de Querétaro, 2018).

Fiala-Butora, J, Stein, MA, and Lord, JE, 'The Democratic Life of the Union: Toward Equal Voting Participation for Europeans with Disabilities' (2014) 55 *Harvard International Law Journal* 83.

Filmer, D, 'Disability, Poverty, and Schooling in Developing Countries: Results from 14 Household Surveys' (2008) 22 *World Bank Economic Review* 141.

FIMA NGO, 'Bases para una Constitución Ecológica en Chile' (2020).

Foro por el derecho a la educación pública, *Informe luz de la situación de la educación en Chile al 2019* (2019).

Fredman, S, *Human Rights Transformed: Positive Rights and Positive Duties* (Oxford, Oxford University Press, 2008).

—— *Intersectional Discrimination in EU Gender Equality and Non-Discrimination Law* (Brussels, European Commission, 2016).

Galdámez, L, 'Constitución y medio ambiente: algunas ideas para el futuro' (2018) 9 *Revista de Derecho Ambiental* 72.

—— 'Los deberes de protección estatal, cláusula presente (aunque dormida) en la Constitución de 1980: una fórmula constitucional frente al cambio climático' in P Moraga (ed), *La protección del medio ambiente: reflexiones para una reforma constitucional* (Chile, Editorial Jurídica de Chile, 2019).

García, JF, 'Minimalismo e incrementalismo constitucional' (2015) 41 *Revista Chilena de Derecho*.

García-Villegas, M, *El país de las emociones tristes. Una explicación de los pesares de Colombia desde las emociones, las furias y los odios* (Bogota, Editorial Planeta Colombiana, 2020).

Gargarella, R, *Latin American Constitutionalism 1820–2010. The Engine Room of the Constitution* (Oxford, Oxford University Press, 2013).

—— 'Diez puntos sobre el cambio constitucional en Chile' (2020) 285 *Nueva Sociedad*.

Gargarella, R, Domingo, P and Roux, T (eds), *Courts and Social Transformation in New Democracies: An Institutional Voice for the Poor?* (Farnham, Ashgate, 2006).

Garretón, MA, 'Chile 1997–1998: The Revenge of Incomplete Democratization' (1999) 75 *International Affairs* 259.

Gauri, V and Brinks, DM (eds), *Courting Social Justice: Judicial Enforcement of Social and Economic Rights in the Developing World* (Cambridge, Cambridge University Press, 2008).

Gerapetritis, G, *New Economic Constitutionalism in Europe* (London, Bloomsbury, 2019).

Gerber, D, 'Constitutionalizing the Economy: German Neo-liberalism, Competition Law and the "New" Europe' (1994) 42(1) *The American Journal of Comparative Law* 25.

Global Education Monitoring Report Team, *A New Generation: 25 Years of Efforts for Gender Equality in Education* (Paris, UNESCO, 2020).

Global Inititiative for Economic, Social and Cultural Rights, *Derechos sociales en Chile: obstáculos y oportunidades constitucionales*. 2020. Webinar recordings. Serie de conversatorios 'Derechos sociales y proceso constituyente: re (imaginando) el Chile del siglo XXI'.

—— *States' Human Rights Obligations Regarding Public Services: The United Nations Normative Framework* (GI-ESCR, 2020).

Global Initiative for Economic, Social and Cultural Rights, Human Rights Centre of the University of Essex and University of Concepción (eds), *Derechos sociales y el momento constituyente de Chile: Perspectivas globales y locales para el debate constitucional* (Santiago, GI-ESCR, 2021).

Góngora Mera, M, 'Discriminación en clave interseccional: tendencias recientes en la jurisprudencia de la Corte Interamericana de Derechos Humanos' in M Morales Antoniazzi, L Ronconi and L Clérico, *Interamericanización de los DESCA. El caso Cuscul Pivaral de la Corte IDH* (Mexico, Instituto Max Planck de Derecho Público Comparado y Derecho Internacional Público Instituto de Estudios Constitucionales del Estado de Querétaro Instituto de Investigaciones Jurídicas Universidad Nacional Autónoma de México, 2020).

González, J et al, *Constituyamos Otra Educación, Una Mejor Sociedad Es Posible: 10 nudos constitucionales en educación y experiencias internacionales destacadas para inspirar el debate nacional* (GI-ESCR et al, 2020).

Guiloff, M and Salgado, C 'El derecho de propiedad privada y la tutela de los bienes públicos' in R Lorca, P Marshall, N Selamé and M Guiloff (eds), *La Hoja en Blanco* (Chile, Editorial La Pollera, 2020).

Guzmán, R, *Derecho Ambiental Chileno* (Chile, Planeta sostenible, 2012).

Halperín, L, Labiaguerre, JA, Delpech, C, González, M, Horen, B, Villadeamigo, JD, Siffredi, L and Müller, G, 'Políticas Sociales En La Argentina: Entre La Ciudadanía Plena y El Asistencialismo Focalizado En La Contención Del Pauperismo' (Universidad de Buenos Aires, Cuadernos del CEPED Número 10, 2008).

Härmä, J, 'Evidence on School Choice and the Human Right to Education' in F Adamson et al (eds), *Realizing the Abidjan Principles on the Right to Education. Human Rights, Public Education and the Role of Private Actors in Education* (Cheltenham, Edward Elgar, 2021).

Harpur, P and Stein, MA, 'Children with Disabilities, Human Rights, and Sustainable Development' in C Fenton-Glynn (ed), *Children's Rights and Sustainable Development* (Cambridge, Cambridge University Press, 2019).

Harris, J, 'Micro-Allocation: Deciding between Patients' in H Kuhse and P Singer, *A Companion to Bioethics* (Blackwell, 2001).

Hayek, F, *Law, Legislation and Liberty* (London, Routledge, 1982).

Heinz, K *Constituting Democracy: Law, Globalisation and South Africa's Political Reconstruction* (Cambridge, Cambridge University Press, 2000).

Henríquez, A, *El principio de protección del alumno en el contexto de la relación educacional* (Santiago, Thomson Reuters, 2018).

—— 'Some Conceptions about Distributive Justice and its Problems about the Enjoyment of the Right to Education' (2018) 17 *Revista de Derecho.*

Henríquez, M, 'La actual Constitución no es compatible con las demandas sociales' *Ciper Académico* (4 February 2020).

Herrera, H, 'Notas preliminares para una lectura no dogmática del principio de subsidiariedad' in P Ortúzar (ed), *Subsidiariedad: más allá del Estado y del mercado* (Santiago, Instituto de Estudios de la Sociedad, 2015).

Hervé, D, *Justicia ambiental y recursos naturales* (Chile, Ediciones Universitarias de Valparaíso, 2015).

Hervé, D and Bascur, D, 'La protección de los derechos de las comunidades indígenas en el SEIA por parte de los tribunales ambientales: ¿avances o retrocesos?' (2019) 11 *Revista Justicia Ambiental* 197.

Hervé, D and López, G 'El medio ambiente y el desafío de una nueva Constitución' in R Lorca, P Marshall, N Selamé and M Guiloff (eds), *La Hoja en Blanco* (Chile, Editorial La Pollera, 2020).

Hervé, D and Pérez, S 'Adecuación de la legislación interna a los estándares impuestos para la administración de los recursos naturales' in J Contesse (ed), *El Convenio 169 de la OIT y el derecho chileno. Mecanismos y obstáculos para su implementación* (Santiago de Chile, Heinrich Boll Foundation, Ediciones UDP, 2012).

Heyer, KC, 'The ADA on the Road: Disability Rights in Germany' (2002) 27 *Law & Social Inquiry* 723.

Heymann, J, and McNeill, K, *Children's Chances: How Countries Can Move from Surviving to Thriving* (Cambridge, MA, Harvard University Press, 2013).

Heymann, J, Sprague, A and Raub, A, *Advancing Equality: How Constitutional Rights Can Make a Difference Worldwide* (Oakland, University of California Press, 2020).

Heywood, M, 'South Africa's Treatment Action Campaign: Combining Law and Social Mobilization to Realize the Right to Health' (2009) 1 *Journal of Human Rights Practice* 14.

Hodgson, TF, 'Bridging the Gap between People and the Law: Transformative Constitutionalism and the Right to Constitutional Literacy' in A Price and M Bishop (eds), *Transformative Justice: Essays in Honour of Pius Langa* (Claremont, Juta, 2015).

Homedes, H and Ugalde, A, 'Privatization of Health Services: The Experiences of Chile and Costa Rica' (2002) 16 *Gaceta Sanitaria* 54.

Hughes, C, *Accidental Logics: The Dynamics of Change in the Health Care Arena in the United States, Britain, and Canada* (Oxford, Oxford University Press, 1999).

Huneeus, C and Undurraga, T, 'Authoritarian Rule and Economic Groups in Chile: A Case of Winner-Takes-All Politics' in V Basualdo, H Berghoff and M Bucheli (eds), *Big Business and*

Dictatorships in Latin America: A Transnational History of Profits and Repression (London, Palgrave, 2021).

Hurley, J, 'Ethics, Economics, and Public Financing of Health Care' (2001) 27 *Journal of Medical Ethics.*

Hurtado, F, 'Índice de acceso a la vivienda (Price Income Ratio)' Cámara Chilena de la Construcción (2019).

Inter-American Commission of Human Rights, Principles of the Inter-American Legal Committee, CJI/RES. 147 (LXXIII-O/08).

—— *Annual Report 2008. Volumen II: Informe Anual de la Relatoría Especial para la Libertad de Expresión* (2008).

—— Office of the Special Rapporteur for Freedom of Expression, The Inter-American Legal Framework regarding the Right to Access to Information, 2010.

—— Resolution 1/2021, Covid-19 Vaccines and Inter-American Human Rights Obligations.

ILGA World, *State-Sponsored Homophobia 2019: Global Legislation Overview Update* (Geneva, ILGA, 2019).

Instituto Nacional de Derechos Humanos, *Resultados de la IV Encuesta Nacional de Derechos Humanos* (Santiago, INDH, 2018).

—— *Informe Anual 2020: Covid y derechos humanos en Chile* (Santiago, INDH, 2020).

International Commission of Jurists, *Corporate Complicity & Legal Accountability* (Geneva, ICJ, 2012).

International Labour Organization, *Social Security and the Rule of Law: General Survey Concerning Social Security Instruments in Light of the 2008 Declaration on Social Justice for a Fair Globalization* International Labour Conference (Geneva, ILO, 2011).

—— Social Protection Floors Recommendation No 202 (2012).

—— *Global Wage Report 2018/19: What Lies Behind Gender Pay Gaps* (Geneva, ILO, 2018).

—— *Implementing the ILO Indigenous and Tribal Peoples Convention No 169: Towards an Inclusive, Sustainable and Just Future* (Geneva, ILO, 2020).

—— *Nota Informativa. Consideraciones sobre seguridad social, seguridad de ingresos, pensiones y el 10% de ahorros de los trabajadores en las AFP en el contexto de la COVID-19 en Chile* (Geneva, ILO, 2020).

International Organization for Migration, *World Migration Report 2020* (Geneva, IOM, 2019).

Jones, MK, 'Does Part-time Employment Provide a Way of Accommodating a Disability?' (2007) 75 *The Manchester School* 695.

Jung, C, Hirschl, R and Rosevear, E, 'Economic and Social Rights in National Constitutions' (2014) 62(4) *American Journal of Comparative Law* 1043.

Kidd, S, 'Citizenship or Charity: The Two Paradigms of Social Protection' (2017) 17 *Pathways Perspectives.*

Kidd, S and Sibun, D, 'What Has the Covid-19 Crisis Taught us about Social Protection?' (2020) 29 *Pathways Perspectives.*

King, J, *Judging Social Rights* (Cambridge, Cambridge University Press, 2012).

—— 'Social Rights in Comparative Constitutional Theory' in G Jacobsohn and M Schor (eds), *Comparative Constitutional Theory* (Cheltenham, Edward Elgar 2018).

—— 'The Future of Social Rights' in K Young (ed), *The Future of Economic and Social Rights* (Cambridge, Cambridge University Press, 2019).

Klare, K, 'Legal Culture and Transformative Constitutionalism' (1998) 14 *South African Journal on Human Rights* 146.

Klein, N, *The Shock Doctrine: The Rise of Disaster Capitalism* (London, Penguin, 2007).

Kowalczyk, A, 'Transnational Capitalist Classes and the State in Chile' (2019) 25 *New Political Economy* 1.

Kymlicka, W, *Contemporary Political Philosophy. An Introduction* (Oxford, Oxford University Press, 2002).

Landau, D, 'Socioeconomic Rights and Majoritarian Courts in Latin America' in C Crawford and D Bonilla Maldonado (eds), *Constitutionalism in the Americas* (Cheltenham, Edward Elgar, 2018).

Landau, D and Dixon, D, 'Constitutional Non-Transformation?' in K Young (ed), *The Future of Economic and Social Rights* (Cambridge, Cambridge University Press, 2019).

Landau, D and Lerner, H (eds), *Comparative Constitution Making* (Cheltenham, Edward Elgar, 2019).

Langford, M, Cousins, B, Dugard, J and Madlingozi, T (eds), *Socio-Economic Rights in South Africa: Symbols or Substance?* (Cambridge, Cambridge University Press, 2014).

Langford, B and Levesque, M, 'Symbolic and Substantive Relevance of Politicians with Disabilities: A British Columbia Case Study' (2017) 40(2) *Canadian Parliamentary Review* 8.

Lanza, E, Ediciones Consejo para la Transparencia, *A 10 años del fallo Claude Reyes: Impacto y desafíos* (Chile, 2016).

Lawson, A, and Waddington, L (eds), *The UN Convention on the Rights of Persons with Disabilities in Practice* (Oxford, Oxford University Press, 2018).

Lazar, J, and Stein, MA (eds), *Disability, Human Rights, and Information Technology* (Philadelphia, PA, University of Pennsylvania Press, 2017).

Liebenberg, S, *Socio-Economic Rights: Adjudication under a Transformative Constitution* (Claremont, Juta, 2010).

—— 'Socio-Economic Rights beyond the Public-Private Divide' in M Langford et al (eds), *Socio-Economic Rights in South Africa: Symbols or Substance?* (Cambridge, Cambridge University Press, 2014).

—— 'The Participatory Democratic Turn in South Africa's Social Rights Jurisprudence' in K Young (ed), *The Future of Economic and Social Rights* (Cambridge, Cambridge University Press, 2019).

Liebenberg, S and Goldblatt, B, 'The Interrelationship between Equality and Socio-Economic Rights under South Africa's Transformative Constitution' (2007) 23 *South African Journal on Human Rights* 335.

Liebenberg, S and Karrisha, P (eds), *Socio-Economic Rights in South Africa: A Resource Book* (University of the Western Cape, Community Law Centre, 2000).

Lobos Palacios, M, 'Panel Derechos Sociales y Una Nueva Constitución' *CEPAL* (2020).

Loo, M, 'La disciplina constitucional del principio de subsidiariedad en Italia y Chile' (2009) 33 *Revista de Derecho de la Pontificia Universidad Católica de Valparaíso* 391.

López, E and Herrera, N, 'Arriendos por las nubes: efecto de la creciente concentración de la propiedad' *Ciper* (2018).

Lord, J, and Stein, MA, 'Prospects and Practices for CRPD Implementation in Africa' (2013) *African Disability Rights Yearbook* 109.

Lord, JE, Stein, MA, and Fiala-Butora, J, 'Facilitating an Equal Right to Vote for Persons with Disabilities' (2014) 6 *Journal of Human Rights Practice* 115.

Loughlin, M, 'What is Constitutionalisation?' in P Dobner and M Loughlin (eds), *The Twilight of Constitutionalism?* (Oxford, Oxford University Press, 2010).

Lovera, D, 'Derechos Sociales en la Constitución del 80 (… y del 89, y del 2005)' in C Fuentes (ed), *En nombre del pueblo: Debate sobre el cambio constitucional en Chile* (Santiago, U DP and Fundación Böll, 2010).

—— 'Derechos sociales en una Nueva Constitución: el constitucionalismo transformador' in J Bassa, JC Ferrada and C Viera (eds), *La Constitución que queremos* (Santiago, LOM, 2019).

McConnachie, C and Brener, S, 'Litigating the Right to Basic Education' in J Brickhill (ed), *Public Interest Litigation in South Africa* (Claremont, Juta, 2018).

Mcnamara, K, 'Rational Fictions: Central Bank Independence and the Social Logic of Delegation' (2002) 25(1) *West European Politics* 47.

Madariaga, A, *Neoliberal Resilience: Lessons in Democracy and Development from Latin America and Eastern Europe* (Princeton, Princeton University Press, 2020).

Mahomed, F, Lord, JE, and Stein, MA, 'Transposing the Convention on the Rights of Persons with Disabilities in Africa: The Role of Disabled Peoples' Organisations' (2019) 27 *African Journal of International and Comparative Law* 338.

Majumdar, S and Villa, V, 'In 2018, Government Restrictions on Religion Reach Highest Level Globally in More than a Decade' (Washington, DC, Pew Research Center, 2020).

Makwetu, K, 'Constitutional Accountability for Public Resources: The Role of the Auditor-General' (2019) 30 *Stellenbosch Law Review* 318.

Maldonado, S, *Trabajo y Discapacidad en el Peru: Mercado Laboral, Politicas Publicas e Inclusion Social* (Lima, Fondo Editorial del Congreso del Perú and Programa de Naciones Unidas para el Desarrollo, 2006).

Mandela, NR, 'Address: On the occasion of the ANC's Bill of Rights conference' in *A Bill of Rights for a Democratic South Africa: Papers and Report of a Conference Convened by the ANC Constitutional Committee, May 1991* (1991).

Mannan, H, McVeigh, J, Amin, M, MacLachlan, M, Swartz, L, Munthali, A, and Van Rooy, G, 'Core Concepts of Human Rights and Inclusion of Vulnerable Groups in the Disability and Rehabilitation Policies of Malawi, Namibia, Sudan, and South Africa' (2012) 23 *Journal of Disability Policy Studies* 67.

Mansuy, D, 'Notas sobre política y subsidiariedad en Jaime Guzmán' (2016) 36 *Revista de Ciencia Política* 503.

Marshall P, Ponce de León, V and Marchant, E, 'Las personas con discapacidad en el proceso constituyente chileno' (2020) 16 *Anuario de Derechos Humanos* 235.

Marshall, TH, *Citizenship and Social Class and Other Essays* (Cambridge, Cambridge University Press, 1950).

Martin, A and Clerico, L, 'El derecho social autónomo a la salud y sus contenidos. El caso Poblete Vilches y el examen de (in)cumplimiento de las obligaciones impostergables y no ponderables' in M Morales Antoniazzi and L Clérico (eds), *Interamericanización del derecho a la salud Perspectivas a la luz del caso Poblete de la Corte IDH* (Querétaro, Instituto de Estudios Comparados del Estado de Querétaro, 2019).

Martinic, S, Huepe, D and Madrid, A, 'Jornada escolar completa en Chile. Representaciones de los profesores sobre sus efectos en los aprendizajes' (2008) 1 *Iberoamerican Journal of Educational Evaluation* 124.

Marzi, D, 'Union Law: Anti-unionism as a Neoliberal Cictory' in JP Bohoslavsky, K Fernández and S Smart (eds), *Pinochet's Economic Accomplices. An Unequal Country by Force* (London, Lexington Books, 2020).

Massai, N and Miranda, B, 'La mitad de la convención: 77 constituyentes electos provienen de listas que impulsan cambios radicales al sistema' *Ciper* (May 2021).

Matus, M, 'Particularismos e imposibilidades de los impuestos a las emisiones en la Constitución Política de Chile. Estudio Preliminar' (2015) 42(3) *Revista Chilena de Derecho* 1035.

Maués, A and Magalhães, B (eds), *O controle de convencionalidade na América Latina: experiências comparadas* (Brazil, Lumen Juris, 2018).

Maye-Rieckh, A and de Greiff, P, *Justice as Prevention: Vetting Public Employees in Transitional Societies* (New York, Social Science Research Council, 2007).

Memoria Viva, *Memoria Viva, Empresa Elecmetal* (online resource).

Menke, C and Turner, C, *Critique of Rights* (Cambridge, Polity, 2020).

Ministerio de Desarrollo Social y Familia, *Informe Final Consejo Asesor para la Cohesión Social. Diagnóstico para una aproximación a la cohesión social en Chile y recomendaciones para fortalecer el aporte de la política social* (Santiago de Chile, 2020).

Ministry of Housing, *Public Accounts 2019*, executive summary (2019).

Mitra, S, and Sambamoorthi, U, 'Wage Differential by Disability Status in an Agrarian Labor Market in India' (2009) 16 *Applied Economic Letters* 1393.

Moeller, J, Singhal, S, Al-Dajani, M, Gomaa, N, and Quiñonez, C, 'Assessing the Relationship between Dental Appearance and the Potential for Discrimination in Ontario, Canada' (2015) 1 *SSM-Population Health* 26.

Möller, K, 'Two Conceptions of Positive Liberty: Towards and Autonomy-based Theory of Constitutional Rights' (2009) 29 *Oxford Journal of Legal Studies* 757.

Montt, G and Coddou, A, 'El Derecho a La Seguridad Social En Chile y El Mundo: Análisis Comparado Para Una Nueva Constitución' 14 *Informes Técnicos* (OIT Cono Sur, 2020).

Moraga, P, Delgado, V and Farías, L, 'Sentencia Corte Suprema 22 May 2018' (2018) Actualidad Jurídica Ambiental.

Moscoso, C, 'The Media during the Dictatorship' in JP Bohoslavsky, K Fernández and S Smart (eds), *Pinochet's Economic Accomplices. An Unequal Country by Force* (London, Lexington Books, 2020).

Mowbray, J, 'Is There a Right to Public Education?' in F Adamson et al (eds), *Realizing the Abidjan Principles on the Right to Education. Human Rights, Public Education and the Role of Private Actors in Education* (Cheltenham, Edward Elgar, 2021).

Muñoz, F, 'Sobre el concepto original de constitución económica y su aplicabilidad al caso chileno', unpublished draft.

National Constituent Assembly of Colombia, report of session plenary dated 18 June 1991.

Navarro, E, 'El estado empresario a la luz de la Constitución de 1980' (2000) 62 *Revista de Derecho Público* 32.

Negretto, G, *Making Constitutions: Presidents, Parties, and Institutional Choice in Latin America* (Cambridge, Cambridge University Press, 2013).

—— 'New Constitutions in Democratic Regimes' in G Negretto (ed), *Redrafting Constitutions in Democratic Regimes: Theoretical and Comparative Perspectives* (Cambridge, Cambridge University Press, 2020).

—— 'Constitution-making and Liberal Democracy: The Role of Citizens and Representative Elites' (2020) 18 *International Journal of Constitutional Law* 206.

Nino, C, *Fundamentos de derecho constitucional: análisis filosófico, jurídico y politológico de la práctica constitucional* (Buenos Aires, Editorial Astrea, 2013).

Nörr, K, 'On the Concept of the "Economic Constitution" and the Importance of Franz Böhm from the Viewpoint of Legal History' (1996) 3(4) *European Journal of Law and Economics* 345.

Nozick, R, *Anarchy, State and Utopia* (Oxford, Basic Books, 1974).

Nussbaum, MC, 'India: Implementing Sex Equality through Law' (2001) 2 *Chicago Journal of International Law* 35.

OAS Special Rapporteur on Economic, Social, Cultural and Environmental Rights, *Business and Human Rights: Inter-American Standards* (OAS, 2019).

Observatorio Nueva Constitución, 'Análisis de las propuestas constitucionales de los (as) candidatos (as) a convencionales ¿Cuáles son los principales temas del debate constitucional?' (May 2021).

O'Connell, P, 'The Death of Socio-Economic Rights' (2011) 74 *Modern Law Review* 532.

OECD, *Sickness, Disability and Work: Breaking the Barriers. A Synthesis of Findings Across OECD Countries* (Paris, OECD, 2010).

—— *Society at a Glance 2019: OECD Social Indicators* (Paris, OECD, 2019).

OECD Data, 'Income Inequality' (retrieved from website).

—— 'Government Spending' (retrieved from website).

OECD-ECLAC, *OECD Environmental Performance Reviews: Chile 2016* (Paris, OECD, 2016).

Organization of the American States, AG/RES 1932 (XXXIII-O/03) *Access to Public Information: Strengthening Democracy* (Resolution adopted at the fourth plenary session, held on 10 June 2003).

—— Principles of the Inter-American Legal Committee CJI/RES 147 (LXXIII-O/08).

—— *Making Decentralisation Work in Chile: Towards Stronger Municipalities* (Paris, OECD Multi-level Governance Studies, OECD, 2017).

Olmos Herrera, C, 'Autonomy in Times of Economic Complicity: Mining Expansion and Water Practices in Northern Chile' in JP Bohoslavsky, K Fernández and S Smart (eds), *Pinochet's Economic Accomplices. An Unequal Country by Force* (London, Lexington Books, 2020).

OSCE/ODIHR, *Guidelines on Promoting the Political Participation of Persons with Disabilities* (OSCE/ODIHR, 2019).

Parra-Vera, O, *Justiciabilidad de los Derechos Económicos, Sociales y Culturales ante el Sistema Interamericano* (Mexico, Comisión Nacional de los Derechos Humanos, 2011).
—— 'La protección del derecho a la salud a través de casos contenciosos ante el Sistema Interamericano de Derechos Humanos' in L Clérico, L Ronconi and M Aldao (eds), *Tratado de Derecho a la Salud* (Buenos Aires, Abeledo Perrot, 2013).
—— 'La justiciabilidad de los derechos económicos, sociales y culturales en el Sistema Interamericano a la luz del artículo 26 de la Convención Americana. El sentido y la promesa del caso Lagos del Campo' in E Ferrer Mac-Gregor, M Morales Antoniazzi and R Pantoja (eds), *Inclusión, Ius Commune y justiciabilidad de los DESCA en la jurisprudencia interamericana. El caso Lagos del Campo y los nuevos desafíos* (Instituto de Estudios Constitucionales del Estado de Querétaro, 2018).
Pautassi, L, 'Indicadores de Progreso para Medir Derechos Sociales: un nuevo escenario para las políticas públicas en América Latina' in B Muñoz-Pogossian and A Barrantes (eds), *Más derechos para más gente. Equidad e inclusión social: superando desigualdades hacia sociedades más inclusivas* (Washington DC, OAS, 2016).
Petition to the Constitutional Assembly by the Ad Hoc Campaign for Social and Economic Rights (19 July 1995).
Picazo, MI, *Las políticas escolares de la Concertación durante la transición democrática* (Santiago, University Diego Portales, 2013).
Pillay, A, 'Toward Effective Social and Economic Rights Adjudication: The Role of Meaningful Engagement' (2012) 10(3) *International Journal of Constitutional Law* 732.
Pinto, M, 'Los derechos económicos, sociales y culturales y su protección en el sistema universal y en el sistema interamericano' (2004) 40 *Revista del Instituto Interamericano de Derechos Humanos* 25.
Pisarello, G, *Los derechos sociales y sus garantías. Elementos para una reconstrucción* (Madrid, Trotta, 2007).
Pistor, K, *The Code of Capital: How the Law Creates Wealth and Inequality* (Princeton, Princeton University Press, 2019).
Pollack, M, 'Gender Equity in the Chilean Health Care System' (2002) Development Finance Series, No 123, CEPAL.
Portilla C, 'Piñera reconoce que estallido social "no lo vi venir" y acusa "ola de violencia sistemática, profesional, organizada"' *La Tercera* (12 December 2019).
Prosser, T, *The Economic Constitution* (Oxford, Oxford University Press, 2014).
Puyol, A, 'Ethics and Prioritisation in Health Waiting Lists' in *Waiting Lists: Can We Do Better?* (2009) 29 *Cuadernos de la Fundació Víctor Grífols i Lucas*, N°18.
Quinot, G, 'Transformative Legal Education' (2012) 129 *South African Law Journal* 411.
Ramírez, N, 'Alarmante impacto de la pandemia: Estudiantes de 6° básico a III medio no alcanzaron el 60% de los aprendizajes en 2020' *EMOL* (26 May 2021).
Ramos, M, 'Hemos llegado a un punto en que el éxito de los colegios privados está produciendo un daño al sistema público de educación' *CIPER* (5 April 2020).
Rattray, S and Lako, E, *Disability Inclusive Development in UNDP: Guidance and Entry Points* (UNDP, 2018).
Raub A, Latz, I, Sprague, A and Stein, MA, 'Constitutional Rights of Persons with Disabilities: An Analysis of 193 National Constitutions' (2016) 29 *HHRJ* 203.
Ravallion, M, 'On the Virus and Poor People in the World' *The Economics of Poverty* (2 April 2020).
Rawls, J, *A Theory of Justice* (Oxford, Oxford University Press, 1971).
—— *Political Liberalism* (New York, Columbia University Press, 1993).
Ray, B, *Engaging with Social Rights: Procedure, Participation, and Democracy in South Africa's Second Wave* (Cambridge, Cambridge University Press, 2016).
Red ONG Infancia y Juventud Chile, *Lista de Cuestiones Previa a la Presentación de Informes (List of issues prior to Reporting) a presentar ante el Comité de Derechos del Niño en el marco de la 88ava sesión* (2019).

Redley, M, Maina, E, Keeling, A, and Pattni, P, 'The Voting Rights of Adults with Intellectual Disabilities: Reflections on the Arguments, and Situation in Kenya and England and Wales' (2012) 56 *Journal of Intellectual Disability Research* 1026.

Repetto, A, 'Gini: ¿Estado o mercado?' (online resource).

Rifo, M, 'Student Movement, Education System and Current Political Crisis in Chile' (2013) 12(13) *Polis* 223.

Rodríguez-Garavito, C and Rodríguez-Franco, D, *Radical Deprivation on Trial: The Impact of Judicial Activism on Socioeconomic Rights in the Global South* (Cambridge, Cambridge University Press, 2015).

Rodríguez Weber, J, 'Promoting and ensuring inequality: the distributive consequences of the dictatorship' in JP Bohoslavsky, K Fernández and S Smart (eds), *Pinochet's Economic Accomplices. An Unequal Country by Force* (London, Lexington Books, 2020).

Roessler, P, Ramaciotti, JP, Bravo, S, and Faiguenbaum, M, *Informe 3: Acceso a la vivienda y condiciones de habilitabilidad de la población migrante en Chile* (Santiago, Servicio Jesuita a Migrantes, 2020).

Roht-Arriaza, N, 'The Belated Centrality of the Economic Dimension in Transitional Justice' in JP Bohoslavsky, K Fernández and S Smart (eds), *Pinochet's Economic Accomplices. An Unequal Country by Force* (London, Lexington Books, 2020).

Ronconi, L, 'Después de mucho andar, los DESC traspasaron las puertas de la Corte IDH y llegaron, ¿para quedarse?' in M Morales Antoniazzi and L Clérico (eds), *Interamericanización del derecho a la salud. Perspectivas a la luz del caso Poblete de la Corte IDH* (Queretaro, Instituto de Estudios Comparados del Estado de Querétaro, 2019).

Rosen, J, *Louis D Brandeis, American Prophet, Jewish Lives* (New Haven, Yale University Press, 2016).

Rosevear, E, Hirschl, R and Jung, C, 'Justiciable and Aspirational Economic and Social Rights in National Constitutions' in K Young (ed), *The Future of Economic and Social Rights* (Cambridge, Cambridge University Press, 2019).

Rossi, J, 'Obligación de progresividad, no regresividad y máximo de los recursos disponibles. Puntos de encuentro y desencuentro entre la Corte Interamericana y el Comité de Derechos Económicos, Sociales y Culturales de las Naciones Unidas' in M Morales Antoniazzi, L Ronconi and L Clérico, *Interamericanización de los DESCA. El caso Cuscul Pivaral de la Corte IDH* (Mexico, Instituto Max Planck de Derecho Público Comparado y Derecho Internacional Público Instituto de Estudios Constitucionales del Estado de Querétaro Instituto de Investigaciones Jurídicas Universidad Nacional Autónoma de México, 2020).

—— 'Punto de inflexión en la jurisprudencia de la Corte Interamericana de Derechos Humanos sobre DESCA. El camino de la justiciabilidad directa: de *Lagos del Campo* a *Asociación Lhaka Honhat*' (2020) 16 Revista Pensar en Derecho.

Rossi, J and Abramovich, V, 'La tutela de los derechos económicos, sociales y culturales en el artículo 26 de la Convención Americana sobre Derechos Humanos' in M Rodríguez-Pinzón and Guevara (eds), *Derecho Internacional de los Derechos Humanos* (Mexico, Fontamara-American University-Universidad Iberoamericana, 2004).

Rossi, J and Filippini, L, 'El derecho internacional en la justiciabilidad de los derechos sociales en Latinoamérica' in P Arcidiácono, N Espejo and C Rodríguez-Garavito (eds), *Derechos sociales: Justicia, política y economía en América Latina* (Siglo del Hombre, Uniandes, CELS and Universidad Diego Portales, 2010).

Rulli, M, 'A Cat with No Bell. The Privatization of the Chilean Pension System during Pinochet's Dictatorship' in JP Bohoslavsky, K Fernández and S Smart (eds), *Pinochet's Economic Accomplices. An Unequal Country by Force* (London, Lexington Books, 2020).

SABC News, 'Corruption has Cost SA close to R1 trillion: Ramaphosa' (15 October 2019).

Sachs, B, 'Lingering Problems of Currency and Scope in Daniels's Argument for a Societal Obligation to Meet Health Needs' (2010) 35(4) *Journal of Medical Philosophy* 402.

Saiz, I, 'Resourcing Rights: Combating Tax Injustice from a Human Rights Perspective' in A Nolan, R O'Connell and C Harvey (eds), *Human Rights and Public Finance: Budgets and the Promotion of Economic and Social Rights* (London, Bloomsbury, 2013).

Salgado, C 'El derecho a la educación' in J Bassa, JC Ferrada and C Viera (eds), *La Constitución chilena* (Santiago, LOM, 2015).

—— 'El derecho a la educación en una nueva Constitución' in J Bassa, JC Ferrada and C Viera (eds), *La Constitución que queremos* (Santiago, LOM, 2019).

Saltman, R, *The Western European Experience with Health Care Reform* (The European Observatory on Health Care Systems, 2002).

Sánchez, H and Albala, C, 'Inequalities in Health. Adult Mortality in Communities of Metropolitan Santiago' (2004) 132 *Revista Médica de Chile* 453.

Sanhueza, JM and Orellana, V, 'Análisis crítico de la reforma educacional de Bachelet (2014–2018)' in V Orellana (ed), *Entre el mercado gratuito y la educación pública* (Santiago, LOM, 2018).

Schippers, A and Waltz, M 'Politically Disabled: Barriers and Facilitating Factors Affecting People with Disabilities in Political Life within the European Union' (2020) 36(4) *Disability & Society* 517.

Schneider, BR, *Hierarchical Capitalism in Latin America: Business, Labor, and the Challenges of Equitable Development* (Cambridge, Cambridge University Press, 2012).

Schur, L, 'Dead end Jobs or a Path to Economic Well being? The Consequences of Non-standard Work for People with Disabilities' (2002) 20(6) *Behavioral Sciences* 601.

Schur, L and Adya, M, 'Sidelined or Mainstreamed? Political Participation and Attitudes of People with Disabilities in the United States' (2013) 94 *Social Science Quarterly* 811.

Schur, L, Kurse, D and Blanck, P, *People with Disabilities: Sidelined or Mainstreamed?* (Cambridge, Cambridge University Press, 2013).

Selles P, 'Carta de organizaciones sociales', *El Mostrador* (Santiago, 31 July 2020).

Sen, A, *Economía de bienestar y dos aproximaciones a los derechos* (Bogota, Universidad Externado de Colombia, 2002).

Sepúlveda, M, 'De la retórica a la práctica: en enfoque de derechos en la protección social en América Latina' Serie de Políticas Sociales 189 (Santiago de Chile, ECLAC, 2014).

—— 'Human Rights Guiding Principles: A Forward-looking Retrospective' in F Adamson et al (eds), *Realizing the Abidjan Principles on the Right to Education. Human Rights, Public Education and the Role of Private Actors in Education* (Cheltenham, Edward Elgar, 2021).

Sepúlveda, M and Nyst, C, *The Human Rights Approach to Social Protection* (Helsinki, Ministry for Foreign Affairs of Finland, 2012).

Servicio Nacional de la Discapacidad, *Segundo Estudio Nacional de la Discapacidad* (2015).

Sibanda, S, 'When Do You Call Time on Compromise? South Africa's Discourse on Transformation and the Future of Transformative Constitutionalism' (2020) 24 *Law Democracy and Development* 384.

Siddique, Z, 'Evidence on Caste Based Discrimination' (2011) 18 *Labour Economics* S146.

Siddle, A and Koelble, TA, *The Failure of Decentralisation in South African Local Government: Complexity and Unanticipated Consequences* (Cape Town, University of Cape Town Press, 2012).

Silva, I, Zuñiga, P, Vergara, F, Millones, Y, Casasco, M, Herrera, M, Silva, V, Contreras, V, *Habitar en dignidad: hacia el derecho a la vivienda en la nueva Constitución* (Santiago, Techo-CHILE, Fundación Vivienda and GI-ESCR, 2020).

Smart, S, 'Extractivism as a Policy: from its Dictatorial Origins to its Democratic Continuity' in JP Bohoslavsky, K Fernández and S Smart (eds), *Pinochet's Economic Accomplices. An Unequal Country by Force* (London, Lexington Books, 2020).

—— 'Privatization and Repression: Two Sides of the Same Coin' in JP Bohoslavsky, K Fernández and S Smart (eds), *Pinochet's Economic Accomplices. An Unequal Country by Force* (London, Lexington Books, 2020).

Soto, E, 'Consideraciones sobre los fundamentos del principio de subsidiariedad' (1986) 39 *Revista de Derecho Público* 33.

South African Human Rights Commission, *Equality Report 2017/2018*.

Sprague, A, Raub, A, and Heymann, J, 'Providing a Foundation for Decent Work and Adequate Income during Health and Economic Crises: Constitutional Approaches in 193 Countries' (2020) 40 *International Journal of Sociology and Social Policy* 1087.

Statistics South Africa, *Poverty Trends in South Africa: An Examination of Absolute Poverty between 2006 and 2015* (2017).

Stein, MA, Stein, PJS, Weiss, D, and Lang, R, 'Health Care and the UN Disability Rights Convention' (2009) 374 *The Lancet* 1796.

Stillerman, J, 'Class Conflict and the Ascent of Globalized Business Groups under Chile's Dictatorship: A Case Study of the Copper Manufacturing Industry' in V Basualdo, H Berghoff and M Bucheli (eds), *Big Business and Dictatorships in Latin America: A Transnational History of Profits and Repression* (London, Palgrave, 2021).

Sunstein, CR, 'Constitutionalism and secession' (1991) 58 *University of Chicago Law Review* 633.

Tobia, R, 'Una mirada comparada sobre los tributos ambientales en Chile y España' (2019) 12 *Revista de Derecho Ambiental* 7.

Tomasevski, K, *Human Rights Obligations: Making Education Available, Accessible, Acceptable and Adaptable* (CLACSO, 2009).

Troncoso, A, 'Dogmática Administrativa y Derecho Constitucional: el caso del servicio público' (1999) 57 *Revista Española De Derecho Constitucional.*

Tushnet, M, 'Comparative Constitutional Law' in M Reimann and R Zimmermann (eds), *The Oxford Handbook of Comparative Law*, 2nd edn (Oxford, Oxford University Press, 2019).

UN Committee on Economic, Social and Cultural Rights, General Comment No 3: States Obligations, UN doc E/1991/23 (1990).

—— General Comment No 4: Right to Adequate Housing, UN doc E/1992/23 (1991).

—— General Comment No 7: Forced Evictions, UN doc E/1998/22 (1997).

—— General Comment No 9: The domestic application of the Covenant, UN doc E/C.12/1998/24 (1998).

—— General Comment No 13: The Right to Education (Art. 13), UN doc E/C.12/1999/10 (1999).

—— General Comment No 19: The Right to Social Security (Art 9), UN doc E/C.12/GC/19 (2008).

—— Concluding Observations: Chile, UN doc E/C.12/CHL/CO/4 (2015).

—— General Comment No 24: State obligations under the International Covenant on Economic, Social and Cultural Rights in the context of business activities, UN doc E/C.12.GC/24 (2017).

—— Concluding Observations: South Africa, UN doc E/C.12/ZAF/CO/1 (2018).

—— Statement on Universal, Affordable Vaccination against Coronavirus Disease (COVID-19), International Cooperation and Intellectual Property (2021).

UN Committee on the Rights of Persons with Disabilities, *General Comment No 7: on the participation of persons with disabilities, including children with disabilities, through their representative organizations, in the implementation and monitoring of the Convention*, UN doc CRPD/C/GC/7 (2018).

UN Committee on the Rights of the Child, General Comment No 1: Article 29(1). Purposes of education, UN doc CRC/GC/2001/1 (2001).

—— Concluding Observations: Chile, UN doc CRC/C/CHL/CO/4-5 (2015).

UN Development Programme, *Orígenes, cambios y desafíos de la brecha social en Chile* (Santiago, United Nations Development Programme, 2017).

UN General Assembly Resolution, Universal Declaration of Human Rights, A/RES/3/217 A.

UN Human Rights Committee, General Comment No 16: Article 17 (Right to Privacy), The Right to Respect of Privacy, Family, Home and Correspondence, and Protection of Honour and Reputation, UN doc HRI/GEN/1/Rev.1 at 21 (1988).

—— General Comment No 22: Article 18 (Freedom of Thought, Conscience or Religion), UN doc CCPR/C/21/Rev.1/Add.4 (1993).

—— General Comment No 28: Article 3 (Equality of Rights between Men and women), UN doc CCPR/C/21/Rev.1/Add.10 (2000).

UN Independent Expert on the effects of foreign debt and other related international financial obligations of States on the full enjoyment of human rights, particularly economic, social and

cultural rights, Guiding Principles on Human Rights Impact Assessments of Economic Reforms, UN doc A/HRC/40/57 (2018).
UN Office of the High Commissioner for Human Rights and Joint United Nations Programme on HIV/AIDS, *International Guidelines on HIV/AIDS and Human Rights* (2006).
—— *Report of the mission to Chile 30 October – 22 November 2019* (2019).
UN Special Rapporteur on adequate housing as a component of the right to an adequate standard of living, and on the right to non-discrimination in this context, Report: Guidance on implementation of the right to housing, UN doc A/HRC/25/54 (2013).
—— Report on the financialization of housing, UN doc A/HRC/34/51 (2017).
—— Report on her mission to Chile, UN doc A/HRC/37/53/Add.1 (2018).
UN Special Rapporteur on Extreme Poverty and Human Rights, Report on mission to Chile, UN doc A/HRC/32/31/Add.1 (2016).
UN Special Rapporteur on the right to education, Report Mission Chile, UN doc A/HRC/35/24/Add.1 (2017).
—— Report on SDG 4 and privatisation, UN doc A/HRC/41/37 (2019).
UN Special Rapporteur on violence against women, its causes and consequences, Multiple and intersectional forms of discrimination and violence against women, UN doc A/HRC/17/26 (2011).
UNDESA/DSPD, *Report of the United Nations Consultative Expert Group Meeting on International Norms and Standards Relating to Disability* (UNDESA/DSPD, 1998).
Undurraga, V, 'Engendering a Constitutional Moment: The Quest for Parity in the Chilean Constitutional Convention' (2020) 18 *International Journal of Constitutional Law* 466.
UNESCO, *Education for All Monitoring Report 2013/2014* (Paris, UNESCO, 2014).
UNESCO et al, *Educación 2030: Declaración de Incheon y Marco de Acción para la realización del Objetivo de Desarrollo Sostenible 4: Garantizar une educación inclusiva y equitativa de calidad y promover oportunidades de aprendizaje permanente para todos*, Document No ED-2016/WS/28 (2016).
Unger, JP et al, 'Chile's Neoliberal Health Reform: An Assessment and a Critique' (2008) 5(4) *PLoS Med* e79.
Unidad de Gestión del Riesgo de Desastres (Colombia), *Recurso de insistencia en contra de la reserva invocada por la Unidad Nacional de Gestión del Riesgo de Desastres (UNGRD) en la respuesta 2021EE00347* (January 2021).
United Nations, *Leaving No One Behind – The Imperative of Inclusive Development: Report on the World Social Situation* (New York, UN, 2016).
Universidad de Chile, Pontificia Universidad Católica de Chile, y Tenemos que Hablar de Chile, '*Resultados Preliminares: Seis Hallazgos de Los Primeros 1.000 Diálogos*' (Santiago de Chile, 2020).
Uprimny, R, 'Las Transformaciones Constitucionales recientes en América Latina. Tendencias y Desafíos' in C Rodríguez-Garavito (ed), *El Derecho en América Latina. Un Mapa para el Pensamiento Jurídico del Siglo XX* (Mexico, Siglo XXI, 2011).
—— *Derechos sociales en Chile: obstáculos y oportunidades constitucionales*, Youtube Video (10 August 2020).
Uprimny, R, Fuentes, A, Botero, C and Jaramillo, JF, *Libertad de prensa y derechos fundamentales. Análisis de la jurisprudencia constitucional en Colombia (1992–2005)*, (Bogota, De Justicia, 2006).
Uprimny, R and Newman, V, *Subreglas para acceder o rechazar el acceso a la información judicial y de seguridad nacional. Sistematización de la jurisprudencia constitucional en Colombia (2006–2012)* (Bogota, De Justicia, 2006).
Vallejo, R, 'La constitución económica chilena: un ensayo en (de)construcción' (2016) 14 *Estudios Constitucionales* 247.
Vallejo, R and Pardow, D, 'Derribando mitos sobre el Estado empresario' (2008) 35 *Revista Chilena de Derecho* 135.
Van Weele, E, 'The UN Convention on the Rights of Persons with Disabilities in the Context of Human Rights Law' in J Anderson and J Phillips (eds), *Disability and Universal Human Rights:*

Legal, Ethical, and Conceptual Implications of the Convention on the Rights of Persons with Disabilities (Utrecht, Netherlands Institute of Human Rights, 2012).
Vanberg, V, *The Constitution of Markets: Essays in Political Economy* (London, Routledge, 2001).
Vega, J et al, 'Chile: Socioeconomic Differentials and Mortality in a Middle-Income Nation' in T Evans et al (eds), *Challenging Inequalities in Health: from Ethics to Action* (Oxford, Oxford University Press, 2001).
Verdugo, S and Prieto, M, 'The Dual Aversion of Chile's Constitution-Making Process' (2021) 19 *International Journal of Constitutional Law* 149.
Vergara, A and Winn, P 'The Employers Do What They Want with Us: Unions and Workers under the Pinochet Dictatorship' in JP Bohoslavsky, K Fernández and S Smart, *Pinochet's Economic Accomplices. An Unequal Country by Force* (London, Lexington Books, 2020).
Vergara, F, 'Pinochet's Repressive Urbanism: The Violent Neoliberalisation of Space in Santiago' in JP Bohoslavsky, K Fernández and S Smart, *Pinochet's Economic Accomplices. An Unequal Country by Force* (London, Lexington Books, 2020).
Vergara, F et al, *Catastro Nacional de Campamentos 2020–2021 Report* (Santiago, Techo-Chile, 2021).
Viera, C, Bassa, J and Ferrada, JC, 'Una aproximación a la idea de 'constitución económica' y sus alcances en la constitución chilena' (2016) 49 *Boletín Mexicano de Derecho Comparado* 1.
Visser, J, Hayter, S and Gammarano, R, *Trends in Collective Bargaining Coverage: Stability, Erosion or Decline?* Labour Relations and Collective Bargaining Issues Brief 1 (Geneva, ILO, 2015).
Vols, M, Kiehl, M and Sidoli del Ceno, J, 'Human Rights and Protection against Eviction in Anti-social Behaviour Cases in the Netherlands and Germany' (2015) 2 *European Journal of Comparative Law and Governance* 156.
Wagstaff, A, Van Doorslaer E and Paci, P, 'Equity in the Finance and Delivery of Health Care: Some Tentative Cross-country Comparisons' (1989) 5(1) *Oxford Review of Economic Policy* 107.
Waldron, J, 'The Core of the Case against Judicial Review' (2006) 115 *Yale Law Journal* 1346.
Waldschmit A, Sturm, A, Karačić, A and Dins, A 'Implementing the UN CRPD in European Countries: A Comparative Study on the Involvement of Organisations Representing Persons with Disabilities' in R Halvorsen, B Hvinden, J Bickenbach, D Ferri and AM Guillén Rodríguez (eds), *The Changing Disability Policy System: Active Citizenship and Disability in Europe* (London, Routledge, 2017).
Walsh, CE, 'Central Bank Independence' in SN Durlauf and LE Blume (eds), *Monetary Economics* (London, Palgrave Macmillan, 2010).
Williams, LA, 'The Role of Courts in the Quantitative Implementation of Social and Economic Rights: A Comparative Study' (2010) 3 *Constitutional Court Review* 141.
Wilson, S, 'Breaking the Tie: Evictions from Private Land, Homelessness and a New Normality' (2009) 126 *South African Law Journal* 270.
—— *Human Rights and the Transformation of Property* (Claremont, Juta, 2021).
Wilson-Kovacs, D, Ryan, MK, Alexander Haslam, S and Rabinovich, A, 'Just Because You Can Get a Wheelchair in the Building Doesn't Necessarily Mean That You Can Still Participate: Barriers to the Career Advancement of Disabled Professionals' (2008) 23 *Disability & Society* 705.
Winn, P, *Victims of the Chilean Miracle. Workers and Neoliberalism in the Pinochet Era, 1973–2002* (Durham, NC, Duke University Press, 2004).
Wintrobe, R, *The Political Economy of Dictatorship* (Cambridge, Cambridge University Press, 1998).
World Economic Forum, *Global Gender Gap Report 2020* (Geneva, World Economic Forum, 16 December 2019).
World Health Organization, *Commission on Social Determinants of Health* (Geneva, WHO, 2009).
—— *Global and Regional Estimates of Violence against Women: Prevalence and Health Effects of Intimate Partner Violence and Non-Partner Sexual Violence* (Geneva, WHO, 2013).
—— A73/CONF./1, *Covid 19 Response* (18 May 2020).
World Health Organization and World Bank, *World Report on Disability* (Malta, WHO, 2011).

Zobairi, A, Atkinson, V, Ouertani, I, *Political Participation of Women and Men with Disabilities in Tunisia: An IFES Assessment* (IFES, 2018).
Zúñiga-Fajuri, A, 'Justice and Health Care Rationing in AUGE. Bioethical Dilemmas Associated with the Distribution of Scarce Resources' (2011) 17(1) *Acta Bioehica* 73.
—— 'Autonomía, salud y responsabilidad: ¿Se puede responsabilizar al enfermo "culpable" de su enfermedad?' in M Gascón, C González and J Cantero (eds), *Derecho sanitario y bioética. Cuestiones actuales* (Valencia, Tirant lo Blanch, 2010).

Index

www.ingramcontent.com/pod-product-compliance
Lightning Source LLC
Chambersburg PA
CBHW071259180926
51613CB00001B/76

* 9 7 8 1 5 0 9 9 5 1 8 9 5 *